# FOOD PROCESSOR MAGIC

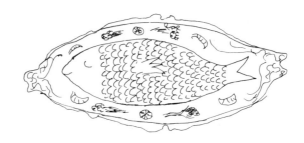

# FOOD PROCESSOR MAGIC

622 Recipes and Basic Techniques

—◆—

by MARY MOON HEMINGWAY

and SUZANNE DE LIMA

*Illustrations by Nina Posnansky*

HASTINGS HOUSE · PUBLISHERS

New York 10016

LIBRARY OF CONGRESS CATALOGING IN PUBLICATION DATA

Hemingway, Mary Moon.
  Food processor magic.

  Includes index.
  1. Cookery. 2. Kitchen utensils. I. de Lima,
Suzanne, joint author. II. Title.
TX652.H42      641.5'89      76-25182
ISBN 0-8038-2321-5

Published simultaneously in Canada by
Saunders of Toronto, Ltd., Don Mills, Ontario

Printed in the United States of America

# CONTENTS

INTRODUCTION   7

TWISTS AND TURNS   13

BASIC PASTRY DOUGHS   23

SAUCES, SALAD DRESSINGS, BUTTERS   31

HORS D'OEUVRE   53

SOUPS   75

EGGS AND CHEESE   103

FISH AND SHELLFISH   119

POULTRY AND STUFFINGS   131

MEATS   143

VEGETABLES   161

SALADS   175

BREADS   183

CRÊPES, PANCAKES, WAFFLES   193

CAKES   201

COOKIES   211

DESSERTS AND DESSERT SAUCES   223

INDEX   239

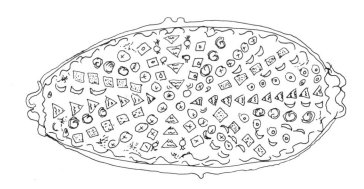

# INTRODUCTION

## What Is the Cuisinart™ Food Processor?

THE CUISINART™ FOOD PROCESSOR is a superbly engineered machine which enables expert or amateur to turn out exceptional dishes without strain or struggle. It's comparable to having a battery of chef apprentices on hand to help out—*sauciers,* vegetable boys, pastry makers, *et al.* It's your *chef du cuisine* at the same time. A labor-saver supreme, it makes possible hitherto extremely difficult, involved dishes.

Taking up no more counter space than a sheet of typing paper, the machine stands always ready to use. It is simple to operate, very easy to clean, and phenomenally quick in producing everything from complex recipes to *pâte à choux,* sausage, vegetables julienne, ground meats, pâtés—all the refinements of *haute cuisine.* In addition, it saves money as well as time by turning out splendid saving graces from leftovers. With it you can translate your imaginative cooking fancies into delicious facts.

For minding your culinary P's and Q's—pastries, pâtés, sauces, soups, savory spreads, quenelles—the Cuisinart™ Food Processor is the *sine qua non* of kitchen appliances. The ½ horsepower motor, which works on 110 volts, is so educated that should it overheat, it will shut off safely of its own accord until it regains its cool. The Lexan plastic bowl is impervious to breakage or extreme temperatures, and can handle small or sizable quantities, or dry or liquid ingredients with efficiency.

This collection of recipes is based on tried and true favorites. Using the basic recipes and techniques included here, innovations, variations, new creations may be concocted agreeably, with a minimum of labor, and in almost no time.

It is wise, however, before taking off to understand the machine. With a little practice you can learn how to chop into coarse or very fine pieces. *Always have the solid ingredients cut into manageable pieces* before processing. *Never crowd the container.* Learn to turn the ma-

7

chine on and off quickly for a coarse chop. Let it run a little longer for medium, still a bit more for fine. *Always scrape down* the ingredients and check to see if the texture is right and that everything has been incorporated.

The more you use the machine, the more accustomed you will become to processing several ingredients together. But rather than make a mush, it is often wise at first to process ingredients separately until you become used to the speed of the blade.

Practice with onions, bread slices, an apple. Don't overprocess unless making a paste or purée.

To whip cream use the plastic blade. Remove the pusher from the tube in order to incorporate more air. Use heavy cream or cream marked "whipping cream." Some "ultra-pasteurized" cream will not whip sufficiently in the processor. Should this occur with any cream, transfer the cream to a bowl and continue to whip with a hand or electric beater until stiff enough for your purposes.

Egg whites can be whipped in the processor, but it will not produce the maximum volume. Use the plastic blade, making sure the blade and the container as well are absolutely free of any grease. For best results use at least 4 egg whites plus ¼ teaspoon of cream of tartar.

The Cuisinart™ Food Processor is a powerhouse, quicker than any device you've worked with before.

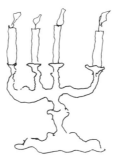

## What does the Cuisinart™ Food Processor do extremely well?

The steel blade chops, mixes, grinds, blends, purées:

1. Chops cooked or raw foods—vegetables, meat, seafood, poultry and ice.
2. Makes foolproof pastry dough, cream puffs, piecrust, cakes and cookies.
3. Grinds nuts, cheese and bread.
4. Produces pâtés, spreads, quenelles and forcemeat.
5. Creates satin-smooth sauces swiftly—béchamel, velouté, mayonnaise, *et al.*
6. Blends flavored butters and frostings.
7. Blends gelatin mixture and ingredients in one operation.

The slicing blade handles hard sausage, vegetables, nuts and cheese, and by reverse slicing turns out julienne strips which may be made by slicing into circles, standing the circles on end in the tube and slicing again.

The shredding blade will grate and shred vegetables, cheese, hard-cooked eggs, citrus rinds, nuts, etc. The shredding blade will also process a very fine julienne.

## General Operating Procedures

1. Treat the machine with respect. The steel blade and discs for the machine are very sharp and must be handled with the same care as any sharp knife.

2. Disconnect from electrical outlet when the machine is not in use, before cleaning it, and before assembling or removing parts.

3. Put the container on the base before inserting the cutting tool on the shaft. Make sure the tool is as far down as it will go; do not use force, but rotate it back and forth until it drops into place.

4. The handle is meant as an aid for pouring. Do not use it as a means of turning the machine on and off. Turn the machine on and off by grasping the feed tube.

5. Place the steel blade in the bowl before adding any ingredients. When using the shredder or slicer, the material must be fed through the tube. Always use the pusher for this. *Never* put your fingers in the tube.

6. When using solids process one cup at a time, cut them, including cheese, into 1-inch pieces. Butter should be broken into pieces as well.

7. When using a combination of ingredients, process the harder ones first before adding the softer ones.

8. Do not use more than 2 cups of liquid at any one time. Add liquids, little by little, through the tube, with the motor running.

9. The container need not always be washed between operations. It is smart to process dry ingredients first—nuts, crumbs, cheese; then set them aside and proceed with the wetter ingredients.

10. *Do not remove the cover from the bowl* until the knife or discs have stopped spinning.

11. Remove the container from the base before removing the cutting tool. This will keep foods from spilling onto the base.

12. When using liquids, pick up the bowl with the steel blade in place so the contents do not seep through the hole. When pouring liquids or soft foods from the container, in order to prevent the blade falling out, grasp the container in the right hand and with the index finger of the left hand press against the knob of the blade.

13. Read the booklet that comes with your machine for complete details, and refer to it for a reminder from time to time. As with any machine, all safety precautions must be scrupulously observed.

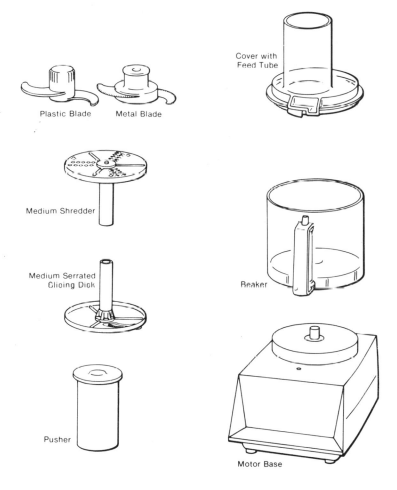

Plastic Blade    Metal Blade

Medium Shredder

Medium Serrated
Slicing Disk

Pusher

Cover with
Feed Tube

Beaker

Motor Base

This illustration was supplied by Cuisinarts Inc.
CUISINART is a trademark of Cuisinarts Inc. of Stamford, Connecticut.

## Cleaning Procedures

1. The *container* and *cover* may be put in a dishwasher, although these parts are easily cleaned with hot soapy water. Do *not* put the *white plunger* in the dishwasher as excessive heat might warp it.

2. Never use abrasive powders or scouring pads.

3. Make sure the base is clean at all times. Wipe it off with a damp cloth as soon as anything is spilled on it, before spilled food has dried.

4. If you are not planning to use the machine immediately, be sure the container and cover are completely dry before reassembling because the machine may sweat from the dampness when it is completely covered.

# TWISTS AND TURNS

---

Make your own peanut butter. Make your own marzipan. Prepare your own bread crumbs. Create condiments and relishes that can't be bought in any store. The Cuisinart™ Food Processor will make these things and many more to enrich your cooking, to insure fresh full-flavored ingredients to add dash to your dishes.

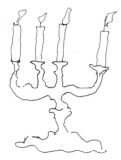

# PEANUT BUTTER

2 cups peanuts, roasted or
  salted
salt

Place peanuts in the container with the steel blade and process, scraping down from time to time, until butter reaches desired consistency. If the peanut butter seems too dry add vegetable or peanut oil, 1 teaspoon at a time. Season with salt to taste.

Other nut butters may be made in the same way and substituted for peanut butter in cookies and spreads.

# PRALINE POWDER

1 cup blanched almonds
1 cup sugar
2 Tbsp. water
⅛ tsp. cream of tartar
1 tsp. vanilla extract

Preheat oven to 300°F. Bake almonds in heated oven until dry but not brown. Boil sugar, water and cream of tartar, shaking the pan in a rotary motion to prevent burning, and cook until the syrup becomes light brown. Add dried almonds and vanilla, and pour onto a large oiled baking sheet. Cool.

When praline becomes hard, break it into small pieces. Process the pieces, little by little, with the steel blade, until all is pulverized. This powder will keep in an airtight container for several weeks. It is a great addition to many desserts and sweet sauces.

## ALMOND PASTE

Almond paste is used for making macaroons and many Scandinavian pastries. Although available in cans, it can easily be made with the food processor.

2 cups blanched almonds
1½ cups confectioners'
    sugar, sifted
2 egg whites
2 tsp. almond extract

Dry the almonds in a low oven (300°F.) until dry but not brown. Grind almonds with the steel blade until pulverized. Mix in sugar, egg whites and almond extract, and process until a paste is formed. Form the paste into a ball, wrap, and let it age in an airtight container for at least 4 days.

## MARZIPAN

1 egg white
1 cup almond paste
½ cup confectioners'
    sugar
2 tsp. vanilla extract,
    or 1 tsp. almond extract

Beat the egg white with the steel blade and process until foamy. Add the almond paste, sugar and flavoring. Process until the mixture holds together. Form the marzipan into any desired shape. The paste may be tinted with food coloring while being processed. If the marzipan is to be used as a sweetmeat by itself, roll the pieces in sugar. Store them in a tightly covered tin. They will keep for a week, but no longer.

## COCONUT

To be sure the coconut is fresh, the liquid should slosh about when the nut is shaken.

*To Open*—Puncture the eyes with an ice pick, and drain out the liquid (this is not coconut milk). Place the nut in a 400°F. oven for 20 minutes. If the shell has not split by then, place it on a board and give it a sharp rap with a hammer. Remove any remaining bits of shell with a knife.

*To Make Grated Coconut*—Pare off the brown outer skin and cut the coconut into pieces to fit the tube. Grate the coconut with the shredding disc.

*To Make Coconut Milk*—Do not remove the brown skin, but cut the meat into pieces to fit the tube; grate with the shredding disc. When all the meat has been processed put it into a fine sieve lined with 2 layers of dampened cheesecloth; set the sieve over a bowl. Pour ¼ cup hot water over coconut shreds and press down with a potato masher or big spoon to press as much liquid as possible from the meat. Gather the cheesecloth together, and squeeze out remaining coconut liquid. Use for "authentic" curries. Refrigerate until used.

————

# CONDIMENTS AND RELISHES

It is worth the effort to make your own condiments and relishes. It makes a surprising difference in variety, and gives you the chance to provide different textures and flavors to suit specific dishes. The combination of ingredients may be of your own choosing, spicy to sweet.

## MANGO CHUTNEY

*2 sweet red peppers, cut up*
*1 green pepper, cut up*
*3 medium-size onions, cut up*
*2 lemons, cut up and seeded*
*¾ cup crystallized orange peel or citron*
*¼ cup crystallized gingerroot*
*½ cup preserved kumquats, cut up (optional)*
*10 to 12 green mangoes*
*3 cups sugar*
*2 cups vinegar*
*1 Tbsp. ground allspice*
*1 Tbsp. ground cinnamon*
*1 Tbsp. ground cloves*
*1 tsp. salt*

Place the peppers in the container with the steel blade and chop coarsely, for 3 to 5 seconds. Set aside in a large bowl. Chop the cut-up onions and lemons coarsely. Add to the peppers. Chop the orange peel or citron, gingerroot and kumquats, for 3 to 5 seconds. Add to other chopped ingredients. Peel the mangoes and cut into pieces to fit the tube; cut into thin slices with the slicing disc. Combine with the chopped ingredients. Place the sugar, vinegar, spices and salt in a big kettle and slowly bring to a boil. Reduce heat and add the prepared vegetables and fruits. Simmer until the mixture is thick and the mango slices transparent but still firm. Pack while hot in sterilized jars, and seal immediately. Makes about 6 pints.

## PEAR CHUTNEY

5 lb. hard pears, peeled
  and cored
4 cups brown sugar
3 cups cider vinegar
4 garlic cloves, peeled
10 oz. preserved gingerroot
2¾ cups seedless raisins
2 Tbsp. mustard seeds
1 Tbsp. salt

Cut the pears to fit the tube, and process with the slicing disc; set aside. Make a syrup of the sugar and vinegar. Chop the garlic and gingerroot. When the syrup just boils, add pears and remaining ingredients and let the mixture come again to a boil. Reduce the heat and let simmer for 5 minutes. Pack while hot in sterilized jars and seal immediately. Makes about 6 pints.

## GRANDMOTHER PAGE'S GREEN TOMATO CHUTNEY

8 quarts (24 lb.) green
  tomatoes, peeled and
  halved
salt
4 quarts (3 lb.) small
  white onions, peeled
¾ cup fresh gingerroot,
  peeled and chopped,
  or 3 oz. chopped
  crystallized gingerroot
1½ cups seeded raisins
½ lb. mustard seeds
1 oz. celery seeds
1 Tbsp. ground black
  pepper
1 Tbsp. ground allspice
1 Tbsp. ground cloves
¾ lb. brown sugar
cider vinegar

Feed the green tomato halves through the tube, and slice with the slicing disc. Place a layer of the tomatoes in a preserving kettle and sprinkle with salt to cover. Add another layer of tomatoes and salt and repeat until all tomatoes are used. Set aside overnight. Rinse and drain the following day. Slice the onions with the slicing disc. Arrange layers of tomatoes and onions, sprinkling each layer with the gingerroot, raisins, spices and sugar. Add vinegar to cover. Simmer for 30 minutes, or until the tomatoes are tender-firm. Pack in sterilized jars while hot, and seal immediately. Makes about 6 quarts.

# PUMPKIN CHIPS

Adapted for the processor from *Two Hundred Years of Charleston Cooking,* University of South Carolina Press, 1976.

2 lb. pumpkin slices
12 lemons
2 lb. sugar

Peel the pumpkin and cut into pieces to fit the tube; process pieces with the slicing disc. Wash and dry the slices thoroughly and weigh out 2 pounds. Grate the rind of 2 lemons with the steel blade; set aside. Cut up and grind all the lemons, and add the pulp and juice to the pumpkin along with the sugar. Boil until the pumpkin is tender, skimming when necessary. When the chips are tender, lift them out of the syrup. Boil the syrup again until it is very thick; about 2 hours altogether is required for the cooking. Return the chips to the syrup for a few minutes, and add the grated lemon rind. Seal in jars, or turn into jelly glasses and seal with paraffin. Makes about 2 pints.

For variation small seeded raisins may be added, also a little fresh gingerroot.

# PICKLED DRIED APRICOTS

2 cups dried apricots
4 cups cider vinegar
1 cup walnuts
3 lemons
3 cups sugar
2 garlic cloves, minced
1 tsp. ground ginger
1 tsp. ground coriander

Soak the apricots in the vinegar for 2 days. Coarsely grind the walnuts with the steel blade, and set aside. Slice the lemons with the slicing disc. Add walnuts, lemons, sugar, garlic and spices to the apricots and vinegar. Bring to a boil and simmer for 1 hour, or until thick. Pour into sterilized jars and seal. Makes 2 to 3 pints.

## CARROT CHIPS

2 lb. carrots, peeled
2 oranges, cut up and
    seeded
1 lemon, cut up and
    seeded
1 inch of fresh gingerroot,
    or 1 tsp. ground ginger
2 lb. sugar
½ cup white vinegar

Slice the carrots with the slicing disc; set aside. Grind the oranges, lemon and gingerroot with the steel blade; set aside. Steam the carrots until just tender; drain. Add sugar, vinegar and ground-up fruit and gingerroot mixture. Cook until mixture is thick. Pack in sterilized jars and seal. Makes about 3 pints.

## ZUCCHINI-RAISIN PICKLE

4 cups zucchini
½ cup salt
1 cup white vinegar
1 cup sugar
6 Tbsp. seeded raisins
1 Tbsp. celery seeds
1 Tbsp. mustard seeds

Slice zucchini with the slicing blade and measure 4 cups. Soak overnight in a solution made of ½ cup salt and 2 quarts water. Drain. Combine vinegar, sugar, raisins and spices. Heat to boiling, add zucchini slices, and boil for 10 minutes. Pack into sterilized jars, seal, and process in boiling-water bath for 5 minutes. Makes about 1½ pints.

## MUSHROOM KETCHUP

3 lb. fresh mushrooms
1½ cups cider vinegar
1 Tbsp. salt
½ tsp. ground allspice
½ tsp. ground cloves
¼ tsp. grated mace
1 Tbsp. dry mustard
2 garlic cloves, minced
½ cup sugar

Trim off tough ends of mushroom stems. Steam the mushrooms in 1 cup of water in a covered kettle until tender. Process them, 1 cup at a time, with the steel blade until puréed. Add remaining ingredients to the purée and boil for 30 minutes. Pour into hot sterilized jars and seal. Makes about 4 pints.

# HOT SAUCE

6 medium-size onions, cut
up
4 canned green chilies,
cut up
10 sweet red peppers, cut
up
2 Tbsp. salt
1 cup water
1 lb. brown sugar
2 cups vinegar
1 Tbsp. mustard seeds
1 Tbsp. prepared
horseradish

Chop the onions, chilies and peppers with the steel blade. Put into a large kettle with the rest of the ingredients except the horseradish. Simmer for 1 hour. Add the horseradish and cook for 10 minutes more. Pack in sterilized jars and seal. Makes about 5 pints.

———

# FLAVORED SHERRIES

Nice to have on hand for flavoring dishes and drinks.

## ONION SHERRY

Use in making cream sauces for fish, seafood and chicken.

2 medium-size onions, cut
up
1 bottle domestic medium-
sweet sherry

Chop the onions with the steel blade, and add to the sherry. Bottle and keep well corked. Allow to age for 2 or 3 days.

## GINGER SHERRY

For Chinese cooking, or desserts.

3-inch piece of fresh
gingerroot
1 bottle domestic dry
sherry

Peel the ginger and slice with the slicing disc. Let it steep in the sherry for 2 or 3 days. Keep well corked.

## SUPER HOT SHERRY

For Bloody Marys, or when a few drops of hot seasoning is indicated.

*1 cup domestic dry sherry*
*1 tsp. crushed dried chili,*
*    or any small dried hot*
*    pepper*

Put sherry and pepper in the container with the steel blade and blend. Let the pepper sit in the sherry until the desired "hotness" is gained. Strain and use carefully.

---

## DUXELLES

This flavoring, called *duxelle* or *duxelles,* was formerly made by chopping mushrooms to a mince by hand. No longer—the food processor does it in a wink. *Duxelles* freezes well, or it will keep in the refrigerator, if well covered, for a week. Use alone as a filling, or add to sauces or stuffings to give flavor and texture.

*1½ lb. mushrooms*
*3 shallots*
*4 Tbsp. butter*
*salt and pepper*

Clean mushrooms, cut off the tough stem ends, and cut up. Place mushrooms in the container with the steel blade and chop for 3 seconds. Press through a cloth or potato ricer, over a bowl, to remove the moisture; save the moisture for stock. Set mushrooms aside. Chop shallots with the steel blade, and sauté them in the butter over moderately high heat, until limp, but do not let them brown. Add minced mushrooms and reduce heat. Sauté until all moisture has evaporated and mushroom mixture is a rich dark brown. Season to taste. Makes about 1 cup.

# BREAD CRUMBS

Bread crumbs can be made in large quantities, packaged in airtight plastic bags, and frozen. They will keep for 1 month or more.

When making bread crumbs use firm bread—French, Italian or a homemade type. Remove the crusts and tear the bread into small pieces. Process, using the steel blade. Do not overcrowd the machine.

There are 3 kinds of bread crumbs: fresh or soft, dried, and golden. Dried crumbs are made from stale or dried bread. One 4-inch-square slice makes approximately ½ cup of crumbs. Golden crumbs are made from fresh or stale bread which has been baked in a preheated 300°F. oven until golden in color, about 1 hour. One 4-inch-square slice makes about ¼ cup of crumbs. Soft fresh bread crumbs are made from fresh bread. One slice of bread makes ¾ cup of crumbs. When measuring, pile them lightly into a cup.

Cracker crumbs are made in the same way as bread crumbs. To make approximately 1 cup of crumbs, use the number of crackers listed in the table that follows.

| Type of Cracker | Coarsely ground | Finely ground |
|---|---|---|
| saltines | 7 | 9 |
| graham | 9 | 11 |
| zwieback | 9 | 12 |
| small vanilla wafers | 22 | 26 |
| 2½-inch chocolate cookies or gingersnaps | 16 | 18 |

# BASIC PASTRY
# DOUGHS

—◆—

All pastries are made with the steel or plastic blade. After the pastry dough is made, wrap it in wax paper and chill for at least 1 hour, or allow to rest in the refrigerator overnight, or freeze it.

When making pastry shells of any size, roll out the dough ⅛ inch thick. Line pastry molds or cover inverted small muffin tins with the dough. Prick the bottom of each shell with a fork and brush with a little butter. Line each tart with wax paper or foil and weigh down with raw rice or dried beans. Chill the pastry in molds before baking. For partially baked shell bake in 400° oven for 10 minutes. Remove foil and weights and bake 10 minutes longer. For fully baked shells continue baking until golden. When using unbaked fillings, bake tarts before filling, for 15 to 20 minutes, until golden. If using hot fillings, partially bake tarts before the final baking for 8 to 10 minutes.

When making cocktail turnovers, roll out the dough very

thin and cut into 2½-inch circles. Place a tablespoon of filling on each circle. Fold the dough over, moistening the edges with egg white or water to seal, and crimp with a fork. If turnovers are to be baked, prick the tops and glaze with a wash made of 1 egg mixed with 1 tablespoon water. If turnovers are to be fried, do not prick or glaze.

When making pinwheels, roll the dough into a thin sheet, making a rectangle. Spread the filling over the dough. Roll up like a jelly roll and chill. Cut into ½-inch slices and place on a greased baking sheet. Bake in a 425°F. oven until golden.

Whenever making any pastry dough, the weather conditions may change the results. If the pastry seems too crumbly, add enough cold water, little by little, with the motor running until a ball forms. If it seems too sticky, add flour, a little at a time, turning the machine on and off until a ball forms.

## STAY-CRISP PASTRY

Excellent for canapés as it does not become soggy.

*3 Tbsp. butter*
*3 Tbsp. olive oil*
*2 cups flour, sifted*
*½ tsp. salt*
*2 egg yolks*
*cold water*

Melt butter with the oil in the top part of a double boiler over hot water. Put the steel blade in the bowl and add sifted flour, salt and egg yolk. Process for 5 to 10 seconds. With the machine running, add the melted butter and oil in a steady stream through the tube, then add enough water until a soft ball of dough forms around the rotating blade. Chill. Roll out the dough on a floured board to about ⅛-inch thickness. Cut into rounds or any desired shapes, prick dough with a fork and place on an ungreased baking sheet. Bake at 400°F. for 15 minutes, or until golden. This amount makes approximately 40 canapés, or a large quiche. This pastry can also be used for miniature quiches, tarts and *barquettes* (boat-shaped tartlets).

## CREAM-CHEESE PASTRY

A simple flaky crust good for tartlets, *empanadas* and other turn-overs, and roll-ups, as well as for piecrust. This pastry becomes soft in a warm kitchen. Use a little at a time, keeping the rest cool until needed. Make half the recipe at a time.

*½ lb. butter (2 sticks)*
*6 oz. cream cheese,*
*. softened*
*¼ tsp. salt*
*2 cups flour, sifted*

Place steel blade in the bowl. Cut the butter and cheese into small pieces and blend in the machine for a few seconds. Turn off the motor, remove the cover, and add salt and flour all at once. Mix until a soft ball of dough forms around the blade. Refrigerate. When ready to use, roll out the dough on a floured surface to ⅛-inch thickness. Bake on a foil-covered cookie sheet in 425°F. oven for 10 to 15 minutes or until golden. This amount of dough will make about 20 tartlets or two 9-inch pie shells.

## COTTAGE-CHEESE PASTRY

A quick satisfying pastry for turnovers or *bouchées*.

*¼ lb. butter (1 stick)*
*½ cup cottage cheese*
*1-2 cups flour, or more*
*to form a ball*

Place steel blade in the bowl. Cut butter into small pieces and put in the machine. Add cottage cheese and blend. With the machine running, gradually add enough flour through the tube to form a ball of dough around the cutting blade. Chill. When ready to use, roll out the dough on a floured surface into a thin sheet. Cut into circles or squares, fill, and fold into turnovers or envelopes. Brush with egg white or water to seal the edges. Bake at 425°F. for 15 minutes, or until light brown. This amount of pastry will make about 15 pieces or one 9-inch shell.

# PÂTE BRISÉE

A classic pastry for tartlets, quiches and pies.

*10 Tbsp. chilled butter*
*1 ¾ cups all-purpose flour*
*1 tsp. salt*
*⅓ to ½ cup ice-cold white*
*wine, vermouth or*
*water*

Combine butter, cut into pieces, with flour and salt in the processor bowl with the steel or plastic blade, and blend. With motor running, gradually add enough cold liquid through the tube to form a dough ball around the blade. Wrap in wax paper and chill for at least 2 hours. Roll out to a thin sheet and line molds or a large quiche pan. Place lined pans in the refrigerator for 1 hour. Preheat oven to 450°F. before baking. Put pastry in oven, then reduce heat to 375°F. Bake for 15 minutes for small shells, or for 35 minutes for a big shell, or until golden.

# TURNOVER PASTRY

Use for turnovers, *empanadas* and *pirozhki*.

*10 Tbsp. butter, in bits*
*3 Tbsp. sour cream*
*1 egg*
*2 cups flour, sifted*
*1 tsp. baking powder*
*1 tsp. salt*

Place the steel blade in the bowl and add the cut-up butter, sour cream and egg. Blend thoroughly. Sift 1 cup of the flour with baking powder and salt. With the machine running, gradually add the flour mixture through the tube. Add just enough of the extra flour to form a well-homogenized ball of dough around the cutting blade. Chill the dough. When ready to use, roll out the dough very thin and cut into 2½-inch circles. Place 1 tablespoon of filling on each circle. Fold over, seal the edges with egg white or water, and press with the tines of a fork. Brush turnovers with 1 egg yolk diluted with 1 tablespoon water (egg wash). Bake for 15 minutes in a 400° oven, or until light brown. These may also be fried, unglazed, in deep fat. This amount of pastry will make about 20 little pies.

# PÂTE À CHOUX (CREAM-PUFF PASTRY)

This pastry dough used for cream puffs, éclairs and Gâteau Saint-Honoré is also used for small unsweetened éclairs or *profiteroles* to be filled with appetizing cocktail food combinations. If filling them with a seafood mixture, try adding ¼ cup cooked mashed shrimps to the dough.

*¼ lb. butter (1 stick)*
*1 cup hot water*
*1 cup flour*
*½ tsp. salt*
*4 eggs*
*1 Tbsp. sugar for sweet fillings*

Preheat oven to 425°F. Combine butter and water in a heavy pot and heat until butter is melted. Mix flour and salt together. When the butter-water mixture comes to a boil, add the flour all at once and stir vigorously with a wooden spoon until the dough forms a firm ball and pulls away from the sides of the pan. Place the dough in the processor with the steel blade, and blend for 10 to 15 seconds. With the motor running, add eggs, one at a time, through the tube. (Add sugar if making dessert puffs.) Process until dough is smooth and shiny. Drop the dough from a teaspoon onto a greased tin, or form into little éclairs. Bake in the preheated oven for 15 to 18 minutes. Reduce oven temperature to 300° and bake for 5 minutes longer, until the puffs are golden. Prick on the side to permit steam to escape. Cool on a rack.

## BASIC PIECRUST

⅔ cup shortening
1 tsp. salt
2 cups flour, sifted
4 Tbsp. ice water
1 egg white

Preheat oven to 425°F. Place shortening, salt and flour in the container with the steel blade, and blend until the mixture resembles cornmeal. With the motor running, pour just enough of the water through the tube to form a ball around the steel blade. Divide the dough into halves. Roll out one circle ⅛ inch thick and about 2 inches larger in circumference than the pie plate. Ease the dough into the pan. Brush dough with egg white. Add filling to the pastry-lined pan. Roll out the top crust, and place on the filling. Make slashes in a design, and crimp or flute the edges together. Bake in the preheated oven for 40 to 50 minutes. Or bake each layer separately to make 2 open-faced pies. Makes 2 crusts.

## FLAKY PIECRUST

1 recipe Basic Piecrust
5½ Tbsp. butter, at room
    temperature

Preheat oven to 425°F. Roll out the pastry ⅛ inch thick. Dot with butter and roll up like a jelly roll. Roll out into a rectangle. Fold the two sides to the center and press together. Fold the ends to the center and seal. Wrap in wax paper and chill.

Divide the dough into halves and roll out ⅛ inch thick to make a 2-crust pie or 2 single shells. Place in a warmed pie tin with moistened edges. Prick the bottom of the shell to prevent puffing. *For a prebaked crust,* bake in the preheated oven for 20 to 30 minutes. *For a filled open-faced pie,* cover the top with foil and bake for 45 minutes; then remove the foil and bake for 10 to 15 minutes more, if necessary.

*For a 2-crust pie,* brush bottom crust with egg white, and fill. Roll out the top crust, and place on the filling. Make slashes in a design, and crimp or flute the edges together. Bake in the preheated oven for 40 to 50 minutes. Makes 2 crusts.

## PÂTE SUCRÉE (SWEET PASTRY)

This is a good pastry for tarts (flan) and turnovers as well as being the traditional dough used for French sweet pies.

*¼ lb. butter (1 stick)*
*1½ cups cake flour*
*¼ cup sugar*
*1 raw egg*
*2 hard-cooked egg yolks*

Cut butter into 6 pieces and put it with the flour and sugar into the container with the steel blade. Blend until crumbly. Add the raw egg and hard-cooked egg yolks, and whir until a ball forms. Wrap the ball in wax paper and chill for at least 1 hour.

Preheat oven to 425°F. Roll out the dough ⅛ inch thick and line the tins (pie, tart, cases). Prick the bottom, line each shell with wax paper or foil, and fill to the top with raw rice or dried beans. Bake in the preheated oven for 10 minutes. Remove the foil and rice or beans and bake until golden. Makes one 9-inch shell, or about 4 small tart shells.

## CRUMB SHELLS

*1½ cups crumbs*
*5½ Tbsp. butter*
*¼ cup sugar*

Preheat oven to 375°F. Make crumbs from any of the following: graham crackers, zwieback, chocolate or vanilla wafers, dried cake, cereal, soda crackers or gingersnaps. Use ½ cup finely ground nuts as a substitute for half of the crumbs if you like. Put the broken-up crumb ingredients in the container with the steel blade, and grind till fine. Add butter and sugar and process for 3 to 5 seconds, to a fine texture. Pat into a buttered pie tin or springform pan. Bake for 8 minutes for a crisp shell, or chill unbaked for 30 minutes before filling. Good with chiffon filling, ice cream or custard fillings. Makes one 9-inch shell.

# NUT CRUST

½ lb. nuts
3 Tbsp. sugar

Preheat oven to 400°F. Place the nuts (pecans, almonds, Brazil nuts or hazelnuts) in the container with the steel blade, and process with the sugar until finely ground. There should be 1½ cups ground nuts. Press against a heavily buttered pie plate. Bake in the preheated oven for 8 minutes. These shells may also be used chilled and unbaked. Makes one 9-inch shell.

# MERINGUE CRUMB SHELLS

1 cup cookie crumbs
¼ lb. nuts (1 cup)
6 egg whites
¼ tsp. cream of tartar
2 cups superfine
   granulated sugar
1 tsp. flavoring extract

Preheat oven to 275°F. Place broken-up cookies (graham crackers, chocolate or vanilla wafers, macaroons) and the nuts (pecans, walnuts or hazelnuts, etc.) in the container with the steel blade, and chop coarsely. There should be an equal volume of nut crumbs and cookie crumbs. Make a meringue by beating egg whites with cream of tartar until stiff but not dry. Add confectioners' sugar gradually, 1 tablespoon at a time. Fold in the nuts, crumbs and flavoring. Spread into 2 buttered and floured 9-inch pie plates, piling meringue high around the edge. Or pile the meringue into buttered and floured 9-inch false-bottom layer pans, or into one 8-inch springform pan. Bake in the preheated oven for 1 to 1½ hours, or until the meringue begins to shrink from the sides of the pan. When baking in a deep springform pan, allow 20 to 30 minutes more. Fill the pies with an airy filling or ice cream. If meringue is in layers or a single cake, it may be frosted with flavored whipped cream. Makes two 9-inch shells.

# SAUCES,
# SALAD DRESSINGS,
# BUTTERS

—◆—

Good stock is the mother of great sauces. With frozen stocks on hand, the repertoire of basic classical sauces is within the reach of anyone. For basic stocks see Chapter 5.

The Cuisinart™ Food Processor is a particularly felicitous appliance for making egg-based sauces—hollandaise, mayonnaise, béarnaise, and all their variations. With speed and efficiency it will produce beautifully homogenized sauces.

Compound butters, so important in some sauces and as an addition to finishing a dish, are blended effortlessly.

Vinaigrette and other salad dressings are melded in the processor in a fraction of the time it would take by hand.

Although not essentially a product for the processor, smooth cream sauces are so easily made in the machine, needing only proper cooking after the ingredients have been blended, that it is a joy to take advantage of the speed and power of the processor for making unfailingly smooth, perfect béchamels and their ilk, in a matter of seconds.

## BROWN SAUCE (SAUCE ESPAGNOLE)

This sauce is a cornerstone of French cooking and the base for many other sauces.

*½ cup chopped suet, or 5 Tbsp. butter and 3 Tbsp. oil*
*3 carrots, cut up*
*2 medium-size onions, cut up*
*1 celery rib, cut up*
*1 garlic clove, cut up*
*½ cup flour*
*2 Tbsp. tomato paste*
*1 tsp. meat glaze or extract (optional)*
*8 cups Beef Stock (see Index)*
*3 parsley sprigs*
*2 fresh thyme sprigs, or ½ tsp. dried thyme*
*1 celery rib with leaves*
*1 bay leaf*
*¼ cup sherry*
*salt and pepper*

If you are using suet, chop it with the steel blade and render it in a heavy skillet over low heat, stirring constantly, until the bits are crisp but not overbrowned. Remove the suet cracklings from the pan with a slotted spoon and discard. Make 1 cup of *mirepoix* by chopping the vegetables in the machine, with the steel blade. Brown *mirepoix* slowly in the suet drippings, or in the butter and oil, stirring to prevent burning. Add flour and continue to brown very slowly. Stir in tomato paste, meat glaze and 4 cups of the stock. Make a *bouquet garni* with the herbs and tie in cheesecloth. Add *bouquet garni* to the saucepan. Bring the mixture to a boil and simmer for 3 hours. Remove the *bouquet garni*. Place the mixture in the container with the steel blade, and purée 2 cups at a time. Let the sauce stand in the refrigerator overnight. Remove the fat and strain, then add remaining 4 cups of beef stock and the sherry and simmer for 2 hours longer. Season to taste. Strain the sauce again and cool. Makes about 5 cups.

## VARIATIONS ON BROWN SAUCE
## (SAUCE ESPAGNOLE)

*Sauce Demi-Glace*—Excellent served with steak. Combine 1 cup Sauce Espagnole, 1 cup beef stock and ½ cup chopped mushrooms. Simmer until thick. Strain and add ½ cup Marsala wine. Keep warm in a double boiler. Makes about 2 cups.

*Sauce Chasseur*—Beautiful with beef. Put 3 tablespoons butter and 3 peeled shallots in the container and process with the steel blade. Slice ½ pound mushrooms with the slicing disc, and sauté them with the shallots and butter. Add ½ cup white wine and 2 cups stock. Reduce by half. Add 2 tablespoons tomato paste and 1 cup Brown Sauce. Season to taste and reheat. Makes about 2 cups.

*Madeira Sauce I*—Classical with ham or filet mignon. Simmer 1½ cups Brown Sauce and reduce to 1 cup. Add 1 tablespoon meat glaze and ½ cup Madeira wine. Stir in 2 tablespoons currant jelly. Keep hot in double boiler and add 1 tablespoon butter. Makes about 1½ cups.

*Madeira Sauce II*—Special for roast poultry. Make Madeira Sauce I with 1½ cups chicken Velouté (see Index) instead of brown sauce, and add 2 cups halved seedless grapes. Makes about 3 cups.

*Sauce Périgourdine*—Excellent with filet of beef. Make Madeira Sauce I; add 2 truffles, peeled and chopped, and 2 tablespoons of their liquor. Heat the sauce, then remove from the heat. Add 2 tablespoons butter, bit by bit. Makes 1¼ cups.

*Sauce Lyonnaise*—Good with leftover meats. Process with the steel blade 2 tablespoons butter and 1 small cut-up onion. Cook the onion butter until golden. Add ¼ cup white vinegar to this. Boil down to half, and add 1 cup of Brown Sauce. Serve with chopped parsley. Makes 1¼ cups.

*Sauce Bordelaise*—Delicious with grilled meats. Process with the steel blade 2 tablespoons butter, 1 small cut-up onion and 2 shallots. Cook onion, shallots and butter until golden. Add 1 cup red wine and ¼ cup garlic vinegar. Boil this down to half, and add 1 cup Brown Sauce. Serve with chopped parsley. Makes about 1½ cups.

*Sauce Diable*—Fine for short ribs and poultry. Blend with the steel blade 2 shallots with ¾ cup dry white wine, 1 tablespoon white vinegar, 1 teaspoon cracked black or green peppercorns and 1 tablespoon A.1. Sauce. Cook all ingredients until they are boiled down by half. Add 1 cup Brown Sauce and strain. Makes about 1½ cups.

*Mustard Sauce*—Blend with the steel blade 1 cut-up onion, 4 tablespoons butter, ¼ teaspoon dried thyme, ¾ cup white wine, 1 tablespoon prepared

Dijon mustard. Season with salt and pepper. Boil down to half. Add to 1 cup Brown Sauce. Makes about 1½ cups.

*Sauce Piquante*—Goes well with pork or previously cooked meats. Combine ½ cup tarragon vinegar, 2 cups Brown Sauce, 1 tablespoon each of minced tarragon, parsley or chervil, capers and chopped sour pickles. Makes about 2 cups.

*Orange Sauce*—Ideal for duck. Combine 2 cups Brown Sauce with ½ cup undiluted frozen orange juice, ¼ cup Triple Sec, 2 tablespoons sugar and 1 tablespoon julienned orange rind (prepared using the shredding disc). Makes about 2 cups.

*Mint Sauce*—For lamb. Combine ½ cup packed fresh mint, 1 tablespoon wine vinegar, 1 tablespoon brown sugar, 1 cup Brown Sauce. Blend together with the steel blade and simmer for 15 minutes. Makes about 1 cup.

# WHITE SAUCES

White sauces can be made in the processor, without first melting the butter and cooking the flour, as long as the sauce is slowly cooked afterwards until thick.

There are three consistencies of white cream sauce or Béchamel—thin, medium and thick.

*Thin*
1 Tbsp. butter
1 Tbsp. flour
1 cup milk

*Medium*
2 Tbsp. butter
2 Tbsp. flour
1 cup milk

*Thick*
3 Tbsp. butter
3 Tbsp. flour
1 cup milk

All recipes in this book call for a medium sauce unless otherwise indicated.

# SAUCE BÉCHAMEL (CREAM SAUCE), MEDIUM

*2 Tbsp. butter*
*2 Tbsp. flour*
*1 cup milk, scalded*
*salt and pepper*

Place butter and flour in the container with the steel blade, and process for 3 to 5 seconds, or until the flour disappears. With the motor running, add scalded milk through the tube and process until smooth. Cook, stirring constantly, until thickened. Season to taste. Makes 1 cup.

## COMPOUND WHITE SAUCES

*Sauce Mornay*—Particularly good for eggs, fish and vegetables. Prepare 2 cups Sauce Béchamel, made with white stock or milk, ¼ cup grated Swiss cheese, ¼ cup grated Parmesan cheese, 2 egg yolks and 1 tablespoon cream. Grate the cheeses with the steel blade. Combine Béchamel, cheeses, egg yolks and cream in the container with the steel blade, and blend until smooth. Heat in a double boiler. For an interesting switch, try Roquefort cheese; marvelous with eggs or chicken. Makes about 2½ cups.

*Sauce Véronique*—Make Béchamel with 1½ cups milk and ½ cup dry white wine. Add ½ cup halved seedless grapes when reheating. Makes 2½ cups.

*Fish Béchamel*—Make 2 cups Béchamel with 1 cup milk and 1 cup fish stock or 1 cup clam juice. Makes 2 cups.

*Sauce Aurore*—Prepare Fish Béchamel and add 3 tablespoons tomato paste. Makes 2 cups.

*Caper Sauce*—Good for chicken, fish or boiled meat such as tongue or mutton. Make Béchamel with the appropriate stock: chicken for poultry; *fumet* for fish; meat stock, or broth in which meat has been cooked, for meat. For a creamier sauce use half cream, half stock. At the end incorporate 6 tablespoons chopped capers, juice of ½ lemon and 2 tablespoons butter into the sauce, turning the machine on and off.

*Cucumber Sauce*—Complementary with fish and vegetables. Peel and seed 3 cucumbers, and chop with the steel blade. Drain cucumbers and sauté them in 6 tablespoons butter until soft. Purée cucumbers with the steel blade. Add purée to 2 cups Béchamel with juice of 1 lemon and 1 teaspoon grated lemon zest. Reheat. Makes about 3 cups.

*Horseradish Sauce*—Tried and true for boiled beef and smoked meats. Grate ½ cup fresh horseradish with the shredding blade. Add to 2 cups of hot Béchamel. (If prepared horseradish is used, drain first.) Makes 2¼ cups.

*Cheese Chive Sauce*—For vegetables, potatoes, noodles or eggs. Prepare ⅓ cup chopped chives or scallions and ½ cup grated Cheddar cheese. Process all together and add to 2 cups Béchamel. Makes about 3 cups.

# SAUCE VELOUTÉ

Sauce Velouté is a cream sauce made with chicken, fish or meat stock.

*2 Tbsp. butter*
*2 Tbsp. flour*
*1 cup stock, hot*
*salt and pepper*

Place butter and flour in the container with the steel blade, and process until the flour disappears, 3 to 5 seconds. With the motor running, add hot stock through the tube and process until smooth. Cook and stir until thick. Season to taste. Makes 1 cup medium velouté. For thicker or thinner veloutés follow the proportions for the Béchamel given on page 34.

## VELOUTÉ VARIATIONS

*Curry Sauce*—Cut up 1 medium-size onion, 2 large cooking apples and 1 garlic clove; melt 3 tablespoons butter. Purée with the steel blade the garlic, onion and apples, and sauté the mixture in the butter. Add 4 tablespoons curry powder, and process with 2 cups Sauce Velouté made with chicken or beef stock. Makes about 3 cups.

*Paprika Sauce*—For chicken or veal. Chop 1 medium-size onion. Sauté the onion in 3 tablespoons butter, blend in 3 tablespoons paprika, add 1 cup heavy cream, and cook gently for 10 minutes. Add this to 1 cup hot Béchamel or Velouté. Makes 2 cups.

*Sauce Bontemps*—For grilled meats and poultry. Chop ½ medium-size onion and cook in 2 tablespoons butter. Season with ½ teaspoon paprika, ½ teaspoon salt and ¼ teaspoon pepper. Add to 1 cup of cider. Over high heat reduce this to ⅔ cup. Stir reduction into 1 cup Velouté or Béchamel. Heat well, and finish with 3 tablespoons butter and 1 teaspoon dry mustard. Makes about 2 cups.

*Herb Sauce*—For veal or fish. Combine 1 tablespoon minced fresh chervil, or ½ teaspoon dried, 6 tablespoons minced parsley, 6 tablespoons minced fresh tarragon, or 1 tablespoon dried, 1 shallot, chopped with the steel blade, and juice of 1 lemon. Blend with 2 cups Velouté or Béchamel, using the steel blade. Reheat. Makes 2½ cups.

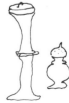

*Mushroom Sauce*—Slice ½ pound mushrooms with the slicing disc, and sauté in 3 tablespoons butter. Add to 2 cups Béchamel or Velouté. For a stronger sauce make Duxelles (see Index), and use the water expressed from the mushrooms as part of the velouté stock. Combine duxelles with mushroom velouté, and add ¼ pound mushrooms, sliced and sautéed, to finish. Makes 3 cups.

*Sauce Suprême*— Perfect with chicken. Simmer 2 cups thick Sauce Velouté, gradually adding ¾ cup heavy cream until the sauce is of a rich consistency. Season with salt and white pepper. Makes about 2½ cups.

*Sauce Allemande*—For sweetbreads, poached chicken, vegetables, eggs. Blend 4 egg yolks with ½ cup light cream and mix with 2 cups hot Sauce Suprême. Finish with 3 tablespoons heavy cream. Makes about 3 cups.

*Ivory Sauce*—For eggs, poultry, sweetbreads. Combine 3 tablespoons meat extract with 1 cup Sauce Suprême. Makes about 1 cup.

*Sauce Poulette*—For vegetables. Add 2 teaspoons lemon juice and 2 teaspoons chopped parsley to 2 cups Sauce Suprême. Makes 2 cups.

*Sauce Bercy*—Fine with fish. Chop 4 shallots and cook in ½ cup white wine until reduced by half. Add to 2 cups thick fish Velouté. Makes about 2¼ cups.

## SAUCE NANTUA

A beautiful sauce for *quenelles, sole en turban,* and other delicate seafood dishes.

*2 cups hot fish Velouté*
*⅓ cup cream, scalded*
*½ cup Fish Stock (see*
*    Index) or clam juice*
*salt and white pepper*
*½ cup Shrimp Butter (see*
*    Index)*

Heat the Sauce Velouté. Pour in the scalded cream and simmer until the sauce is reduced to 1½ cups. Add fish stock or clam juice, and seasonings to taste. Strain through a fine sieve or cheesecloth. Stir until smooth. Remove from heat and stir in the shrimp butter. Use at once or refrigerate, covered with plastic. When ready to serve, heat in a double boiler. Makes about 3 cups.

# EGG-AND-OIL-BASED SAUCES

## MAYONNAISE

Mayonnaise, although generally used cold, may be served warm; also it may be modified with innumerable seasonings or additions. This sauce can be used in a variety of dishes as well as for salads and cold plates.

*2 egg yolks*
*½ tsp. salt*
*1 tsp. dry mustard*
*3 Tbsp. lemon juice or*
*    vinegar*
*1¼ cups vegetable or*
*    olive oil*

Put all ingredients except the oil in the container with the steel or plastic blade. Process for a few seconds. Turn off the machine and scrape down the sides. With the machine running, add the oil through the tube in a thin stream. Blend until thick. Makes 1 cup.

## MAYONNAISE VARIATIONS

*Emerald Mayonnaise*—Process ¼ cup snipped chives, 4 parsley sprigs, ½ teaspoon dried tarragon, ½ teaspoon dried thyme, 1 cut-up scallion, ½ packed cup of spinach, watercress or sorrel, and ½ teaspoon dry mustard with 2 tablespoons tarragon vinegar, using the steel blade. Add 1½ cups mayonnaise and whisk together. Makes about 1½ cups

*Tomato Anchovy Mayonnaise*—Blend with the steel blade ¼ cup tomato purée, 2 tablespoons chives, 2 or 3 anchovy fillets and ½ cup mayonnaise. Fold into 1 additional cup mayonnaise. Makes about 1¾ cups.

*Horseradish Mayonnaise*—Whip ½ cup heavy cream with the plastic blade, and blend in ¼ cup grated fresh horseradish, grated with the shredding disc, or ½ cup drained prepared horseradish. Fold into 1 cup mayonnaise. Try adding ¼ cup applesauce plus 1 teaspoon brandy to the horseradish mix for a sweet-sour fillip. Makes about 2 cups.

*Mustard Mayonnaise*—Whip 1 cup heavy cream with the plastic blade, and fold it into 1 cup mayonnaise. Stir in 2 teaspoons prepared mustard. Makes about 3 cups.

*Sauce Tartare*—Chop 3 small sweet pickles with 2 tablespoons capers, 1 teaspoon prepared mustard, 1 tablespoon chives, using the steel blade, and fold into 1 cup mayonnaise. Makes 1 cup.

*Sauce Rémoulade*—Make Sauce Tartare, and add ½ teaspoon anchovy paste or 2 minced anchovies. Makes about 1 cup.

*Curry Mayonnaise*—Particularly good with artichokes and *crudités*. Add 1 or more tablespoons curry powder, to taste, to 1 cup mayonnaise. Makes about 1 cup.

*Banana Mayonnaise*—For fruits. Chop 4 tablespoons dry-roasted peanuts, with the steel blade, blending in 1 cut-up small banana. Fold into 1 cup mayonnaise. Makes about 1½ cups.

*Mayonnaise Indienne*—For seafood salads. Mix 1 cup mayonnaise, ¼ teaspoon ground coriander, ¼ teaspoon ground cuminseed, 2 tablespoons capers and 1 teaspoon ground turmeric. Makes about 1 cup.

*Piquant Mayonnaise*—For fish mousse or seafood salads. Blend all together 1 cup mayonnaise, 3 tablespoons chili sauce, 1 teaspoon Worcestershire sauce, ¼ cup heavy cream, 1 teaspoon garlic salt, 2 tablespoons chopped pickles. Makes 1½ cups.

*Sauce Louis*—Mix together 1 cup mayonnaise, 2 tablespoons drained capers, 1 tablespoon prepared mustard, ½ teaspoon dried tarragon, ¼ teapoon dried chervil, ¼ cup chopped fresh chives. Makes about 1 cup.

## HARD-COOKED-EGG MAYONNAISE (SAUCE GRIBICHE)

2 hard-cooked eggs, separated
1 whole raw egg
1 cup oil
2 medium-sweet pickles
2 Tbsp. capers (optional)
1 tsp. salt
½ tsp. white pepper
pinch of ground saffron (optional)

Put the hard-cooked egg yolks in the processor with the steel blade, and blend by turning the machine on and immediately off. Scrape down and add the whole raw egg. Process for 3 seconds; scrape down. With the motor running, slowly pour the oil through the tube. Check the consistency of the mayonnaise; if it seems thin add a little more oil and again check. Continue to add oil until the desired thickness is achieved. Set aside. Process the remaining ingredients with the steel blade for 3 seconds, and incorporate them in the mayonnaise. Makes about 2 cups.

# HOLLANDAISE

The queen of egg sauces can be used with all sorts of dishes when combined with a variety of subtle flavorings.

*6 egg yolks*
*4 Tbsp. lemon juice*
*1 tsp. salt*
*dash of cayenne*
*½ lb. butter (2 sticks), cut up*

Place in the container with the steel blade the egg yolks, lemon juice, salt and cayenne. Switch the processor on and immediately off. Heat the butter to the boiling point. With the motor running, pour the hot butter through the tube in a steady stream. As soon as all butter is used, turn off the motor. Thicken the sauce over hot but not boiling water. If the sauce curdles, whisk in 2 tablespoons hot water, little by little. Makes 1½ cups.

## VARIATIONS ON HOLLANDAISE

*Sauce Mousseline*—A lighter version of Hollandaise. Fold in 1 cup whipped cream, whipped with the plastic blade, to 2 cups Hollandaise. Makes 3 cups.

*Shrimp Hollandaise*—Appetizing with fish or cauliflower. Substitute Shrimp Butter (see Index) for a part of the plain butter in 2 cups Hollandaise. Makes 2 cups.

*Anchovy Hollandaise*—For broiled tomatoes, broccoli, baked eggs. Substitute Anchovy Butter (see Index) for a part of the plain butter in 2 cups Hollandaise. Makes 2 cups.

*Sauce Maltaise*—A natural for asparagus. Add 4 tablespoons fresh orange juice and the grated zest of ½ orange to 2 cups Hollandaise. Makes 2¼ cups.

*Almond Hollandaise*—Dresses vegetables and fish. Add ½ cup chopped or slivered almonds, toasted in butter, to 2 cups Hollandaise. Makes 2¼ cups.

*Duxelles Hollandaise*—For fish or chicken dishes. Fold ¾ cup Duxelles (see Index) into 2 cups Hollandaise. Makes 2½ cups.

## BÉARNAISE SAUCE

*4 Tbsp. white wine*
*4 Tbsp. white vinegar*
*4 tsp. minced shallots*
*2 tsp. dried tarragon*
*6 egg yolks*
*½ lb. butter (2 sticks)*
*white pepper*

Cook together the white wine, vinegar, shallots and tarragon until the mixture is reduced by one third. Place it in the container with the steel blade, and process with the egg yolks, switching the machine on and immediately off. Heat the butter to boiling. With the motor running, pour butter through the tube in a steady stream until it is all used. Season with pepper to taste. Thicken as for Hollandaise. Makes 1½ cups.

## VARIATIONS ON SAUCE BÉARNAISE

*Sauce Choron*—For grilled and sautéed meats. Add 6 tablespoons tomato paste to 2 cups Béarnaise Sauce.

*Sauce Foyot*—For meats. Add 2 teaspoons meat extract to 2 cups Béarnaise Sauce.

*Sauce Beauharnaise*—Pleasing with grilled fish. Add 2 tablespoons tarragon butter (see Green Butter) to 2 cups of Béarnaise.

## CREOLE SAUCE

*1 cup cut-up onion*
*2 celery ribs, cut up*
*½ cup cut-up green*
*pepper*
*2 garlic cloves*
*1 Tbsp. oil*
*2 Tbsp. butter*
*2 cups canned tomatoes,*
*drained*
*1 Tbsp. tomato paste*
*1 tsp. chili powder*
*1 tsp. brown sugar*
*1 bay leaf*
*¼ tsp. dried thyme*
*½ cup sliced stuffed olives*
*(optional)*
*2 cups stock (fish, meat,*
*or poultry)*

Chop the onion, celery, green pepper and garlic with the steel blade, and sauté them in the oil and butter. Add tomatoes and other ingredients. Simmer for 1 hour, stirring from time to time. Makes about 3½ cups.

# BOLOGNESE MEAT SAUCE

2 onions, cut up
1 celery rib, cut up
1 carrot, cut up
6 slices of bacon, cut up
½ lb. raw lean beef,
　cubed
salt and pepper
¼ tsp. grated nutmeg
2 cups canned tomatoes
1½ cups Beef Stock (see
　Index)
½ cup dry white wine
1 cup mushrooms,
　quartered
1 Tbsp. butter

Chop the vegetables together with the steel blade. Fry the bacon in a heavy kettle. Remove bacon pieces and drain off half of the fat. Add the processed vegetables, and cook together until vegetables are soft. Remove them with a slotted spoon and set aside. Grind the beef and bacon with the steel blade for 5 to 8 seconds. In the pan in which the vegetables were cooked quickly sauté the meat until beef loses its color. Season with salt and pepper to taste, and nutmeg. Add tomatoes, stock, processed vegetables and wine, and simmer uncovered for 2 to 3 hours. Slice the mushrooms with the slicing disc. Sauté them in butter and add to the sauce. Simmer for 30 minutes longer. Makes about 2½ cups.

# VEGETABLE SAUCE FOR MEAT OR POULTRY

½ cup cut-up carrot
¼ cup cut-up onion
½ cup cut-up celery
4 Tbsp. butter
4 lettuce leaves, torn up
1 cup white stock (chicken
　or veal)
½ cup cut-up cooked
　broccoli
½ cup cooked or canned
　lima beans, or 1 cup
　cooked black-eyed peas
¾ cup dry white wine
salt and pepper

Process carrot, onion and celery with the shredding disc. Sauté them in butter and add lettuce leaves. Add the stock (see Index), broccoli, beans and wine. Season to taste. Heat to serve. Very good with ham steaks. Makes about 2 cups.

## MEXICAN FISH SAUCE

*1 green pepper, cut up*
*1 onion, cut up*
*1 garlic clove*
*4 Tbsp. vegetable oil*
*2 tsp. flour*
*⅛ tsp. ground cloves*
*⅛ tsp. ground cinnamon*
*½ tsp. chili powder*
*2 tsp. sugar*
*1 Tbsp. wine vinegar*
*½ lemon, sliced*
*1 Tbsp. celery leaves*
*1 Tbsp. cilantro (optional)*
*2 cups tomato sauce*
*1 hard-cooked egg,*
*chopped*
*salt and pepper*

Process green pepper, onion and garlic together with the steel blade for 5 to 7 seconds. Cook vegetables in the oil until soft. Add the flour, and let it brown a bit. Add remaining ingredients except the hard-cooked egg. Simmer for 30 minutes. When ready to serve, gently stir in the egg, and season to taste. Makes 1½ cups.

## PLUM SAUCE

This sauce is excellent for game or fresh ham.

*2 cans (16 oz. each)*
*purple plums, cut up*
*1 medium-size onion, cut*
*up*
*¼ lb. butter (1 stick)*
*½ cup lemon juice*
*½ cup brown sugar*
*½ cup currant jelly*
*1 tsp. ground ginger*
*1 Tbsp. wine vinegar*

Drain the plums and reserve the juice. Pit the fruit and purée in the processor with the steel blade. Set aside. Chop the onion and sauté it in 2 tablespoons butter until golden. Add the plum purée, the rest of the butter, the remaining ingredients and the plum juice. Simmer until thickened. Makes about 3 cups.

# AVOCADO SAUCE

Delightful with vegetable aspics and cold seafood.

*1 Tbsp. lime juice*
*2 Tbsp. heavy cream*
*4 drops of Tabasco*
*1 medium-size avocado,*
  *cut up*
*1 tsp. mild mustard*

Process all ingredients together with the steel blade for 3 to 5 seconds. Serve cold. Makes about 1 cup.

# DILL SAUCE

*1 hard-cooked egg yolk*
*1 raw egg yolk*
*½ cup salad oil*
*1 Tbsp. vinegar*
*dash of Worcestershire*
  *sauce*
*½ tsp. dry mustard*
*¼ tsp. salt*
*¼ tsp. sugar*
*pepper*
*¼ cup heavy cream*
*2 Tbsp. fresh dill, or 1*
  *tsp. dried dill*

Process with the steel blade the cooked and raw egg yolks, slowly adding the oil through the tube. Add the vinegar, Worcestershire and seasonings, turning the machine on and off. Before serving, fold in the cream, whipped with the plastic blade, and add the dill. Serve cold. Makes about 1 cup.

# COLD CUCUMBER SAUCE

*4 Tbsp. snipped chives*
*1 cucumber, cut up*
*½ tsp. dried tarragon*
*1 Tbsp. chopped onion*
*1 cup yogurt*
*½ cup cottage cheese*
*1 Tbsp. vinegar*
*salt and pepper*

Process all the ingredients together with the steel blade for 3 to 5 seconds. Serve with seafood, vegetables or fish aspics. Makes about 1½ cups.

## WHITE BUTTER SAUCE

Superb with fish.

4 parsley sprigs
½ lb. sweet butter (2
    sticks), cut up
    and softened
⅓ cup lemon juice
⅓ cup clam juice
⅓ cup heavy cream
salt and pepper

Put the parsley sprigs in the container with the steel blade and blend with the softened cut-up butter until thoroughly mixed. With the motor running, slowly pour lemon and clam juices through the tube, then add the cream. Continue to blend until the sauce thickens. Season to taste. Makes about 1 cup.

## CHAUD-FROID

The handsome sauce for masking cold dishes.

2 cups hot Sauce Velouté
    (see Index)
2 envelopes unflavored
    gelatin
½ cup stock

Make the velouté, using the stock appropriate to the dish (chicken, veal, fish, vegetable). Soften the gelatin in ½ cup stock, and dissolve it in the hot velouté. Whisk. Set the mixture in a pan over ice. When thick, brush or spoon the *chaud-froid* on the food to be masked. If the sauce becomes too set, set the bowl over hot water for a bit until sauce becomes manageable again. Chill the coated pieces until set. Makes 2 cups.

## CRESS SAUCE

For grilled meats and hamburgers.

3 cups cut-up watercress
1 green pepper, cut up
2 scallions, cut up
4 Tbsp. olive or salad oil
1 tsp. tarragon vinegar

Process all together with the steel blade for 5 seconds. Makes about ½ cup.

# SALAD DRESSINGS

With the food processor salad dressings are smoother. Also all manner of marvelous ingredients can be homogenized into the mixture for splendid results.

## OIL AND VINEGAR DRESSING

*¼ cup vinegar*
*1 cup oil*
*½ tsp. salt*
*¼ tsp. pepper*

Place all ingredients in the container with the steel blade, and homogenize. Makes 1¼ cups.

## OIL AND VINEGAR PLUS

Blend with basic Oil and Vinegar Dressing.

*Chutney Dressing*—For fruit or chicken. Add ½ cup chutney chopped.

*Blue Cheese and Bacon Dressing*—For plain greens. Add 4 tablespoons blue cheese and 3 slices of bacon, cooked and crumbled.

*Watercress Dressing*—For vegetable salad. Add ½ cup watercress and 2 hard-cooked egg yolks.

*Anchovy Dressing*—For celery, endive, cooked vegetables. Add 2 anchovy fillets.

*Onion Curry Dressing*—For celeriac (celery root) or apple. Add 1 tablespoon minced onion sautéed in oil and 1 teaspoon curry powder.

*Mustard Cream Dressing*—For celeriac (celery root), ham salad, chef's salad. Add 3 tablespoons heavy cream and 1 tablespoon prepared mustard.

*Caper Dressing*—For potato or seafood salads. Add 1 hard-cooked egg, cut up, 1 tablespoon capers and 6 drops of Tabasco.

*Caviar Dressing*—For avocados, endive, beet and fish salads. Add 2 tablespoons red caviar and 1 hard-cooked egg, cut up.

*Sour Cream and Cheese Dressing*—For tomatoes, chicken or green salads. Add 7 tablespoons sour cream and 2 tablespoons grated sharp cheese.

*Chiffonade Dressing*—For greens, endive, citrus salads. Add 3 hard-cooked eggs, cut up, 1 cooked beet, cut up, and 1 tablespoon minced parsley.

*Garlic Dressing*—For greens, tomatoes, vegetable salads. Add 1 or 2 garlic cloves, ¼ teaspoon dry mustard and ¼ teaspoon cayenne.

*Honey Dressing*—For fruit salads. Add ¼ cup honey.

## SAUCE VINAIGRETTE

Good with fish, artichokes, cold asparagus.

*¼ green pepper, cut up*
*1 tsp. minced chives*
*1 tsp. minced parsley*
*1 tsp. minced fresh basil*
*½ Tbsp. minced capers*
*2 small pickles, cut up*
*1 cup Oil and Vinegar*
 *Dressing*
*salt and pepper*

Blend all together with the steel blade for 3 to 5 seconds. Makes about 1 cup.

————

# CREAMY DRESSINGS

Creamy dressings can be made with a base of sour cream, cream cheese, cooked dressing or sweet cream.

## COOKED DRESSING

*2 eggs*
*1 tsp. sugar*
*1 tsp. dry mustard*
*3 Tbsp. vinegar*
*1 Tbsp. heavy cream*
*salt and pepper*

Put the steel blade in the container and blend all ingredients. Add salt and pepper to taste. Cook in the top part of a double boiler over simmering water until dressing thickens. Makes about 1 cup.

## COOKED DRESSING PLUS

Blend with cooled cooked dressing.

*Tropical Dressing*—For fruits. Add ½ cup crushed pineapple and 2 tablespoons lemon juice.

*Siennese Dressing*—Good for tomatoes or green vegetables. Add 3 tablespoons minced fresh basil, or 1 teaspoon dried, 1 garlic clove, 1 tablespoon grated Parmesan cheese and black pepper to taste.

*Pimiento Dressing*—For cold fish or raw vegetables. Add 1 pimiento, minced, and 1 tablespoon minced parsley.

## SOUR-CREAM DRESSING

2 Tbsp. sugar
¼ cup white vinegar
2 eggs
1 cup sour cream
½ tsp. salt
½ tsp. dry mustard

Put the steel blade in the container and blend all ingredients. Cook in the top part of a double boiler over simmering water, stirring constantly, until just thick. Dilute with cream or fruit juice, if needed. Makes about 2 cups.

## SOUR-CREAM DRESSING PLUS

Blend with the cooled basic recipe, using the steel blade.

*Cucumber Dressing*—For potato salad, fish, cucumbers. Add 1 cucumber, seeded and cut up, and 1 teaspoon dried dill, or 2 tablespoons minced fresh dill.

*Onion Dressing*—For greens, potato salad, cold vegetables. Add 1 Tbsp. minced onion and a pinch of sugar.

*Green Pepper Dressing*—For aspics. Add ¼ cup watercress and ¼ green pepper.

*Vermouth Dressing*—For fish or fruits. In the basic recipe use dry vermouth instead of vinegar.

# GREEN GODDESS DRESSING

For green salads and seafood.

*1 egg yolk*
*½ tsp. salt*
*2 Tbsp. tarragon vinegar*
*4 anchovy fillets*
*1 cup salad oil*
*¼ cup heavy cream*
*1 Tbsp. lemon juice*
*¼ cup snipped chives*
*2 Tbsp. minced fresh*
  *tarragon, or ½ tsp.*
  *dried*
*2 scallions, cut up*

Place the steel blade in the container and add egg yolk, salt, vinegar and anchovies; blend. With the motor running, pour in the oil, then add remaining ingredients. Makes about 1 cup.

This dressing can be made by incorporating the chopped greens in 1½ cups Mayonnaise (see Index).

# PROCESSOR CAESAR DRESSING

The advantage of this dressing is that it can be made ahead. Although it is not the dramatic do-it-on-the-spot original recipe, it is a delicious approximation.

*2 egg yolks*
*½ cup olive oil*
*¼ cup wine vinegar*
*1 garlic clove*
*6 anchovies*
*1 tsp. prepared mustard*
*pepper*
*½ cup grated Parmesan*
  *cheese*

Place all ingredients in the container with the steel blade and blend until smooth. Serve with romaine or other greens, and sautéed croutons. Makes about 2 cups.

# RAVIGOTE DRESSING

For cold artichokes, shrimps, tossed greens.

*1 cup oil*
*¼ cup vinegar*
*1 shallot*
*1 Tbsp. prepared mustard*
*1 hard-cooked egg, cut up*
*1 Tbsp. capers*
*1 tsp. each of dried*
  *tarragon, chives, and*
  *chervil, or 1 Tbsp. each*
  *of fresh herbs*

Place all ingredients in the container with the steel blade and blend together for 4 or 5 seconds. Makes about 1½ cups.

# CREAM-CHEESE DRESSING

Very good with asparagus, also with bacon-spinach salad and cold cooked vegetables.

*3 oz. cream cheese*
*1 tsp. salt*
*½ tsp. paprika*
*1 Tbsp. lemon juice*
*1 Tbsp. minced chervil*
*1 egg yolk*
*¼ cup oil*

Place in the container with the steel blade all ingredients except the oil; blend. With the motor running, pour the oil through the tube. Makes about 1 cup.

Any one of the soft French herb-flavored cheeses can be substituted for the cream cheese.

———

# COMPOUND BUTTERS

Compound butters give the dullest canapés verve and are often good enough to serve alone as a dip or as a spread with honest-to-goodness bread or special crackers. These butters freeze beautifully. They can be used in cooking to perk up simple dishes, finish sauces, or glorify vegetables. Also, compound butters, mixed with puréed hard-cooked egg yolks, are excellent for binding stuffed eggs.

## COMPOUND BUTTER METHOD

Process with the steel blade ¼ pound (1 stick) softened butter with the desired flavoring. Do not overprocess; 10 seconds should be enough.

*Anchovy Butter*—Spread on toast as a base for hard-cooked egg or tomato slices, topped with mashed tuna or salmon. Use with fish dishes, green vegetables or pasta.

Process ¼ pound (1 stick) cut-up butter with the steel blade, with 3 tablespoons anchovy paste or 2 anchovy fillets.

*Bovril Butter*—For toasted bread canapés, and to finish meat sauces. Spread this butter on thin white bread fingers and bake in 350°F. oven until golden; these canapés may be kept in an airtight box for 2 weeks.

Process ¼ pound (1 stick) cut-up butter, with 1 tablespoon Bovril, using the steel blade.

*Green Butter*—Use as a base for fish or chicken canapés or under vegetable spreads. Dress cooked vegetables or fish, chicken dishes or rice with this.

Using the steel blade, process ¼ pound (1 stick) cut-up butter with 6 parsley sprigs, 2 tablespoons fresh tarragon or ½ teaspoon dried, a small handful of chives and 2 shallots, or use the herbs of your choice—basil for beef, mint for lamb, tarragon for chicken.

*Horseradish Butter*—For roast beef or fish appetizers and in cold meat sandwiches.

Process 4 tablespoons (½ stick) butter with 2 tablespoons prepared horseradish, using the steel blade.

*Piquant Butter*—To spark ham or beef canapés on dark breads.

Process ¼ pound (1 stick) butter with 1½ teaspoons dry mustard, 1 tablespoon Worcestershire sauce or A.1. Sauce, and 1 teaspoon grated onion.

*Shrimp Butter*—Cover ½ pound *unpeeled* raw shrimps with boiling water and cook uncovered for 5 minutes. Chop the shrimps, shells and all, in the container with the steel blade; blend well. Turn off the machine, scrape down the sides, and process again until you have a purée or mush. Add the purée to 2 tablespoons hot water and ¼ pound (1 stick) unsalted butter and cook in the top part of a double boiler over simmering water for 10 minutes. Season to taste with salt and white pepper. Strain through a fine sieve or cheesecloth into a bowl, cover, and refrigerate until ready to use. Discard the liquid that forms underneath the hardened butter.

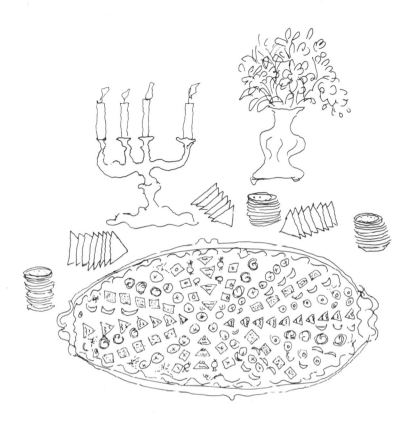

# HORS D'OEUVRE

━━◆━━

Here is where the Cuisinart™ Food Processor wins a blue ribbon. You can begin with fresh ingredients or invent with what's on hand—cheese ends, bits of cooked meat, leftover sauces, nuts, vegetables. Some of the more memorable, never-to-be-repeated dips and spreads may come into being through the magic of processing. With a flick of the switch, you can turn out melt-in-the-mouth cocktail pastries, make steak tartar, compound butters.

As Escoffier said, "Sufficient has been said to allow of any cook, with a little taste and inventiveness, easily making an endless variety of combinations."

# CHEESE ROUNDS

2 oz. Parmesan cheese, approximately
1½ cups cubed sharp cheese
1 Tbsp. Cognac
¼ tsp. salt
⅜ lb. butter (1½ sticks) cut up
1 to 1½ cups flour

Place the steel blade in the bowl and grate enough cheese to make ¼ cup. Add the cubed sharp cheese, the Cognac, salt and cut-up butter. Blend until smooth. With the motor running, gradually add flour through the tube until a ball of dough forms around the blade. Chill the dough for 1 hour or more. Roll out dough on a floured surface into a rectangle ¼ inch thick. Cut into rounds. Lay the rounds on a lightly greased cookie sheet. Place in a *cold* oven. Set the temperature at 400°F. and bake for 10 to 15 minutes. Watch carefully as these burn easily. They will keep in a tightly covered tin.

# PARMESAN CHEESE DROPS

½ cup grated Parmesan cheese
½ cup sifted flour
1 cup heavy cream
½ tsp. salt

Preheat oven to 450°F. Grate the cheese in the processor with the steel blade; set aside. Put flour, cream and salt in the processor bowl; blend until just smooth. Add grated cheese and whir for 3 seconds. Drop by teaspoon, 2 inches apart, on a greased cookie sheet. Bake for 8 to 10 minutes.

# CHEESE AND ALMOND FINGERS

¼ cup almonds
4 Tbsp. butter
3 Tbsp. light cream
½ cup grated Swiss or Cheddar cheese
salt and pepper

Chop the almonds with the steel blade, and sauté them in 1 tablespoon of the butter until golden; set aside. Blend other ingredients in the machine, using the steel blade. Season to taste. Spread cheese mixture on toast circles or points. Sprinkle with almonds and bake in a hot oven until bubbly.

## BAKED SHRIMP PASTE

½ cup toasted almonds
½ lb. cooked shrimps
8 oz. cream cheese, cubed
1 Tbsp. milk
3 shallots
1 tsp. prepared
   horseradish

Chop almonds in the processor, using the steel blade; set aside. Process all the other ingredients, until smooth. Put the paste in a 2-cup baking dish, and sprinkle the top with the almonds. Bake in a 375°F. oven for 15 minutes. Serve hot or cold with Melba toast.

## SHRIMP TOAST

½ lb. cooked fresh
   shrimps
½ lb. fat pork
6 water chestnuts
3 egg whites
1 inch of fresh gingerroot,
   peeled, cut up
1 tsp. sherry
salt and pepper
6 slices of bread, crusts
   removed, cut into
   squares or triangles
oil

Place first 6 ingredients in the processor; using the steel blade, blend to a paste. Season to taste. Spread mixture on bread. With a knife dipped into water, cut bread into small squares or triangles. Heat oil until it begins to smoke (375°F.) and fry the pieces, shrimp side down. Turn and fry the uncooked side. Drain on paper towels.

## CARL'S QUENELLE CANAPÉS

Cut thin white bread into rounds and sauté in butter. Lightly spread them with Fish Quenelle forcemeat (see Index). Press a small cooked shrimp into the center of each canapé. Using a pastry tube, pipe more quenelle forcemeat around the edge of the bread round. Spoon a thick dollop of Sauce Aurore (see Index) over the shrimp. Place canapés on a foil-lined cookie sheet, and bake in a preheated 375°F. oven for 10 to 15 minutes. These may be frozen before baking; place in one layer on a cookie sheet until frozen, then store in a covered container in the freezer. Thaw before baking. Makes about 6 dozen.

## CHICKEN-LIVER TOAST

½ cup cut-up Gruyère
    cheese
8 chicken livers
3 Tbsp. butter
3 anchovy fillets with oil
salt
toast squares, buttered
½ cup dried bread
    crumbs

Grate cheese with steel blade and set aside. Sauté livers in the butter. Put them in the processor with the anchovies and a little of their oil. Using the steel blade, purée the mixture until a spreadlike consistency is reached. Season with salt to taste. Spread on buttered toast squares. Top with crumbs and the grated cheese, and bake at 350°F. until crumbs are browned.

## MINIATURE POTATO PANCAKES

6 medium-size potatoes (2
    lb.), peeled and cut up
2 eggs
1 small onion, quartered
⅓ cup flour
1 tsp. salt
bacon fat or cooking oil

Preheat oven to 300°F. Using the shredding blade, put the peeled cut-up potatoes, a few at a time, in the tube. Press down with the plunger and continue adding potatoes until all are grated. Cover immediately with cold water to prevent discoloration. Put the steel blade in the bowl. Put eggs, onion, flour and salt into processor and blend for 10 seconds. Drain the potatoes and pat dry. Stir the batter into the potatoes. Drop batter by teaspoons into spitting hot (375°) fat or vegetable oil, and cook on both sides until crisp and lacy. Make a few at a time and transfer them to a heatproof platter in a 300°F. oven to keep warm. Serve with a side dish of sour cream or lingonberry preserves.

## GOUGÈRE

Prepare Cream-Puff Pastry (see Index) and incorporate into the dough ⅔ cup grated Swiss cheese and 1 teaspoon dry mustard, moistened with a little vinegar. Bake in the same fashion as cream puffs. These may be eaten *sans* filling, but they are doubly delectable when filled with anything that has an affinity for cheese and mustard.

# BOUCHÉES ANCHOIS

Prepare Cream-Puff Pastry (see Index). Substitute 1 cup of hot clam juice for the hot water, and add 1 tablespoon anchovy paste to the butter. Bake like small éclairs or in boat-shaped molds. These are good filled. Lobster, crab meat, minced clams or fish fillings bound with mayonnaise or sour cream—all suit these well.

## BENNE (SESAME SEED) WAFERS

*⅜ lb. butter (1½
   sticks) cut up
2 cups flour
1 tsp. salt
dash of cayenne pepper
ice water
1 cup sesame seeds
additional salt*

Preheat oven to 375°F. Put the steel blade in the container. Put in the cut-up butter with the flour, salt and cayenne. Blend until mealy. With the motor running, slowly add ice water through the tube until the ingredients form a ball of dough around the cutting blade. Roll out the dough on a floured board ⅛ inch thick, and cut into small round wafers. Sprinkle with sesame seeds, patting them down. Place on a cookie sheet, prick the dough and bake in the preheated oven for 15 to 20 minutes. While the wafers are still hot, sprinkle with salt. These may be kept in a covered tin and reheated in a slow oven to crisp.

## HOT TARTS AND CREAM PUFFS

Use Stay-Crisp Pastry or Cream-Cheese Pastry (see Index). Make tiny tart shells, partially bake them, then fill and bake again in a 425°F. oven for 10 to 15 minutes. Make Cream-Puff Pastry and shape tiny puffs. Bake, let them cool, then fill them, and heat through only until hot.

# MUSHROOM FILLING

½ lb. fresh mushrooms
1 garlic clove
3 Tbsp. butter
2 oz. brandy
½ teaspoon salt
pepper
½ cup sour cream

Trim off the tough ends of the stems, and quarter the mushrooms. Coarsely chop mushrooms and garlic in the processor, using the steel blade. Sauté the mixture in the butter until mushrooms are tender. Pour in the brandy and cook over high heat until brandy has evaporated. Season with the salt, and pepper to taste. Remove from the heat and add sour cream. Fill puffs or tarts.

# CREAM-CHEESE FILLING

Using cream cheese as a base, there are many possibilities for contriving different delicious fillings for hot tartlets. Let your imagination soar. Process smoked fish with cucumbers, or sardines with capers. Mix in anchovies, minced clams and water chestnuts. Use up leftovers, meat, chicken, or ham seasoned with your choice of bottled mustard, horseradish, beef extract, curry powder—whatever tickles your taste.

6 oz. cream cheese
2 Tbsp. butter
¼ cup sour cream
salt and pepper

Place cheese, butter and sour cream in the processor and blend with the steel blade. Season to taste. Using this as a base, make any of the following fillings.

### BACON-OLIVE FILLING

4 scallions, cut up
¾ cup pitted ripe olives
6 slices of bacon, cooked
  and crumbled

Place the steel blade in the bowl and chop the cut-up scallions with the ripe olives. Add the cream-cheese mixture and blend. Fold in the crumbled cooked bacon.

### MUSHROOM FILLING

½ lb. mushrooms,
  quartered
2 Tbsp. butter
2 egg yolks, beaten

Chop the mushrooms coarsely in the machine, using the steel blade. Cook mushrooms in the butter. Add beaten egg yolks and fold into the cream-cheese mixture.

CHUTNEY-CHEESE
   FILLING

*½ cup peanuts*
*⅓ cup chutney*
*1 ½ tsp. curry powder*

Chop peanuts fine in machine, using the steel blade; set aside. Chop chutney fine. Add chutney and curry powder to cream-cheese mixture and blend quickly. Fill the tarts, and sprinkle with the chopped peanuts.

## FLORENTINE FILLING

In menu language, "Florentine" means a spinach-based dish. Here are some bite-size Florentine delights as succulent an idea for finger food as they are for the customary entrées.

## SPINACH PURÉE

*1 ½ lb. fresh spinach, or 2*
   *pkg. (10 oz. each)*
   *frozen chopped spinach*
*½ cup light cream*
*pinch of grated nutmeg*
*salt*

Wash fresh spinach very well. Put in a large skillet but do not add water. Steam for 6 to 8 minutes, until the spinach is wilted, or cook frozen according to directions on the package. Drain and press dry. Put the spinach in the container with the steel blade, and add the cream, nutmeg, and salt to taste. Blend until puréed. Spoon spinach purée into baked tart shells, half filling them. Top with one of the following:

*Chopped cooked chicken livers*—dressed with any prepared bottled mustard sauce, sprinkled with minced parsley.
*Chopped smoked or canned salmon*—mixed with crumbled hard-cooked egg and moistened with Mayonnaise (see Index).
*Minced smoked fish*—masked with mayonnaise flavored with capers.
*Tiny shrimps*—dusted with lemon rind (which has been processed with the shredding disc in the machine), with a dollop of sour cream on top.

Tarts with Florentine filling can be served hot or cold, or a large single shell can be prepared for a luncheon dish.

# PIROZHKI

These little Russian pies are members of the international family of filled pastries—called *empanadas* in Spanish America, turnovers or pasties in England, *chaussons* in France, and egg rolls or won ton in the Orient. They are thin skins of flaky pastry filled with a variety of savory mixtures, then baked or fried and often served piping hot. When small, they make perfect appetizers; larger versions become satisfying entrées; cold turnovers are great picnic fare, either small or large.

For cocktail fare, the pastry can be cut into 2½-inch rounds, filled in the center, then topped with another round; the edges are sealed with egg white or water and crimped. Or they may be cut into 4-inch rounds to be folded over, sealed, and either baked or fried. If they are to be baked, glaze them with egg wash as in the Turnover Pastry recipe (see Index). These are delicious mouth-watering morsels which take to a variety of fillings.

## PIROZHKI OR TURNOVER FILLINGS

Use Turnover Pastry or Cream-Cheese Pastry (see Index). Be sure the fillings are cool before spooning onto the dough. Then fold over, or top with another circle of dough. Seal the edges with egg white or water, crimp, and then bake or fry.

## SHRIMP FILLING

*1 cup cooked shrimps*
*1 cup cooked rice*
*½ cup light cream*
*3 Tbsp. dry vermouth*

Using the steel blade, process shrimps in the machine for 3 to 5 seconds; set aside. Fold in remaining ingredients and spoon onto the dough.

## BEEF FILLING

*1 medium-size onion, cut up*
*½ lb. raw beef, cubed*
*3 Tbsp. butter*
*salt*
*3 Tbsp. sour cream or chili sauce*
*2 Tbsp. minced fresh dill*
*2 hard-cooked eggs*

Chop the onion with the beef cubes in the processor using the steel blade, and grind to hamburger consistency. Sauté onion and beef in the butter and add salt to taste. Put the sour cream or chili sauce, dill and hard-cooked eggs in the container and blend for 3 seconds. Fold the egg mixture into the meat; adjust seasoning to taste.

## PORK AND SHREDDED CABBAGE FILLING

*1 medium-size onion, quartered*
*1 lb. lean raw pork, cubed*
*½ lb. cabbage, cut up*
*4 Tbsp. butter or peanut oil*
*2 Tbsp. soy sauce*

Place quartered onion and the cubed pork in the processor with the steel blade, and grind for 8 to 10 seconds; set aside. Using the shredding disc, place wedges of cabbage in the tube. Press down with the plunger and continue adding wedges until all the cabbage is finely shredded. Mix onion, pork and cabbage, and lightly sauté in butter for 8 to 10 minutes, until the pork is no longer pink. Season with soy sauce; add more to taste if you like.

## COTTAGE CHEESE AND VEGETABLE FILLING

*½ cup cut-up carrots*
*¼ cup cut-up celery*
*½ green pepper, cut up*
*½ lb. cottage cheese*

Chop the cut-up vegetables together, using the steel blade. Fold them into the cottage cheese.

## EMPANADA FILLING

½ lb. raw top round of
  beef, cubed
1 garlic clove
½ cup cut-up onion
3 Tbsp. olive oil
1 Tbsp. flour
½ cup Beef Stock (see
  Index)
12 pitted ripe olives
½ cup raisins, plumped in
  hot water or sherry
½ tsp. chili powder
¼ tsp. ground cuminseed

Process the beef with the steel blade until it is coarsely ground; set aside. Chop garlic and onion. Sauté onion, garlic and beef in the oil. Add the flour and stir. Add beef stock and simmer for a few minutes. Chop the olives, and add with raisins, chili powder and cuminseed to the beef. Cool. Make empanada pastry, roll out, and fill. Fry or bake the filled turnovers.

## COLD SPREADS AND COLD FILLINGS

Spreads, although generally used in sandwiches or on toast or crackers, have a special appeal when served on a raw vegetable base—cucumber or zucchini rounds or wide flat carrot strips—or as stuffing for celery, endive or cooked artichoke leaves. Many can be used as tart or cream-puff fillings, or can be thinned to dip consistency by using more cream, mayonnaise, cream cheese—whatever the binder.

## LIPTAUER CHEESE

*8 oz. creamed cottage
  cheese*
*8 oz. cream cheese, cut
  up*
*¼ lb. butter (1 stick), cut
  up*
*½ cup sour cream*
*4 anchovies*
*2 Tbsp. paprika*
*3 Tbsp. capers*
*1 Tbsp. onion*
*2 tsp. caraway seeds*
*1 garlic clove*
*¾ tsp. dry mustard*
*2 Tbsp. gin*
*6 radishes, sliced*
*4 Tbsp. chopped chives*

Combine all ingredients except radishes and chives. Process them with the steel blade, 1 cup at a time, until well blended. Pack the mixture into a mold, and let it ripen in the refrigerator for 1 week. Slice the radishes, using the slicing disc. Just before serving, garnish mixture with the chopped chives and sliced radishes. Serve with thin slices of brown bread.

## BEER CHEESE SPREAD

*1 lb. Cheddar cheese, cut
  up*
*4 oz. blue cheese*
*¼ lb. butter (1 stick), cut
  up*
*1 cup beer*
*1 Tbsp. Worcestershire
  sauce*
*4 drops of Tabasco*
*2 tsp. wine vinegar*
*1 garlic clove*
*1 tsp. dry mustard*

Combine all ingredients loosely in a bowl. Put half of the mixture in the processor with the steel blade, and blend well. Blend remaining half. Pack the mixture in a crock or bowl. Cover and refrigerate. Port wine, ½ cup, may be substituted for the beer.

## BROILED CHEESE SPREAD

½ lb. store cheese, cut up
2 hard-cooked eggs, cut
  up
¾ cup stuffed olives
1 tsp. dry mustard
1 small onion,
  cut up

Place all the ingredients in the machine with the steel blade, and process until smooth. Spread the mixture on toasted bread rounds and brown quickly under the broiler.

## BRANDIED BLUE CHEESE

¼ cup walnuts
½ cup blue cheese
1½ Tbsp. cream
4 Tbsp. butter
2 Tbsp. brandy or
  Armagnac
salt and pepper

Grind the walnuts with the steel blade. Add the remaining ingredients and blend for 5 to 7 seconds. Season to taste. Serve with French bread.

## AVOCADO BLUE-CHEESE SPREAD

½ cup blue cheese
1 small ripe avocado,
  peeled and cut up
juice of ½ lemon

Place the ingredients in the container with the steel blade, and process until blended. Use as a dip or a spread with corn chips or Melba toast.

## PEANUT-BUTTER AND CREAM-CHEESE SPREAD

½ cup Peanut Butter (see
  Index)
3 oz. cream cheese
½ cup seedless raisins
¼ cup preserved
  gingerroot

Process all ingredients in processor with the steel blade. Spread on broad carrot slices or toast.

## TONGUE SPREAD

½ lb. cooked tongue, cut
  up
3 oz. cream cheese
2 Tbsp. sherry
½ cup raisins, plumped in
  boiling water or sherry

Place all ingredients in machine with the steel blade, and blend until smooth. Use as a filling for cream puffs or scooped-out, small crusty rolls. When using rolls, chill them after filling, then slice them into rounds, ¼ inch thick.

## CHICKEN SPREAD

½ cup nuts (almonds,
  pistachios), toasted
1 cup cut-up cooked
  chicken meat
1 Tbsp. curry powder
¼ cup Mayonnaise (see
  Index)

Grind toasted nuts in the processor with the steel blade. Add cut-up chicken and curry powder and blend for 5 to 8 seconds. Add the mayonnaise and turn the machine on and immediately off. Good on bread and very intersting as a filling for celery ribs or endive leaves.

## CHICKEN-TARRAGON SPREAD

1 large breast of chicken,
  poached, cut up
¼ cup almonds
4 oz. whipped cream
  cheese
½ tsp. dried tarragon
salt and pepper

Grind the chicken breast in the processor, using the steel blade; set aside. Grind the almonds. Put all the ingredients in the container and blend with the steel blade. Season. Fill cream puffs, or mound the mixture on pastry rounds, or serve with tiny Baking Powder Biscuits (see Index).

## CHICKEN LIVER PÂTÉ

1 lb. chicken livers
1 medium-size onion, cut
  up
2 Tbsp. butter
2 Tbsp. vermouth
2 hard-cooked eggs, cut
  up
salt and pepper
2 Tbsp. chopped parsley

Drop chicken livers into boiling water to cover and simmer until barely done. Drain. Chop the onion in the machine, using the steel blade. Add remaining ingredients except hard-cooked eggs and parsley, and blend until smooth. Fold in the eggs. Season to taste, and garnish with chopped parsley. Melba toast is the classic accompaniment.

## KIPPERED HERRING SPREAD

In place of kippered herring, try using other smoked fish, or use two 3¼-ounce cans of sardines in mustard sauce, one 7½-ounce can of crab meat, or two 3¾-ounce cans of smoked oysters in place of the smoked fish.

1 can (7 oz.) kippered
  herring, or ½ lb.
  smoked fish, flaked
3 oz. cream cheese
2 inch strip of lemon rind
black pepper

Grind kippered herring or other seafood, with any liquid from the can, with the steel blade. Add cheese and lemon rind, and process until smooth. Season with pepper to taste. Serve on crackers.

## TARAMASALATA

3 thin slices of white
  bread
¼ cup water
4 oz. tarama (carp roe) or
  red caviar, chilled
2 cups olive oil
1 egg yolk, beaten
6 Tbsp. lemon juice

Remove crusts from bread and soak bread in water; drain. Place tarama or caviar in processor and blend with the steel blade by flicking the machine on and off. Add the drained bread; whir. With the motor running, add the oil slowly through the tube, a few drops at a time. Continue to run the motor and add the beaten egg yolk and lemon juice. Blend with the steel blade until mixture is light and fluffy. Serve on sesame crackers or in Syrian bread wedges.

## EGGPLANT CAVIAR

*2 medium-size eggplants*
*2 medium-size onions, cut*
*up*
*3 garlic cloves*
*juice of 1 lemon*
*2½ Tbsp. olive oil*
*½ Tbsp. salt*
*1 tsp. black pepper*
*½ cup chopped parsley*

Bake whole eggplants in 350°F. oven for 1 hour, or until cooked through. Cool, halve, and scoop out the pulp; set aside. Put onion and garlic in the bowl; using the steel blade, process until finely minced. Add the eggplant pulp and remaining ingredients, and blend. Chill. Serve on crackers or as a dip.

## RAW TURNIP AND CARROT SPREAD

*1 cup cut-up sweet white*
*turnip*
*1 cup cut-up carrots*
*¼ cup Mayonaise (see*
*Index)*
*¼ cup sour cream*

Shred carrots and turnips in the machine, using the shredding blade. Mix with mayonnaise and sour cream. Serve on raw zucchini rounds.

## STEAK TARTAR

The food processor is superb for making very fresh steak tartar, ground to your taste.

*2 lb. raw filet of beef or*
*top sirloin, cubed*
*1 medium-size onion, cut*
*up*
*¼ cup parsley sprigs*
*salt and pepper*

Process cubes of meat, 1 cup at a time, until desired texture is obtained; set aside. Chop onion and parsley in the machine. Mix all the ingredients together. This is marvelous served with buttered black bread or toasted French bread.

## STEAK TARTAR, SCANDINAVIAN STYLE

6 anchovy fillets
2 tsp. prepared Dijon
  mustard
⅓ cup Cognac
1 raw egg yolk

Using preceding recipe, add these additional ingredients, except the egg yolk, with the final go-round of the meat. Shape into a large patty. Make a well in the center. Just before serving, drop the raw egg yolk into the depression. Mix the egg yolk and meat when offering the delicacy. Accompany with side dishes of chopped onion, parsley and capers. Have a pepper grinder on hand. Rye bread or pumpernickel is indicated.

---

# MEAT AND SEAFOOD BALLS

Meat or seafood balls are universally satisfying, found in all of the world's cuisines. In bite sizes, they perform admirably at cocktail parties—satisfying but not surfeiting. The food processor makes them in a wink.

## ALBANIAN MEATBALLS

½ lb. uncooked lamb,
  cubed
2 eggs, beaten
2 cups fresh bread
  crumbs
½ Tbsp. cornstarch
2 Tbsp. chopped fresh
  mint, or 2 tsp. dried
  mint
½ tsp. ground cinnamon
½ Tbsp. salt

Put lamb in the container with steel blade and process until the meat is of fine texture. Add the other ingredients and blend for 5 to 10 seconds. Shape into small balls. Fry in deep oil heated to 375°F. until brown. Drain. Serve alone or with mint sauce.

## IRAQI MEATBALLS

*1 lb. uncooked lamb or
beef, cubed
3 Tbsp. fresh bread
crumbs
1 Tbsp. curry powder
4 small onions, cut up
1 tsp. salt
¼ tsp. pepper
3 Tbsp. flour or cornmeal
⅓ cup oil*

Put the meat in the bowl and grind with the steel blade. Add bread crumbs, curry powder, cut-up onions, and salt and pepper. Process briefly. Form small balls with 2 teaspoons. Roll in flour or cornmeal, and sauté in oil. Typically served with a curry sauce, these are good with a Stroganoff sauce, or with a bourbon, brown sugar and ketchup dip.

## YANKEE MEATBALLS

*1 lb. cooked corned beef
or tongue, cut up
2 cups golden bread
crumbs
3 eggs
1 tsp. dry mustard
½ cup parsley
1 can (16 oz.) cranberry
sauce
½ cup currant jelly
¼ cup apple jack (optional)
⅓ cup oil*

Grind the meat in the processor with the steel blade. Add 1 cup bread crumbs, eggs, mustard and parsley, and blend until mixed. Form into balls. Roll in remaining crumbs and saute in oil and drain on paper towels. Heat cranberry sauce with the jelly and apple jack and serve with the meatballs. These go well with pickled Brussels sprouts and dilled carrots.

## CODFISH BALLS

*1 cup shredded, prepared
codfish
2 cups mashed potatoes
2 Tbsp. cream
1 Tbsp. minced chives
1 tsp. grated onion
2 eggs
½ tsp. salt
¼ tsp. black pepper
¼ cup chopped parsley*

Soak codfish in water for 3 hours. Drain. Place in the processor with the steel blade. Add the mashed potatoes, cream, chives, onion, eggs, seasonings and parsley. Blend, scraping down if necessary. Shape into balls and fry in deep fat heated to 375°F. Their usual accompaniment is a sharp seafood cocktail sauce, but tartare sauce or a Newburg sauce makes a nice change.

# FAR EAST SHRIMP BALLS

1 lb. cleaned raw shrimps
2 Tbsp. pork fat
1 slice of fresh white
   bread
2 Tbsp. water
1 egg yolk
1 tsp. salt
4 water chestnuts
1 knob of fresh
   gingerroot, peeled and
   cut up, or ¼ tsp.
   ground ginger
1 egg white
3 cups peanut oil

Preheat oven to 300°F. Place shrimps and pork fat in the bowl and process with the steel blade until they become an homogenized paste. Add the bread which has been broken up and soaked in the water. Run the machine for 10 to 15 seconds. Add the egg yolk, salt, water chestnuts and cut-up gingerroot, and process. Scrape down. Beat the egg white until foamy and stir into the mixture. Pour the oil into a deep skillet or wok, and heat until a smoky haze forms over the pan (375°F.). Form the mixture into balls with 2 wet teaspoons, to prevent sticking, and with a slotted spoon drop the balls into the hot oil. Do not fry more than 6 balls at one time, and dip spoons into water after each use. Turn balls gently for 3 to 4 minutes. Drain on a cookie sheet lined with paper towels, and keep hot in a 300°F. oven. Serve plain or with a sweet-and-sour sauce.

# CHICKEN-LIVER AND CHESTNUT BALLS

1 lb. chicken livers
5 Tbsp. butter, cut up
8 water chestnuts
salt and pepper
chopped parsley
3 scallions, cut up
2 Tbsp. soy sauce

Sauté chicken livers in 3 tablespoons of the butter until brown but still soft. Place the livers along with the remaining ingredients in the machine. Using the steel blade, process for 5 seconds. Season to taste. Form into small balls and roll in chopped parsley. Chill. Serve with food picks.

# COLD VEGETABLE HORS D'OEUVRE

## STUFFED RAW MUSHROOMS

*1 lb. medium-size
  mushrooms
⅓ cup sour cream
2 Tbsp. fresh dill, or ½
  Tbsp. dried dill
1 Tbsp. lemon juice*

Remove stems from mushrooms and cut off tough ends. Place stems in processor bowl with the sour cream, dill and lemon juice. Using the steel blade, blend all together for 5 to 10 seconds. Stuff mushroom caps with the mixture and chill.

If a spread is desired, chop both mushroom caps and stems. Add a little more sour cream to thin, and serve in thick scooped-out cucumber slices. Chopped, marinated raw vegetables also make a delicious filling for raw mushrooms.

## BEET HORS D'OEUVRE

*2 cans (16 oz. each)
  whole beets
1 can (16 oz.) sliced beets
1 Tbsp. capers
1 Tbsp. sour cream
2 hard-cooked eggs,
  crumbled*

Hollow out the whole beets, leaving enough edge to make firm shells. Add the pulp to the canned sliced beets. Process the beets, capers and sour cream in the processor with the steel blade until just melded. Fill hollowed-out beets with the mixture and sprinkle with crumbled hard-cooked egg. A mixture of 1 cup of finely chopped cooked green beans, or carrots or raw cucumbers, may be used in place of the processed beets. Instead of filling beets, fill cherry tomatoes with the mixture, or spread on sweet turnip rounds.

# VEGETABLE MACÉDOINE

24 radishes
2 scallions
1 large cucumber or
   carrot
Curry Mayonnaise (see
   Index)

Place the shredding disc in the processor bowl. Layer radishes in the tube, press down with the plunger, turn on the machine, and shred. Repeat with the scallions and cucumber or carrot, which have been cut into pieces to fit in the tube. Bind the vegetables together with curry mayonnaise. Serve on raw vegetable rounds or pumpernickel.

# DIPS

## SALSA VERDE

An out-of-the-ordinary dip for shellfish: shrimps, crab chunks, scallops.

1 small bunch of parsley
1 small bunch of chives
1 garlic clove
2 Tbsp. capers
1 Tbsp. anchovy paste
½ tsp. strong prepared
   mustard
1 Tbsp. lemon juice
½ cup olive oil
4 spinach leaves

Process all the ingredients, using the steel blade, and chill overnight. Instead of olive oil and lemon juice, 1 cup of mayonnaise may be used for a thicker sauce. A little *salsa verde* may be blended with hard-cooked egg yolks, a little at a time, to get the right consistency for cocktail deviled eggs.

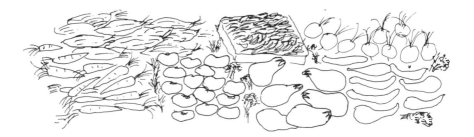

## SCALLOPS WITH SALSA VERDE

For a different seafood appetizer, poach 1½ pounds bay scallops in 2 cups white wine or dry vermouth. If sea scallops are used, cut into small pieces. Cool overnight in juice and serve with *salsa verde*.

## BAGNA CAUDA

A splendid Italian classic dip for raw vegetables.

¾ cup olive oil
3 Tbsp. butter
4 garlic cloves
8 anchovy fillets

Process all ingredients. Cook in a skillet until the flavors are melded and the consistency is creamy. Keep hot in a candle-heated earthenware dish. Use for dunking raw broccoli, zucchini, raw artichoke leaves, endive leaves, sweet pepper strips, carrot sticks, small asparagus spears. Accompany with crusty bread chunks.

## TAPENADE

A cold anchovy-tuna sauce to accompany a platter of raw vegetables.

8 or 9 anchovy fillets
1 can (7 oz.) tuna fish
⅓ cup capers
18 pitted ripe olives
3 garlic cloves
½ cup olive oil
¼ cup brandy
1 tsp. lemon juice

Process all together, adding more oil if necessary to thin sauce to mayonnaise consistency. Season to taste.

## SOUTH SEA DIP

3 scallions, cut up
½ tsp. curry powder
2 tsp. preserved candied
  gingerroot, or 1-inch
  piece of peeled fresh
  gingerroot, cut up
4 water chestnuts
1 cup cottage cheese
½ cup light cream

Process all ingredients together, using the steel blade. Serve with endive leaves, zucchini spears, crisp wafers or salt sticks.

## GUACAMOLE

½ small onion, cut up
2 large ripe avocados, cut
  up
1 canned chili (optional)
juice of 1 lemon
pinch of sugar
1 tsp. salt
¼ tsp. pepper
1 medium-size tomato,
  peeled, seeded, cut up

Chop onion in the processor with the steel blade. Add avocados, chili, lemon juice, sugar and seasonings, and process for 5 to 10 seconds. Add the tomato and turn the machine on and immediately off. If not served immediately, cover with plastic wrap and refrigerate to prevent darkening of the surface. Fry split tortillas cut into bite-size wedges (tostados) for scoops, or use packaged corn chips.

## AVOCADO-RUM DIP

A slight switch on the usual Mexican concoction.

2 ripe avocados, cut up
1 cup Mayonnaise (see
  Index)
2 Tbsp. lime juice
¼ cup light rum

Process with the steel blade for 5 to 10 seconds. When thinned with more mayonnaise, this becomes a superb sauce for shrimps or crab or cooked marinated scallops.

# SOUPS

—◆—

Thin soups, thick soups, splendid soups, surprising soups may be made in the Cuisinart™ Food Processor with a flick of the wrist. Glorious combinations can be concocted from both fresh and leftover ingredients. All manner of leftovers may be used for unique soups by homogenizing them and adding the resulting purée to different types of stock. It is not always feasible to make the entire soup in the machine, but it is the best way to make the basic purée, using some of the stock or sauce for liquid, which may then be incorporated into the required additional amount of liquid.

The food processor makes marvelous garnishes for soups, from the julienne of vegetables for Consommé Printanier to tiny *profiteroles,* forcemeat balls, dumplings or quenelles, sliced mushrooms and sausages.

# STOCK

A good stock makes the difference between a superb soup and a thin nonentity. With the food processor, stocks are not as complicated as they sound, and their preparation is speeded up. All soup stock should be carefully skimmed during the boiling period and thoroughly defatted before using. If you want to have a beautiful clear soup, the stock must be clarified. For every 5 cups of defatted stock, add 3 stiffly beaten egg whites. Simmer over moderate heat, stirring until the egg whites rise. Do not let the stock boil. Remove from the heat and allow the stock to settle for 15 minutes. Strain the stock through several layers of dampened cheesecloth.

Why not set aside a day for making different stocks, and then freeze them for future use? They will last for 6 months in the freezer but for not more that 1 week in the refrigerator. If stored but not frozen, bring to a boil before using.

## BEEF STOCK

3 lb. beef knuckle, cracked
3 lb. raw lean beef, cubed
4 quarts cold water
1 large carrot, cut up
3 celery ribs, cut up
1 turnip, cut up
1 large onion, studded with 6 whole cloves
1 parsley sprig
1 bay leaf
8 peppercorns
1 Tbsp. salt

Have the butcher crack the bones. Cube the meat and place 1 cup at a time in the container with the steel blade, and chop. Place the meat and bones in a large kettle and cover with the cold water. Let the meat and bones soak for 30 minutes to extract the juices, then bring slowly to the boil, frequently skimming the surface. Partially cover the kettle and simmer for 1 hour. Process all the vegetables except the onion in the machine with the steel blade. Tie parsley sprig and bay leaf in cheesecloth for *bouquet garni*. Add the vegetables, *bouquet garni*, peppercorns and clove-studded onion to the stock kettle. Partially cover and gently simmer for 3 to 4 hours. Cooking may be stopped at any point and contintued later. Strain the stock through dampened cheesecloth; add the salt. Let stock cool uncovered, then refrigerate. Remove fat before using. Makes about 2 quarts.

# BROWN STOCK

Brown stock is made in the same way as beef stock, but first brown the bones in a 400°F. oven for 1 hour. Cook the bones with the meat, add the vegetables, and proceed as for beef stock.

# VEAL STOCK

Veal stock is used for more delicate broths, and in velouté soups or sauces.

*3 lb. veal bones, cracked*
*1½ lb. raw veal shank meat or veal trimmings, cubed*
*1 lb. chicken necks, or 1 chicken carcass (optional)*
*3 carrots, cut up*
*2 medium-size onions, cut up*
*1 celery rib, cut up*
*1 garlic clove, cut up*
*1 bay leaf*
*4 parsley sprigs*
*pinch of thyme*
*2 tsp. salt*
*½ tsp. white pepper*

Have the butcher crack the bones. Grind the cut-up meat with the steel blade. Put the meat and bones in a large stockpot and cover with water. Let the meat, bones and chicken parts soak for 30 minutes to extract the juices. Combine vegetables and garlic to make a *mirepoix*. Process *mirepoix* ingredients all together in the processor using the steel blade. Tie herbs in cheesecloth to make a *bouquet garni*. Add *mirepoix* and *bouquet garni* to the stockpot. Partially cover and cook for 3 to 4 hours, skimming off the scum as it forms. Cooking may be stopped at any time and continued later. Remove *bouquet garni* and strain stock through dampened cheesecloth. Add the salt and pepper. Cool the stock, uncovered, then chill. Remove the fat before using. Makes about 2 quarts.

# CHICKEN STOCK

*4 lb. raw chicken pieces, or one 4-lb. fowl, cut up (do not use liver)*
*4 quarts cold water*
*1 cup cut-up celery*
*1 cup cut-up carrots*
*1 cup cut-up leeks, (optional)*

Put the chicken in a large kettle and cover with the cold water. Bring to a boil and simmer for 1 hour, skimming the surface as the scum rises. Process the vegetables except onions, using the steel blade. Tie herbs in cheesecloth to make a *bouquet garni*. Put vegetables, clove-studded onions and *bouquet garni* in with the chicken and simmer, partially covered, for 1½ hours. Remove

2 medium-size onions,
 each studded with 3
 cloves
1 bay leaf
4 parsley sprigs
pinch of dried thyme
2 tsp. salt
½ tsp. white pepper

bouquet garni and onions and strain the stock through dampened cheesecloth. Add seasonings. Cool and refrigerate. Defat and clarify the broth before using. Makes about 2 quarts.

## FISH STOCK (FUMET)

Fish fumet is the best base for making chowders and fish sauces.

1 cup cut-up onions
½ cup cut-up carrots
½ cup cut-up celery
1 Tbsp. oil
1 Tbsp. butter
salt and white pepper
4 cups water
4 lb. uncooked fish heads
 and bones
2 cups dry white wine

Process the vegetables with the slicing blade, and sauté them in the oil and butter until soft, adding salt and white pepper to taste. Add the water, fish heads and bones, and wine. Bring to a boil and skim the stock as necessary. Simmer, partially covered, for 30 minutes. Strain through dampened cheesecloth. Correct seasonings. Allow to cool and then refrigerate. Makes 1½ quarts.

## VEGETABLE STOCK

This stock may be served by itself as a light delicate broth, or it can be used as a base for sauces or as a poaching liquid.

4 carrots
4 scallions
2 medium-size onions
1 celery rib
4 leeks, green and white
 parts, washed
 (optional)
2 Tbsp. butter
1 bay leaf
4 parsley sprigs
2 tsp. salt
½ tsp. pepper

Process the vegetables with the slicing disc, and sauté them in butter until soft. Cover the vegetables with water and bring to a boil, skimming off the scum as necessary. Tie bay leaf and parsley in cheesecloth to make a bouquet garni. Add bouquet garni, salt and pepper, and simmer the stock for 2 hours. Remove bouquet garni, and strain stock through dampened cheesecloth. Season. Makes about 1½ quarts.

# THIN SOUPS

Clear soups and consommés may be enriched with other liquids and garnished for color, texture and variety. When homemade stock is not on hand, canned bouillon or chicken stock may be substituted.

## BEEF CONSOMMÉ

*1½ lb. raw lean beef,
  cubed
1 medium-size onion, cut
  up
2 carrots, cut up
2 celery ribs, cut up
2 large tomatoes, seeded
whites and shells of 2
  eggs
3 quarts Beef Stock (see
  Index)
salt and pepper*

Grind the cubed meat, 1 cup at a time, in the processor with the steel blade to a coarse texture, and set aside. Process the vegetables, 1 cup at a time, using the steel blade. Add meat, vegetables, egg whites and shells to the stock. Bring to a boil and simmer for 1 hour. Strain through dampened cheesecloth. Season to taste. Cool uncovered and refrigerate. Makes about 2 quarts.

To enrich the flavor of consommé, bring it to a boil and add any of the following; them simmer for 15 minutes to meld the flavors.

*Consommé à l'Orange*—Use 2 parts consommé to 1 part orange juice.
*Lemon Consommé*—Use juice and shredded rind of 1 lemon to 2 cups consommé. Good hot or cold.
*Tomato Bouillon*—Use equal parts of consommé and tomato juice. Good hot or cold.
*Wine Consommé*—To 1 quart consommé add ½ cup of wine—Madeira, port, Marsala or sherry. Good hot or cold.

## CONSOMMÉ MADRILÈNE

*1½ lb. fresh tomatoes,*
  *peeled and seeded*
*1 cup red wine*
*½ tsp. minced chervil*
*3 cups Beef Stock (see*
  *Index)*

Chop the tomatoes with the steel blade. Add them to the wine, chervil and beef stock, and simmer for 15 minutes. Strain. To jelly the soup add 2 tablespoons unflavored gelatin, soaked, then dissolved in ½ cup hot consommé. Chill. Makes about 6 cups.

## CHICKEN CONSOMMÉ

Chicken consommé is nothing more than clarified chicken stock. It is a delicious base for many interesting combinations, being more delicate than its beef counterpart. This consommé can be used to make many other soups.

## HERB BROTH

*2 Tbsp. each of fresh*
  *herbs (chervil, parsley,*
  *chives, tarragon or*
  *whatever herbs are*
  *available)*
*6 cups clarified Chicken*
  *Stock (see Index)*

Mix the herbs with 1 cup of chicken stock and process, using the steel blade. Add to the remaining stock. Simmer for 15 minutes. Makes 6 cups.

## CONSOMMÉ VERT-PRÉ

*3 scallions*
*½ cup watercress*
*5 lettuce leaves*
*½ cup spinach*
*4 Tbsp. butter*
*6 cups clarified Chicken*
  *Stock (see Index)*

Cut up the vegetables, then process them, using the steel blade. Wilt them in the butter. Combine greens and chicken stock and simmer for 15 minutes. Makes about 6 cups.

## CONSOMMÉ PAYSANNE

½ cup each of cut-up
  celery root or celery,
  carrot and turnip
¼ head of cabbage
½ head of lettuce
2 leeks, washed
6 Tbsp. butter
6½ cups clarified Chicken
  Stock (see Index)
salt and pepper

Julienne the celery root or celery, carrot and turnip in the processor, using the slicing disc; set aside. Process the cabbage, lettuce and leeks, using the slicing disc. Braise all the vegetables in the butter and ½ cup of the chicken stock. When vegetables are tender, add remaining stock and simmer for 15 minutes. Season to taste. Makes about 6 cups.

## COCK-A-LEEKIE

2 lb. leeks, trimmed
6 cups clarified Chicken
  Stock (see Index)
½ tsp. ground allspice

Slice leeks with the slicing blade, and wash thoroughly. Cover with water and simmer until tender, about 10 minutes. Process leeks and stock, 2 cups at a time, with the steel blade. Season with the allspice. Makes about 6 cups.

## CONSOMMÉ FORESTIÈRE (MUSHROOM BROTH)

1½ lb. mushrooms
6 cups clarified Chicken
  Stock (see Index)
salt and pepper
butter

Trim the tough ends off the stems of the mushrooms and cut the mushrooms into quarters. Add mushroom caps and stems (except 3 caps for garnish) to the stock, bring to a boil, and simmer for 8 minutes. Process the mushrooms and stock, 2 cups at a time, using the steel blade, until homogenized. Season to taste. Reheat and garnish with thin slices of the reserved 3 caps, lightly sautéed in butter. Makes about 2 quarts.

## CHICKEN EGG-FLOWER SOUP

*1 cup cut-up cooked*
  *chicken*
*3 cups clarified Chicken*
  *Stock (see Index)*
*1 tsp. salt*
*¼ tsp. white pepper*
*½ cup frozen green peas*
*3 Tbsp. cornstarch*
*3 Tbsp. water*
*1 egg, well beaten*
*1 tsp. sesame oil*
*4 scallions*

Using the steel blade, process the chicken and set aside. Bring the stock to a boil and add salt, pepper and peas. Mix cornstarch with 3 tablespoons water and add to the soup, stirring vigorously. Remove from the heat and slowly add 1 cup of hot soup to the beaten egg. Stir the egg mixture back into the soup and add the sesame oil and the chicken. Chop the scallions. Place 1 tablespoon scallions in each bowl and pour the hot soup over them. Serves 4.

# VEGETABLE SOUPS

## RUSSIAN BEET SOUP

*3 large cooked beets,*
  *halved*
*2 cucumbers, seeded*
*1 small onion, cut up*
*3 celery ribs, cut up*
*3 Tbsp. butter*
*1 Tbsp. vinegar*
*1 tsp. sugar*
*2 tsp. salt*
*¼ tsp. pepper*
*5 cups Chicken Stock (see*
  *Index)*
*pumpernickel rounds*
*sour cream*

Julienne the cooked beets, using the shredding disc; set aside. Process the cucumbers, using the shredding disc; set aside. With the steel blade chop the onion and celery, and sauté in the butter until soft. Add the vinegar, sugar, salt and pepper. Combine this mixture with the stock, beets and cucumbers. Simmer for 20 minutes. Garnish with toasted pumpernickel rounds and sour cream. Makes 6 cups.

# PISTOU SOUP

*1 cup fresh or frozen lima
    beans*
*2 quarts boiling water*
*6 potatoes*
*½ lb. green beans*
*1 lb. zucchini*
*3 leeks, washed, or 1
    large onion, cut up*
*3 Tbsp. butter*

Cook lima beans in the boiling water. While they are cooking, slice the potatoes and green beans in the processor, using the slicing disc. When lima beans are cooked, about 15 minutes, add potatoes and green beans. Slice the zucchini with the slicing disc; set aside. Chop the leeks or onion with the steel blade, and sauté in butter until translucent. Add zucchini to leeks or onion and toss lightly; cook until all vegetables are tender. Purée the potatoes, green beans and lima beans with some of their stock, about 2 cups at a time, in the processor with the steel blade. Add zucchini and leeks or onion to the purée. Makes about 2 quarts.

PISTOU

*6 garlic cloves*
*10 fresh basil leaves, or 2
    tsp. dried basil*
*3 Tbsp. chopped parsley*
*1½ cups grated Gruyère
    cheese*
*4 tsp. tomato paste*
*¾ cup olive oil*

Make the *Pistou*. Place first 5 ingredients in the container with the steel blade, and process until they are homogenized. With the motor running, drizzle the oil through the tube until a thick paste forms. Do not overprocess. The *pistou* may be served separately or stirred into the hot soup. Makes about 2 cups.

# LIGHT ONION SOUP

*2 cups onions*
*4 Tbsp. butter*
*2 tomatoes, peeled,
    seeded, and chopped by
    hand*
*6 cups Chicken Stock (see
    Index)*
*1 cup white wine*
*1 tsp. salt*
*¼ tsp. pepper*
*French bread*
*6 Tbsp. grated Swiss
    cheese*

Slice the onions in the processor, using the slicing disc, and sauté them in the butter in a kettle until they are soft. Add tomatoes and simmer for 5 minutes more. Pour in the chicken stock and cook slowly for 30 minutes. Add the wine. Season. Pour the soup into an ovenproof casserole or individual bowls, and place slices of toasted French bread on the top. Sprinkle with cheese, grated with the shredding disc, and place under broiler until the cheese melts. Makes 6 cups.

## MINESTRONE

6 Tbsp. olive oil
2 medium-size onions
1 medium-size eggplant,
   peeled and cut up
4 carrots
8 celery ribs
½ lb. green beans
2 medium-size zucchini
4 cups cut-up cabbage
1 can (28 oz.) stewed
   tomatoes and juice
8 cups Beef Stock or Beef
   Consommé (see Index)
salt and pepper
1 can (20 oz.) cannellini
   beans
Parmesan cheese, grated

Heat the oil in a heavy kettle. Quarter the onions and chop coarsely in the processor, using the steel blade. Sauté onions in the hot oil until soft. Chop the eggplant, 1 cup at a time, with the steel blade for 10 to 20 seconds, and add to the onions in the kettle. With the slicing disc, process the carrots, celery, beans and zucchini, and put them in the kettle. Process the cabbage with the slicing disc and add it with the tomatoes and stock or consommé to the kettle. Season to taste, and simmer for 2½ hours. Before serving, add the drained cannellini beans and reheat for 15 minutes. Serve with grated Parmesan cheese, grated with the steel blade. Makes about 3 quarts.

## SOPA VERDE

2 leeks, cut up and
   washed
2 scallions, cut up
1 cup cut-up celery
1 cup watercress
2 parsley sprigs
1 head of lettuce,
   quartered
6 Tbsp. butter
6 cups Chicken Stock (see
   Index)
salt and pepper
2 egg yolks
garlic toast rounds

With the steel blade, process the cut-up leeks, scallions, celery, watercress and parsley; set aside. With the slicing disc, process the lettuce wedges. Wilt all the vegetables in the butter. Simmer them in the chicken stock in a large kettle for 20 minutes. Put the soup in the processor with the steel blade, 2 cups at a time, and homogenize. Season to taste and reheat. Using the steel blade, process the 2 egg yolks with a small amount of the hot liquid, then whisk this into the soup. Serve with garlic toast rounds. Makes about 2 quarts.

## PEASANT SOUP

*3 carrots, cut up*
*2 turnips, cut up*
*2 onions, cut up*
*3 celery ribs, cut up*
*½ cup parsley*
*½ cup cut-up cabbage*
*6 cups stock, Chicken*
   *or Vegetable (see*
   *Index)*
*1 cup cooked rice*
*2 egg yolks*
*1 cup heavy cream*
*salt and pepper*
*4 Tbsp. butter*

Process the vegetables, 1 cup at a time, with the steel blade, for 3 to 5 seconds. Cook them in the stock for 20 minutes. Add the rice. Purée in the processor, 2 cups at a time. When ready to serve, reheat in a double boiler. Blend egg yolks and cream with the steel blade, and whisk the mixture into the soup. Season to taste. Finish with the butter. Makes 2 quarts.

_____

# THICK SOUPS

Purées, cream and velouté soups are very easily and smoothly made in the food processor. Some puréed soups are based on thick purées of vegetables, meat, poultry or seafood, thinned with a stock or cream to the desired consistency. Many low-calorie, yet creamy-tasting, soups can be made this way by using stock and purées with no other thickening. True cream soups combine a purée of meat, vegetables, poultry or seafood with a medium cream sauce. Additional cream may be added for a richer soup.

Rich velouté soups are also based on puréed ingredients, which are then combined with béchamel sauce made with chicken, veal or fish stock, plus the additional *liaison* of egg yolks and cream.

_____

# PURÉES

Many vegetable purées are thickened with potatoes and are often as good cold as hot. Cold soups, however, may need a stronger-flavored garnish.

## POTATO-THICKENED VEGETABLE SOUP

*1½ cups peeled potatoes*
*6 cups stock—chicken,*
*    meat, vegetable (see*
*    Index)*
*2 cups cooked vegetables*
*3 Tbsp. heavy cream*
*2 Tbsp. butter*
*salt and pepper*

Place the slicing disc in the processor and slice the potatoes. Cook potatoes in 2 cups of the stock until tender. Add the cooked vegetables and put them in the container along with the potatoes and the stock, 2 cups at a time. Blend with the steel blade until smooth, and add this purée to any remaining stock. Heat, and whisk in the cream and the butter. Season to taste. Makes about 6 cups.

## VARIATIONS WITH POTATO-THICKENED VEGETABLE SOUP

*Celery*—Use 2 cups chopped celery, blanched, and garnish with slivered toasted almonds.

*Celery Root (Celeriac)*—Use 2 cups chopped celery root, blanched, and garnish with sliced radishes.

*Lettuce*—Use 2 cups shredded lettuce, wilted in 2 tablespoons butter, and garnish with buttered croutons.

*Chicory*—Use 2 cups chopped chicory, wilted in 2 tablespoons butter, and garnish with chopped hard-cooked egg.

*Watercress*—Use 2 cups chopped watercress, wilted in 3 tablespoons butter in a covered pan, and garnish with diced ham.

*Carrot*—Use 1 pound carrots, sliced, blanched, and sautéed in 3 tablespoons butter; garnish with a dollop of sour cream.

*Broccoli*—Use 2 cups chopped broccoli, blanched, and garnish with toasted slivered almonds.

*Spinach*—Use 1 pound spinach, blanched and chopped, and garnish with crumbled bacon.

# VEGETABLE PURÉES

These soups depend on a vegetable base alone for the thickening. A dandy way to use leftover vegetables, separately or in combinations. Also, cooked and raw vegetables may be used together for a subtle texture variation.

## FRESH PEA PURÉE (SAINT-GERMAIN)

*4 cups cooked fresh peas*
*4 to 5 cups Veal Stock or*
*Chicken Stock (see*
*Index)*
*salt and pepper*
*4 Tbsp. butter*
*1 tsp. minced chervil or*
*mint*

Set aside 4 tablespoons of the peas for garnish. Put remaining peas in the container with the steel blade, and add 2 cups of stock. Blend, and add mixture to remaining stock. Bring to a boil and remove from heat. Season to taste. Beat in the butter, 1 tablespoon at a time, and garnish with reserved peas and minced chervil or mint. Good hot or cold. Makes about 6 cups.

## PUMPKIN OR WINTER SQUASH PURÉE (PURÉE POTIRON)

*1 large onion, cut up*
*2 Tbsp. butter*
*2 lb. cooked pumpkin or*
*winter squash, cut up*
*6 cups Chicken Stock (see*
*Index)*
*¼ tsp. grated nutmeg*
*1 tsp. grated fresh ginger-*
*root, or ¼ tsp. ground*
*ginger*
*1 tsp. salt*
*2 Tbsp. butter*
*1 cup light cream*

Place the cut-up onion in the container with the steel blade, and process. Sauté onion in the butter in a heavy soup kettle. Add cut-up pumpkin or squash, chicken stock, spices and salt. Bring to a boil and simmer until pumpkin or squash is soft. Put the soup, 2 cups at a time, in the container with the steel blade, and purée. Adjust seasoning. Reheat; remove from heat and whisk in the butter and cream. Makes 6 cups.

## CHESTNUT SOUP

*1 lb. fresh chestnuts, or 1 can (16 oz.) chestnuts unsweetened, or ½ lb. dried chestnuts, soaked overnight*
*6 cups Chicken Stock (see Index)*
*3 carrots, cut up*
*2 medium-size onions, cut up*
*1 celery rib, roughly cut*
*1 garlic clove*
*2 Tbsp. oil*
*salt and pepper*
*¾ cup light cream*

If fresh chestnuts are used, slit each one on the flat side. Cover with water and boil for 5 minutes. Drain, and remove shells and inner skins. Cook fresh or soaked dried chestnuts in the chicken stock until tender. If canned chestnuts are used, do not cook them, just heat them in the stock. Place the vegetables and garlic (to make a *mirepoix*) in the container with the steel blade, and chop. Brown the *mirepoix* in the oil and combine with chestnuts and stock. Purée the mixture, 2 cups at a time, with the steel blade. Season to taste. Reheat, and add the light cream. Makes 6 cups.

## CUBAN BLACK-BEAN SOUP

*1 lb. dried black beans*
*1 onion, cut up*
*1 green pepper, cut up*
*2 garlic cloves*
*3 Tbsp. olive oil*
*2 cups hearty red wine*
*2 bay leaves*
*salt and pepper*
*1 onion, chopped*

Soak the beans overnight. Drain and remove the floaters. Cover with fresh water and simmer until soft, 1 to 2 hours, adding water to keep beans just covered. (Note: Salt should not be added until beans are cooked because it tends to toughen them.) Place the *cut-up* onion, green pepper and garlic in the container with the steel blade, and chop. Sauté vegetables in the oil until limp, and add them to the beans. Pour in 1 cup of the wine and add the bay leaves. Simmer until creamy thick, adding more wine if necessary. Discard the bay leaves. Purée, 2 cups at a time, with the steel blade. If necessary, thin with water or more wine and reheat. Season to taste. Serve sprinkled with *chopped* onion as garnish.

The beans may be served unpuréed along with, or mixed with, rice, to make the famous Cuban dish—"Moors and Christians." Makes 2½ quarts.

## BLACK BEAN SOUP II

*1 lb. dried black beans*
*1 large onion, cut up*
*1 carrot, cut up*
*1 celery rib, roughly cut*
*3 Tbsp. butter*
*6 cups water*
*4 cups Chicken or Beef*
*Stock (see Index)*
*salt and pepper*
*sherry*
*2 hard-cooked eggs, or 10*
*lemon slices*

Soak the beans overnight and skim off the floaters. Drain. Place the onion, carrot and celery in the container with the steel blade, and chop. Sauté vegetables in the butter. Add vegetables to the beans with the water and stock. Cook covered for about 2 hours, until tender. Add salt and pepper to taste. Place in the container, 2 cups at a time, and purée. Reheat and add sherry, if desired. Garnish with chopped hard-cooked eggs or lemon slices. Makes about 2½ quarts.

## POTATO AND LEEK SOUP

No matter what it is called, and it comes with many fancy names, potato and leek soup stands on its own. It is also a grand base for soups, hot or cold, when combined with vegetables from A to Z (Asparagus to Zucchini). With sorrel, it becomes *Potage Germiny;* with the additional blessing of cream and chives, it becomes Vichyssoise; with carrots it's called *Potage Crécy.*

*4 leeks*
*3 Tbsp. butter*
*3 cups peeled potatoes*
*4 cups Chicken Stock (see*
*Index)*
*1½ cups light cream*
*salt and pepper*
*2 Tbsp. butter*
*parsley*
*croutons*

Trim the leeks and slice them with the slicing disc. Wash them thoroughly and drain, then sauté them in the butter until they are limp. Slice the potatoes with the slicing disc, and cook them in the chicken stock until tender. Put leeks, potatoes and some of the stock in the container and purée 2 cups at a time with the steel blade. Add the rest of the stock and the cream. Season to taste. Reheat and stir in the butter by spoonfuls. Garnish with minced parsley and croutons. Makes 6 cups.

# JADE SOUP

*1 lb. spinach, cut up*
*1 head of chicory, cut up*
*1 bunch of watercress, cut up*
*1 bunch of parsley*
*6 cups Veal or Vegetable Stock (see Index)*
*1 onion*
*4 medium-size potatoes*
*salt and pepper*
*¾ cup light cream*
*chopped chives*

Process the green vegetables with the steel blade, and simmer them in 2 cups of the stock. Place the slicing disc in the container and slice onion and potatoes. In a separate pot cook onion and potatoes together in remaining 4 cups of stock until they are soft. Combine potatoes, onions, cooked greens and all of the stock. Purée 2 cups at a time with the steel blade. Season to taste. Add the cream and reheat, but do not boil. Sprinkle with chopped chives. Good hot or cold. Makes 2 quarts.

# PURÉE OF DRIED LEGUMES

*1 lb. dried legumes (lentils, pea beans, yellow or green split peas)*
*2 ham hocks*
*2 quarts stock or water*
*2 onions, cut up*
*1 garlic clove*
*1 carrot, cut up*
*2 parsley sprigs*
*1 celery rib*
*1 bay leaf*
*pinch of dried thyme*
*6 peppercorns*
*1 clove*
*½ lb. salt pork, diced by hand*
*salt and pepper*
*2 frankfurters*

Put legumes and ham hocks in a large pot with the stock or water. Put 1 onion, the garlic and carrot in the container with the steel blade, and chop. Tie herbs and spices in cheesecloth to make a *bouquet garni*. Add to the stockpot with the chopped vegetables, and season to taste. Bring to a boil and simmer until legumes are tender. Chop remaining onion with the steel blade, and put it in a heavy saucepan with the salt pork. Fry until onion and pork pieces are golden brown, then add them to the legumes and simmer for 15 minutes. Remove ham hocks and *bouquet garni*. Purée the soup, 2 cups at a time, with the steel blade. Season to taste. Reheat, and serve with thin slices of frankfurter, sliced with the steel blade.

Another version of this may be made by omitting the ham hocks, seasoning the soup with ground cuminseed, and garnishing it with browned onion rings and lemon slices. Makes about 6 cups.

# CREAM SOUPS

Cream soups are smoother and often richer than purées. The thickening element is béchamel (cream sauce). The proportions for a cream soup are ½ béchamel, approximately ¼ part solid ingredient, ¼ white stock or milk. The amount of the solid ingredient will depend on the strong or mild flavoring desired as well as the texture preferred.

## VEGETABLE CREAM SOUP

*1 lb. prepared vegetables, chopped, sliced or shredded*
*2 cups thin Sauce Béchamel (see Index)*
*1 cup stock*
*salt and pepper*
*1 cup light cream*
*3 Tbsp. butter*

It is necessary to blanch some fibrous vegetables such as artichoke hearts, celery and asparagus, before combining them with sauce and stock, or sautéing them in butter. Combine 2 cups béchamel, 1 cup complementary stock (chicken, vegetable or beef) and the drained vegetables. Simmer for 12 minutes. Put the steel blade in the container and blend 2 cups at a time. Season to taste. Reheat and whisk in the cream. Finish with butter. If a thinner soup is desired, dilute with more stock. Makes about 6 cups.

## SUGGESTED PURÉES FOR VEGETABLE CREAM SOUPS

ARTICHOKE PURÉE

*8 canned artichoke hearts, or 1 pkg. (9 oz.) frozen*
*3 Tbsp. butter*

If canned artichokes are used, slice them and sauté in butter. If frozen artichokes are used, blanch them before sautéing. This soup is good served hot or cold.

### FRESH ASPARAGUS PURÉE

*1 lb. asparagus, reserving*
*a few tips for*
*garnishing*
*3 Tbsp. butter*

Peel the asparagus to about 1 inch from the tips. Cut the stalks into pieces. Blanch them, then sauté lightly in butter.

### CELERY PURÉE

*2 cups celery pieces*
*3 Tbsp. butter*

Blanch the celery, then sauté in butter.

### BRUSSELS SPROUTS PURÉE

*1 lb. Brussels sprouts*
*3 Tbsp. butter*

Cut the sprouts into halves. Parboil, and sauté in butter.

### ONION PURÉE

*2 cups onions*
*3 Tbsp. butter*

Slice the onions with the slicing disc, and sauté in butter until limp.

### CAULIFLOWER PURÉE

*1 head of cauliflower*
*3 Tbsp. butter*

Divide cauliflower into flowerets, Blanch, then sauté lightly in butter.

### SPINACH PURÉE

*1 lb. spinach, or 2 pkg.*
*(10 oz. each) frozen*
*spinach*
*3 Tbsp. butter*

Wash fresh spinach, or defrost frozen spinach, and chop with the steel blade. Sauté spinach in butter until all the liquid has evaporated.

### GREEN-BEAN PURÉE

*1 lb. green beans*
*3 Tbsp. butter*

Slice beans with the slicing disc, and cook until crisp-tender. Sauté in butter.

### LEEK PURÉE

*6 leeks*
*3 Tbsp. butter*

Slice leeks with the slicing disc, wash carefully, and blanch. Sauté in butter.

WATERCRESS PURÉE

2 bunches of watercress
3 Tbsp. butter

Wilt the watercress in the butter. This soup is good hot or cold.

MUSHROOM PURÉE

1½ lb. mushrooms
2 shallots
3 Tbsp. butter

Trim the mushrooms, then slice them with the slicing disc, reserving a few for garnish. Chop the shallots with the steel blade, and sauté in the butter. Add the mushrooms and sauté together until limp.

## CREAM OF CORN SOUP

2½ cups canned creamed
  corn, or 2½ cups
  kernels cut from the cob
1 cup milk (for fresh corn)
2 to 3 cups thin Sauce
  Béchamel (see Index)
salt and pepper

If fresh corn is used, simmer the corn in 1 cup milk until tender. Add 2 cups sauce béchamel plus the milk in which the corn was cooked. If canned corn is used, combine it with 3 cups béchamel. Place in the container with the steel blade, and purée 2 cups at a time. Season to taste. For pungent variety, add a soupçon of curry powder. Makes 6 cups.

## CREAM OF TOMATO SOUP

1 small onion, quartered
3 Tbsp. butter
2 tsp. brown sugar
2 cups fresh tomatoes,
  peeled, seeded, and
  chopped, or canned
  tomatoes
4 cups thin Sauce
  Béchamel (see Index)
salt and pepper
whipped cream

Place the onion in the container with the steel blade and chop. Sauté onion lightly in the butter, and add brown sugar. Add tomatoes and cook for 15 minutes. Strain the mixture into the béchamel. Season to taste. Reheat and decorate with a dollop of whipped cream. Serve with souffléed crackers. Makes 6 cups.

# VELOUTÉS

Veloutés are the richest of the creamy soups. Some are excellent served hot or chilled. Chicken, veal, fish or vegetable stock is generally used instead of milk. A regular cream soup, made with one of these stocks, may be translated into a velouté with a final *liaison* of butter, egg yolks and cream.

To make a *liaison,* put 3 egg yolks and ½ cup cream into the container and process, using the steel blade. With the machine running, gradually pour 1 cup of hot soup through the tube. After mixture is homogenized, whisk this into the remaining soup. When serving the soup hot, reheat but do not boil.

## POTAGE BAGRATION—VEAL

*1 lb. lean raw veal, cubed*
*7 Tbsp. butter*
*4 cups thin Sauce Velouté*
  *(see Index), made with*
  *veal or chicken stock*
*3 egg yolks*
*½ cup heavy cream*
*salt and pepper*
*Parmesan or Gruyère*
  *cheese, grated*

Coarsely grind the veal in the processor, using the steel blade. Sauté the meat in 3 tablespoons butter. Add the meat to the sauce velouté, and simmer gently for 20 minutes. Purée in the processor, 2 cups at a time, using the steel blade. Add the *liaison* of egg yolks and cream to the last 2 cups of potage, and blend. Season to taste. Gradually finish off with remaining 4 tablespoons butter. Serve with a side dish of grated Parmesan or Gruyère cheese. Makes about 6 cups.

## POTAGE BAGRATION—FISH

Make 4 cups Sauce Velouté (see Index), using fish stock. Following the same method as for the veal soup, substitute 1 pound of any good white fish, steamed, for the meat. Serve with lemon slices.

## POTAGE GERMINY

Excellent hot or cold.

4 packed cups sorrel
2 Tbsp. butter
6 cups Chicken or
    Vegetable Stock (see
    Index)
8 egg yolks
½ cup light cream
salt and pepper

Place the sorrel in the container with the steel blade, and chop, then wilt sorrel in the butter. Add sorrel to the stock and simmer for 20 minutes. When ready to serve the soup, thicken it. Place egg yolks and cream in the container with the steel blade, and whir. With the motor running, pour in 1 cup of strained hot soup through the tube, and blend. Stir the *liaison* into remaining sorrel soup. Season to taste, and gently reheat or serve cold. Makes 6 cups.

---

# BISQUES

Bisque cream soups are generally based on fish stock, puréed shellfish and sauce béchamel.

## OYSTER BISQUE

1 small onion, cut up
5 Tbsp. butter
1 Tbsp. paprika
1 quart oysters in their
    liquor
3 Tbsp. cornstarch
salt and pepper
1½ cups milk, scalded
½ cup heavy cream,
    scalded

Chop the onion with the steel blade. Sauté in 3 tablespoons butter and add paprika; set aside. Cook the oysters in their liquor to the boiling point. Drain, saving the liquor and setting oysters aside. Moisten cornstarch with a little of the oyster liquor and add to the sautéed onion. When frothy, add the rest of the oyster liquor and simmer for 10 minutes. Keep hot in the top part of a double boiler over barely simmering water. Purée the oysters with the steel blade, and reheat in the oyster liquor. Season to taste. When ready to serve, add the scalded milk and cream. Float remaining 2 tablespoons butter on the surface, and dust with more paprika. Makes about 6 cups.

1 quart of Cherrystone clams may be substituted for the oysters.

# LOBSTER BISQUE

2 live lobsters, 1½ lb.
  each, or 1 large
  lobster, 3 lb.
1¼ cups uncooked rice
4 cups Fish Stock (see
  Index)
3 carrots, cut up
2 medium-size onions, cut
  up
1 celery rib, cut up
1 garlic clove
3 Tbsp. butter
2 Tbsp. oil
1 Tbsp. brandy
white wine
salt and pepper
1 Tbsp. tomato paste
¾ cup heavy cream
½ cup sherry, or 2 Tbsp.
  brandy (optional)

Have your fish market split the live lobsters and chop into chunks. Cook rice in fish stock until soft. Drain, and save both rice and stock. Combine vegetables and garlic to make a *mirepoix*. Process the *mirepoix* all together with the steel blade. Sauté *mirepoix* with lobster chunks, flesh side down, in the butter and oil in a heavy kettle until the shells turn red. Add 1 tablespoon brandy and cover with wine. Simmer until vegetables are mushy. Remove lobster chunks from the pan and pick out the meat, saving a few pieces for garnish. Drain the *mirepoix* and save it and cooking liquid. Pour the *mirepoix* liquid into the rice stock. Put the *mirepoix,* rice and lobster meat into the container with the steel blade, and purée to a paste. Season to taste. Heat the mixture of reserved liquids, and whisk in the tomato paste. Combine with the lobster mixture. Just before serving, heat the cream, but do not boil, and add it to the lobster soup. Finish with ½ cup sherry or 2 tablespoons brandy. Makes about 6 cups.

1½ pounds shrimps in their shells, 6 hard-shell crabs, broken up, or 2 dozen cracked crayfish, also cooked in their shells, may be substituted for the lobster.

# BILLI-BI

Superb hot or chilled.

3 quarts mussels
1 cup dry white wine
4 cups Fish Stock (see
  Index)
2 egg yolks
½ cup heavy cream,
  scalded
salt and white pepper

Scrub the mussels and remove the beards. Soak them in cold water to get rid of any sand. Put mussels and wine in a large kettle. Cover and cook until the shells open, about 5 to 10 minutes. Set aside the mussels, and strain the cooking liquid into the fish stock. Remove the mussels from their shells and set a few of them aside for garnish. Put remaining mussels and strained cooking liquid into the container, 1 cup at a time, and purée with the steel blade. Put purée in the top part of a double boiler and heat over simmering water. Place egg yolks and cream for *liaison* in the processor with the steel blade, and whir. With the motor running, pour 1 cup of the soup through the tube and blend. Stir all together. Season to taste. Drop a few whole mussels into each cup and pour in the soup. Makes about 6 cups.

―――――

# COLD SOUPS

Cold soups, often jellied or creamy, may also be refreshing thin broths. It should be noted that some of the preceding soups have been marked, "Good hot or cold."

## COLD AVOCADO SOUP

3 ripe avocados, cut into
   pieces
2 cups Chicken Stock (see
   Index)
1 cup sour cream
1 cup light cream
¼ tsp. chili powder
salt and white pepper
3 Tbsp. light rum
   (optional)
pimientos, chopped

Process half of the ingredients in the container with the steel blade, and set aside. Process remaining ingredients. Mix all together and chill. Garnish with finely chopped pimientos. Makes 6 cups.

## COLD BROCCOLI SOUP

½ cup cut-up scallions
2 cups cut-up cooked
   broccoli
6 cups Chicken Stock (see
   Index)
8 oz. cottage cheese
salt and pepper
cherry tomatoes, sliced
   thin

Place scallions and broccoli in the processor with the steel blade and purée. Add the mixture to the chicken stock. Pour the soup, 1 cup at a time, into the container with the cheese and whir. Season to taste. Whisk all together and chill. Garnish with thin slices of cherry tomatoes. Makes 6 cups.

## COLD BISQUE CREOLE

1½ lb. raw shrimps
3 cups water
1 garlic clove
1 bay leaf
½ lemon, sliced
1 medium-size green
   pepper, cut up
2 tomatoes, peeled and
   seeded
1 small onion, quartered
2 Tbsp. oil
1 Tbsp. tomato paste
4 cups thin Sauce Velouté
   (see Index), made with
   shrimp cooking liquid
½ tsp. salt
dash of cayenne pepper
1 cup light cream
1 tsp. gumbo filé
   (optional)

Poach shrimps in the water with the garlic, bay leaf and lemon slices. Simmer until shrimp shells have turned pink, approximately 10 minutes. Drain shrimps and save the cooking liquid. Shell the shrimps and devein; set aside. Chop pepper, tomatoes and onion with the steel blade for 3 seconds, and sauté in the oil; set aside. Place the shrimps and tomato paste in the container with the steel blade, and process until puréed. Make sauce velouté, using reserved shrimp cooking liquid for stock. Mix sauce with puréed shrimps. Season. Add sautéed vegetables, cream and gumbo filé. Chill. Makes about 2½ quarts.

## COLD BORSCHT

4 cups raw beets, peeled
1 large onion, cut up
2½ quarts Vegetable
   Stock (see Index) or
   water
2 Tbsp. sugar
2 tsp. salt
2 Tbsp. red-wine vinegar
1 cup sour cream

Place the shredding disc in the container and grate the beets and onion. Cover them with the stock or water and bring to a boil, then simmer, partially covered, for 30 minutes. Skim off the scum when necessary. Add the sugar, salt and vinegar; cool. Stir in the sour cream and mix well. For a change of texture and flavor, add 1 cup peeled, seeded and shredded cucumbers; use the shredding disc to process cucumbers; drain well. Makes 2½ quarts.

# GAZPACHO

5 medium-size tomatoes,
  red or green, cut up
2 medium-size cucumbers,
  cut up
1 large onion, cut up
1 green pepper, cut up
3 garlic cloves
3 cups coarsely crumbled
  French or Italian
  bread, no crusts
¼ cup red-wine vinegar
4 Tbsp. olive oil
4 cups cold stock or water
2 Tbsp. tomato paste
salt and pepper

Peel, seed, and coarsely chop the tomatoes with the steel blade. Place remaining vegetables in the container and coarsely chop. In a deep bowl, combine all the vegetables, the bread, vinegar, oil, stock or water and tomato paste. Ladle the mixture into the processor, 2 cups at a time, and blend until it becomes a purée. Season to taste. Chill. Serve with side dishes of chopped cucumbers, peppers, hard-cooked eggs, scallions, croutons and chopped parsley. Makes 2½ to 3 quarts.

# COLD CUCUMBER SOUP

2 medium-size cucumbers,
  cut up (if waxed, peel)
1 garlic clove
1 can (11½ oz.) condensed
  pea soup, undiluted
1½ cups Chicken Stock
  (see Index)
1 cup sour cream
salt and pepper
chopped chives

Put the cut-up cucumber and garlic in the container with the steel blade, and chop. Add remaining ingredients except seasoning and chives, and process until smooth. Season. Serve very cold, and garnish with chopped chives. Makes 6 cups.

## CARAWAY SQUASH BISQUE

Adapted for the processor from *The Four Seasons Cookbook*.

*1 small onion, cut up*
*1 celery rib, cut up*
*1 carrot, cut up*
*4 Tbsp. butter*
*2 yellow crookneck squash, each about ¾ lb.*
*1 medium-size potato*
*6 cups Beef Stock (see Index)*
*2 tsp. caraway seeds*
*¾ cup heavy cream*
*salt and pepper*

Put the onion, celery and carrot in the container with the steel blade, and chop. Sauté vegetables in the butter until soft but not browned. Cut the squash and potato into workable pieces. Add them to the stock along with the sautéed vegetables and caraway seeds. Cook until the squash is very tender, about 30 minutes. Place the vegetables and stock, 2 cups at a time, in the container with the steel blade, and blend. Mix in the cream and seasonings to taste. Chill. Makes about 2 quarts.

## COLD SHRIMP BISQUE

*½ lb. raw shrimps, unshelled*
*6 Tbsp. butter*
*2 Tbsp. salad oil*
*1 cup cut-up leeks, washed*
*1 large onion, cut up*
*4 carrots, cut up*
*2 oz. brandy*
*2 cups dry white wine*
*2 cups clam juice*
*salt and pepper*
*2 cups light cream*

Sauté shrimps in the butter and oil until shells turn pink. Remove shrimps with a slotted spoon, peel, and set aside. Process the vegetables with the steel blade, and sauté them in the pan in which the shrimps were cooked. Return the shrimps to the pan. Heat the brandy and pour over the shrimps. Ignite and stir until flame disappears. Add wine and clam juice, bring to a boil, and simmer for 10 minutes. Put shrimp-vegetable mixture, 2 cups at a time, into the container with the steel blade, and purée. Season to taste. Stir in the cream and chill. Makes 2 quarts.

## COLD SOUP CRÉCY

*1 lb. carrots, cut up*
*1 large onion, cut up*
*4 Tbsp. butter*
*½ tsp. curry powder*
*1 Tbsp. grated lemon rind*
*4 cups Chicken Stock (see Index)*
*salt and white pepper*
*1 cup light cream*

Place carrots and onion in the container with the steel blade, and chop. Sauté the vegetables in the butter until onion is translucent. Add curry powder and grated lemon rind, and combine vegetables with stock. Simmer until carrots are tender. Purée, 2 cups at a time, with the steel blade. Add salt and pepper to taste. Stir in the cream and chill. Makes 6 cups.

## COLD FISH SOUP

*1 recipe Potato and Leek Soup (see Index)*
*1 lb. white fish*
*1 Tbsp. lemon juice*
*1 bay leaf*
*4 peppercorns*
*salt and pepper*
*chopped fresh dill*

Prepare potato and leek soup and set aside. Tie the fish in cheesecloth and place in simmering water to cover to which the lemon juice, bay leaf and peppercorns have been added. Simmer for 8 to 10 minutes. Remove bay leaf and drain fish. Cut fish into pieces and place in the container with the steel blade. Add 2 cups of potato and leek soup and blend. Combine the fish mixture with the remaining soup. Season to taste. Chill. Serve with chopped fresh dill. Makes 2 quarts.

# EGGS AND CHEESE

## STUFFED HARD-COOKED EGGS

The Cuisinart™ Food Processor is a natural for blending egg yolks with different ingredients to make tasty fillings for hard-cooked eggs. Hard-cooked eggs can stand on their own as an hors d'oeuvre, but dressed with a sauce they can become a delicious first course or entrée.

### STUFFED HARD-COOKED EGGS, COLD

Cut hard-cooked eggs lengthwise into halves, and carefully remove the yolks, setting the white halves aside. Prepare fillings by processing all the ingredients with the yolks, using the steel blade. Scrape down the sides from time to time. Blend until smooth, and season. If necessary, correct the consistency, either with a thinning agent or a bread-crumb thickener.

## STUFFINGS FOR COLD HARD-COOKED EGGS

Use 9 eggs to serve 6; combine hard-cooked yolks with these extra ingredients.

*Olives*—Add 8 pitted green or ripe olives, chopped, moistened with mayonnaise.

*Shrimp and Water Chestnuts*—Add 4 water chestnuts, cut up, and 6 cooked shrimps, cut up. Thin with mayonnaise.

*Bacon and Chutney*—Add 2 strips of bacon, cooked and crumbled, 1 tablespoon minced chutney and ½ teaspoon curry powder. Moisten with cream or milk.

*Sardine*—Add 3 sardines and 1 scallion, cut up. Moisten with a little white wine or vermouth.

*Blue Cheese and Walnut*—Add 2 tablespoons crumbled blue cheese and 6 walnuts, chopped. Thin with mayonnaise.

*Corn Chips*—Add 8 corn chips, broken up, and 1 teaspoon chili powder. Moisten with taco sauce or tomato paste.

*Chives*—Add ½ cup snipped chives and 2 tablespoons sour cream.

*Anchovy*—Add 2 anchovies and rind of ½ lemon, cut up. Moisten with anchovy oil from the can.

*Tapenade*—Mix in 3 tablespoons Tapenade (see Index).

## STUFFED HARD-COOKED EGGS, HOT

Follow the procedure for cold stuffed hard-cooked eggs. Place the filled eggs in a buttered shallow baking dish and mask well by spooning the sauce over and around the eggs. The dish may be prepared well in advance up to this point. Just before serving, heat in a 425°F. oven for 20 minutes, or until bubbly.

### STUFFINGS AND SAUCES FOR HOT HARD-COOKED EGGS

Use 9 eggs to serve 6.

*Eggs Chimay*—Mix equal parts of Duxelles (see Index) and egg yolks. Mask with Sauce Mornay (see Index). Sprinkle the top with ½ cup grated Swiss cheese.

*Eggs with Peas and Chicken Livers*—Sauté 3 chicken livers, cut up, in 3 tablespoons butter, and purée with 1 cup cooked green peas. Bind with 1 table-

spoon cream or softened butter, and mix with the yolks. Cover with
Mushroom Sauce (see Index).

*Eggs with Tuna Fish*—Flake ½ cup canned tuna, and mix with ¼ teaspoon celery seeds, 4 tablespoons mayonnaise and 1 tablespoon prepared mustard.
Mix with yolks. Mask with Caper Sauce (see Index).

*Eggs with Bacon and Onion*—Cook 4 slices of bacon, and crumble; mix with 1
medium-size onion, chopped, and sautéed in 1 tablespoon bacon fat until
lightly browned. Mix with yolks. Cover with Cheese Chive Sauce (see
Index) and buttered bread crumbs.

*Eggs with Ham*—Mix ½ cup cut-up cooked ham and 1 teaspoon prepared mustard with yolks. Bake in Bontemps Sauce (see Index).

*Hungarian Eggs*—Mix 1 green pepper, cut up, ¼ teaspoon caraway seeds and
1 teaspoon paprika with yolks. Cover stuffed eggs with Paprika Sauce (see
Index).

*Eggs with Smoked Fish*—Blend ½ cup smoked fish, 2 tablespoons sour cream
and 1 teaspoon lemon juice with yolks. Mask stuffed eggs with Hot Cucumber Sauce (see Index).

*Parsley Eggs*—Blend ½ cup packed parsley with 2 tablespoons butter and
yolks. Place each egg half on a slice of tomato. Cover with Sauce Allemande or Hollandaise (see Index), and dust with grated Parmesan cheese.

## OMELETS

Uncommonly good omelets can be made in the food processor,
incorporating all manner of appetizing ingredients with the eggs,
rather than having them as extracurricular additions. The chunkiness
of the ingredients will be determined by the length of time you process them. Sometimes it makes a more interesting dish to have the extra
ingredients in larger pieces—peppers, mushrooms, ham, chicken livers,
etc. This varies the texture and at the same time retains more of the taste
of the chunky pieces.

### PLAIN OMELET

*8 eggs*
*4 Tbsp. water*
*salt and pepper*
*2 Tbsp. butter*

Place ingredients in the container with the steel
blade. Add any of the following combinations,
and process with the eggs for few seconds. Cook
in an omelet pan in 2 Tbsp. of butter until
just set. Serves 4.

## OMELET VARIATIONS

*Fines Herbes*—Add 4 tablespoons each of parsley, tarragon, chives, etc.

*Fines Herbes with Cheese*—Add 4 tablespoons parsley, 1 cut-up scallion and 3 tablespoons cut-up Cheddar or Swiss cheese, or any leftover hard cheese.

*Parmesan*—Add ¾ cup cut-up Parmesan cheese and 2 tablespoons cream.

*Duxelles*—Add 1 cup Duxelles (see Index), or 1 cup cut-up mushrooms, sautéed with 2 minced shallots and 1 teaspoon curry powder (optional) in 2 tablespoons butter.

*Ham*—Add 1 cup cubed ham, ½ cup pickles, and ½ tablespoon dry mustard.

*Salmon*—Add 7¾ ounces canned salmon, drained, 2 tablespoons capers, 2 tablespoons heavy cream and juice of 1 lemon.

*Western*—Add 1 green pepper and 1 onion, cut up, and ½ cup cubed ham.

*Pimiento*—Add 1 canned pimiento, 1 tomato, peeled, seeded, cut up and drained, 1 garlic clove and 4 parsley sprigs.

*Sorrel or Spinach*—Add 1 cup sorrel or spinach leaves, wilted in 1 tablespoon butter.

———

# PANCAKE OMELETS

These egg dishes are more substantial than regular omelets as they have more solid ingredients. They are marvelous for using leftovers. They are cooked over low heat and must be finished on both sides. Therefore they are firmer. Serve in wedges, like a cake.

## OMELET SAVOYARD

*1 cup cut-up Gruyère cheese*
*4 cups potatoes, peeled*
*1 large onion, cut up*
*3 Tbsp. butter*
*1 Tbsp. oil*
*8 eggs*
*salt and pepper*

Grate the cheese with the steel blade and set aside. Shred the potatoes with the shredding blade, and place them in cold water until used. Chop the onion with the steel blade, and sauté in the butter and oil. Drain and dry the potatoes. Add them to the skillet with the onion and fry, turning often, until a good crust is formed. With the steel blade process the eggs and seasonings to taste, and pour over the potato mixture. Cook until firm. Sprinkle with grated cheese and put under the broiler until just set. Serves 6.

## ZUCCHINI FRITTATA

6 small zucchini
8 eggs
3 parsley sprigs
3 Tbsp.oil
salt and pepper
½ cup grated Parmesan
    cheese

Shred the zucchini with the shredding disc. Drain, and set aside. Put the eggs and parsley in the container with the steel blade, and blend for 3 seconds. Sauté zucchini in the oil. Season to taste. Pour egg mixture over zucchini and cook until just set. Sprinkle with the cheese and put under the broiler until golden. Serves 6.

## CROUTON FRITTATA

1½ cups croutons
¼ lb. butter (1 stick)
8 eggs
2 Tbsp. cream
salt and pepper

Croutons should be enough to cover bottom of an 8- or 9-inch skillet. Toast croutons in the butter. Blend eggs with cream. Add salt and pepper to taste, and pour egg mixture over croutons. Cook until just set. Put under the broiler until golden. Serves 6.

With plain croutons, the addition of 3 tablespoons sugar and 1 teaspoon ground cinnamon makes a cinnamon toast omelet, which may be dusted with more cinnamon sugar or accompanied with a fruit sauce.

Hard sausage, sliced thin with the slicing disc, can be layered in Crouton Frittata and topped with grated cheese for a hearty dish.

## PEASANT FRITTATA

1 lb. Sausage Meat (see
    Index)
4 cups potatoes, peeled
1 large onion
8 eggs
½ tsp. poultry seasoning

Fry sausage until crumbly; remove from pan with a slotted spoon and set aside; leave 3 tablespoons fat in pan. Slice the potatoes and onion with the slicing blade. Cook in the sausage fat until crisp. Return sausage to the pan. Pour the eggs beaten with the poultry seasoning over vegetables and sausage. Cook until set, then put under the broiler until crusty. Serves 6.

# ENTRÉE SOUFFLÉS

The food processor, which homogenizes so simply and surely, turns out a soufflé base in a breeze. The cream sauce base can be prepared in the machine and cooked over hot water, or very carefully over direct heat, until thickened. The egg yolks are then processed with any other ingredients and added to the sauce base. This may be done ahead of time, and the beaten egg whites can be folded in just before baking. Soufflés can be cooked in individual as well as larger dishes. Vegetable soufflés are attractive baked in a ring mold and served with a cream sauce. (For dessert soufflés, see Chapter 16.)

## CHEESE SOUFFLÉ

*1 cup cut-up cheese*
*3 Tbsp. butter*
*3 Tbsp. flour*
*1 ½ cups hot liquid (milk, stock, wine, etc.)*
*6 egg yolks*
*8 egg whites*
*salt and pepper*

Preheat oven to 375°F. Use Gruyère, Emmental, Cheddar, or ⅔ cup of any one plus ⅓ cup grated Parmesan cheese. Grate the cheese with the steel blade. Add the butter and flour to the container and process for 3 to 5 seconds. With the machine running, add the hot liquid through the tube. Cook the sauce in the top part of a double boiler over hot water, or over direct heat, stirring constantly. Beat egg yolks into the sauce; blend well. When the sauce is cool, fold in the egg whites which have been beaten stiff but not dry. Spoon the mixture into a buttered 8-cup soufflé dish, and bake in the preheated oven for 25 minutes, or until the soufflé is puffed and golden. Serves 4 to 6.

### VARIATIONS ON CHEESE SOUFFLÉ

*Soft Cheese*—Use 1 cup cubed Brie or Camembert cheese in place of the hard cheese, plus 3 tablespoons grated Parmesan.

*Florentine*—Use 2 packages (10 oz. each) frozen chopped spinach, cooked and well drained. Purée the spinach with 3 tablespoons butter and ¼ teaspoon grated nutmeg, using the steel blade. Spread the spinach mixture over the bottom of a 8-cup soufflé dish, and mound a cheese soufflé mixture on top of the spinach.

*Extra-Light*—Substitute ½ cup creamed cottage cheese and 3 ounces cream cheese for the usual harder cheeses.

*Green Cheese*—Blend together ½ cup packed parsley, ½ teaspoon tarragon, 2 teaspoons chives and 2 tablespoons shallots or 2 cut-up green onions. Sauté in 3 tablespoons butter, and add to the Extra-Light soufflé mixture or to the regular cheese soufflé recipe.

*Chicken and Mushroom*—Fold 1 cup cubed cooked chicken, chopped, and 1 cup Duxelles (see Index) into a plain or cheese soufflé mixture, and serve with Sauce Suprême (see Index).

*Leftover Fish*—Blend ¼ cup fresh dill and the cut-up rind of ½ lemon with 1½ cups cooked flaked fish, using the steel blade. Fold the fish into the soufflé base. Serve with a complementary sauce.

*Leftover Meat*—Chop 2 shallots or 2 scallions with 1½ cups cubed cooked meat, using the steel blade, and add to cheese soufflé or a plain soufflé base. Serve with a tomato-flavored sauce.

## PLAIN SOUFFLÉ BASE

*3 Tbsp. butter*
*4 Tbsp. flour*
*1½ cups milk, hot*
*pinch of grated nutmeg*
*salt and pepper*
*6 egg yolks*
*1½ to 2 cups puréed or
    chopped vegetables,
    meat, fish or seafood*
*8 egg whites*

Preheat oven to 375°F. Place butter and flour in the container with the steel blade, and process until just blended, for 3 to 5 seconds. With the machine running, add the hot milk through the tube, and add seasonings to taste. Add egg yolks and blend for 3 to 5 seconds. Cook in the top part of a double boiler over hot water, or over direct heat, stirring constantly, until thick. Add the chopped or puréed ingredients to the sauce. Fold in the beaten egg whites. Spoon the mixture into a buttered 8-cup soufflé dish. Bake in the preheated oven for 25 minutes, or until the soufflé is high and mighty. Serves 4 to 6.

## VARIATION

*Soufflé Véronique*—Purée 1 cup cooked filet of sole or other white fish. Substitute ¾ cup white wine for half of the milk. Add 1 teaspoon lemon juice and fold in 1½ cups seedless white grapes, halved. Serve with Sauce Véronique (see Index). Serves 6.

# SOUFFLÉED SPECIALTIES

These soufflés are easy to make, requiring no sauce base, being only a combination of egg yolks, egg whites and purées.

## SEAFOOD SOUFFLÉ

1 can (7 oz.) minced
  clams
½ lb. raw lobster tails,
  shrimps or scallops
5 egg yolks
5 egg whites

Preheat oven to 375°F. Put clams with their liquid and the cut-up shellfish in the container with the steel blade, and process until a thick paste is obtained. Add the egg yolks and whir again. Fold in the stiffly beaten egg whites. Set baking dishes in a pan of hot water. Bake individual ramekins in the preheated oven for 20 minutes, or a large dish for 30 to 35 minutes. Serves 4 to 6.

## CHICKEN-LIVER AND WATER-CHESTNUT SOUFFLÉ

1 lb. chicken livers
3 Tbsp. butter
1 cup water chestnuts,
  sliced
5 eggs, separated
½ cup sherry

Preheat oven to 375°F. Sauté chicken livers in butter until cooked through but still soft. Slice water chestnuts with the slicing disc and set aside. Purée chicken livers, egg yolks and sherry with the steel blade. Fold in water chestnuts and the stiffly beaten egg whites. Spoon into 4 buttered individual molds. Bake in the preheated oven for 20 minutes. Serves 4.

## SUCCOTASH SOUFFLÉ

1 cup cooked whole-
  kernel corn
1 cup lima beans, cooked
5 egg yolks
2 Tbsp. butter

Preheat oven to 375°F. Use canned corn, or cooked freshly cut green corn. Process the cooked vegetables, egg yolks, butter and seasonings with the steel blade. Fold in the stiffly beaten egg whites, and pile in a buttered 5-cup mold. Set

*1 tsp. salt*
*1 tsp. sugar*
*6 drops of Tabasco*
*6 egg whites*

mold in a pan of hot water, and bake in the preheated oven for 30 to 35 minutes. Serves 4 to 6.

# ROULADE

A roulade is a "jelly-roll" soufflé which can be filled with all manner of puréed or chopped delicacies—clams to ham. Lovely for a party.

## ROULADE SOUFFLÉ

*butter for pan*
*4 Tbsp. butter*
*6 Tbsp. flour*
*2 cups milk, hot*
*4 eggs, separated*
*1 tsp. salt*
*⅛ tsp. cayenne pepper*
*1 Tbsp. brandy*
*1 Tbsp. sour cream*

Preheat oven to 375°F. *Generously* butter a jelly-roll pan, 15 × 10 inches. Line the pan with wax paper, leaving an overhang of 2 inches at each end. Butter the paper as well. Place 4 tablespoons butter and the flour in the container and process until just incorporated. With the machine running, add the hot milk through the tube. Cook the mixture in the top part of a double boiler over hot water, or over direct heat, until thick and smooth. Cool. Place egg yolks, salt, cayenne, brandy and sour cream in the container with the steel blade, and whir. Whir the egg-yolk mixture with the cooled sauce. Beat the egg whites until they stand in soft peaks. Mix one third of the egg whites into the sauce mixture, then lightly fold in the remainder. Spread the batter into the prepared pan, smoothing it out with a spatula. Bake in the preheated oven for 20 to 25 minutes, or until golden on top. Place a clean towel on the counter and turn out the roulade onto it. Strip off the wax paper carefully and trim off the crisp edges. Spread the surface of the roulade with the filling and roll up. Reheat in foil or on an ovenproof platter.

## FILLING FOR ROULADE SOUFFLÉ

Extra filling may be thinned to make a sauce, or a special sauce may be served, to complement the filling.

*1 cup thick Sauce Béchamel, or ½ cup sour cream mixed with 1 cup Mayonnaise (see Index)*
*2 cups cut-up cooked vegetable, meat, poultry, fish, or similar purée*

Chop or purée the solid ingredients, using the steel blade, and fold into the sauce or sour-cream and mayonnaise.

### FILLING VARIATIONS

*Duxelles and Salmon*—Moisten with hollandaise in place of béchamel.
*Chicken and Broccoli*—Bind with sour cream and mayonnaise in place of béchamel.
*Tongue and Spinach*—Mix with mustard-flavored béchamel.
*Seasoned Ground Meat*—Moisten with sour cream and dill instead of béchamel; serve with Dill Sauce (see Index).

---

# TIMBALES

Timbales are light custardy delights, in texture between a mousse and a soufflé. They have the advantage of having a bit more substance than a soufflé, and they can be reheated. Timbales are usually cooked in their individual molds or in muffin tins, then turned out and dressed with a sauce, but they can be cooked in one large dish, a ring mold or any interesting mold. Timbales have an especially appetizing appeal when treated to a garnish of chopped parsley and buttered bread crumbs.

# CUSTARD TIMBALES

*1½ cups warm milk, or 1
cup warm chicken stock
and ½ cup light cream*
*4 eggs*
*1½ cups cooked
vegetable, fish, poultry
or meat*
*salt*

Preheat oven to 325°F. Place the ingredients, with salt to taste, in the container with the steel blade and blend for 10 to 20 seconds. Spoon the mixture into 6 buttered custard cups or molds or into one 6-cup mold. Cover the mold with foil. Set the mold or molds on a rack in a pan of hot water. Bake in the preheated oven for 25 to 30 minutes, or to the point when a knife inserted in the center comes out clean. Remove timbales from the oven and allow them to stand for a few minutes to set. Run a knife around the edges and unmold.

If time is important, the molds can be placed on a rack in a pressure cooker, with ½ cup water in the cooker. Cover molds securely with foil and cook at 15 pounds pressure for 3 minutes. Reduce the pressure quickly. Serves 6.

## FLAVORINGS FOR CUSTARD TIMBALE

*Cheese*—Add 1 cup grated cheese to custard base. Serve with bacon curls and toast points. Serves 4 or 5.

*Vegetable*—Fold in 1½ cups puréed asparagus, broccoli, cauliflower, peas, well-drained shredded zucchini, or sautéed chopped onions or mushrooms. Serve with Sauce Hollandaise or a complementary sauce—Poulette or Herb Sauce (see Index for sauce pages). Serves 4.

## CHICKEN-LIVER TIMBALES

*2 slices of bread without
crusts*
*milk*
*¾ cup chicken livers*
*1 tsp. prepared Dijon
mustard*
*1 shallot*
*½ cup heavy cream*
*3 eggs, separated*
*salt*

Preheat oven to 325°F. Soak bread in milk and squeeze dry. Put bread and other ingredients except salt and egg whites in the machine. Process with the steel blade for 7 seconds. Season with salt to taste. Beat egg whites until they form soft peaks, then fold egg whites into the liver mixture. Spoon mixture into buttered molds, cover with foil, and set on a rack in a pan of hot water. Bake in the preheated oven for 30 minutes, or to the point when a knife inserted in the center comes out clean. Unmold and serve with Mushroom Sauce (see Index); garnish with parsley or other chopped herbs. Serves 5 or 6.

## TIMBALES BASED ON BÉCHAMEL SAUCE

*4 cups cut-up cooked meat, fish, poultry or vegetables*
*2 cups Sauce Béchamel (see Index)*
*4 whole eggs*
*4 egg yolks*
*salt and pepper*
*½ cup heavy cream*

Preheat oven to 350°F. Place the solids in the container with the steel blade, 2 cups at a time, and purée. Add remaining ingredients except the cream and blend well, scraping down the sides of the bowl from time to time. Season with salt and pepper to taste. Stir in the cream. Fill 12 well-greased individual molds. Set in a shallow pan containing about 1 inch of hot water. Bake in the preheated oven for 25 to 30 minutes, or until a knife comes out clean when inserted into the center of the timbales. Serve with a complementary cream sauce or a variation of hollandaise (see Index for sauces). Serves 12.

# QUICHES

The most famous of these open custard tarts, *Quiche Lorraine,* should not have any cheese in the filling—just good cream, eggs, ham or smoky bacon. Pâte Brisée is a classic pastry for making the quiche shell. The shells can be filled with all manner of mixtures. A quiche is light enough for a first course, substantial enough for a main dish; a quiche makes a satisfying hors d'oeuvre if prepared in individual tart pans. See Chapter 4 for examples of hors d'oeuvre tarts.

## QUICHE SHELL

Prepare Pâte Brisée (see Index), line a 9-inch pie pan or deep quiche pan, and prebake according to directions on page 23.

## CUSTARD FILLING FOR QUICHE

Use a layer of cheese, bacon, mushroom, onions, etc., and a partially baked quiche shell.

*3 eggs*
*¼ tsp. salt*
*1½ cups light cream*
*salt and pepper*
*¼ tsp. grated nutmeg*

Preheat oven to 375°F. Place the layer of cheese, bacon, etc., on the partially baked shell. Put the custard ingredients in the container with the steel blade, and blend. Pour the custard into the shell, and finish baking in the preheated oven for 35 minutes. Serves 6.

## FIRMER QUICHE FILLING

Use puréed or chopped ingredients and a partially baked quiche shell.

*1½ cups cooked solids,*
*chopped, puréed or*
*sliced*
*3 eggs*
*1 cup light cream or milk*
*¼ tsp. grated nutmeg*
*salt and pepper*

Preheat oven to 375°F. Process solids with proper blade or disc. Blend liquid ingredients in the processor with the steel blade, and fold in the processed solids along with the seasonings to taste. Pour into the partially baked shell, and finish baking in the preheated oven for 30 to 35 minutes or until a knife comes out clean. Serves 6.

## WHITE QUICHE

*1 deep quiche shell, or*
*9 inch pan*
*6 slices of bacon, cooked*
*until limp*
*4 oz. cream cheese*
*3 eggs, separated*
*½ cup heavy cream*
*1 Tbsp. parsley*
*salt and pepper*

Preheat oven to 400°F. Lay the limp bacon on the bottom of the partially baked shell. Process remaining ingredients together except the egg whites with the steel blade and place the mixture in a bowl. Beat the egg whites until stiff but not dry and fold into the cheese mixture. Pour into the shell and bake in the preheated oven for 20 minutes. Reduce oven temperature to 350°F. and bake for 10 more minutes, or until puffy. Serves 6.

## SPINACH QUICHE À LA GRECQUE

2 pkg. (10 oz. each)
  frozen chopped spinach
½ cup cottage cheese
½ cup cut-up Feta cheese
6 scallions, cut up
1 tsp. minced basil
salt and pepper
1 Tbsp. lemon juice
3 eggs
1½ cups light cream or
  milk
1 deep quiche shell, or
  9 inch pan

Preheat oven to 400°F. Cook spinach and drain. Put spinach, cheeses, scallions, seasonings to taste and lemon juice in the container with the steel blade. Process until just mixed, about 10 seconds. Scrape down the sides and add the eggs and milk. Blend for 3 to 5 seconds. Spoon the mixture into the partially baked shell. Bake in the preheated oven for 20 minutes. Reduce oven heat to 350°F. and bake for 10 minutes more. Serves 6.

## BLUE CHEESE QUICHE

4 oz. blue cheese
8 oz. cream cheese, cubed
2 Tbsp. butter
3 eggs
1½ cups sour cream
dash of cayenne
salt and pepper
1 deep quiche shell, or
  9 inch pan
1 cup walnuts
butter

Preheat oven to 400°F. Blend cheeses, butter, eggs, sour cream, and seasonings to taste with the steel blade. Pour into the partially baked quiche shell. Chop the nuts with the steel blade, and sprinkle them on top of the cheese mixture. Dot with butter. Bake in the preheated oven for 20 minutes. Reduce oven heat to 350°F. and bake for 10 minutes more. Serves 6.

## LEEK QUICHE

2 lb. leeks, white part
  only
4 Tbsp. butter
1 cup cubed cooked ham
1 deep quiche shell, or
  9 inch pan
3 eggs
1 cup light cream
butter
salt and pepper

Preheat oven to 350°F. Slice leeks with the slicing disc. Wash and drain. Sauté leeks in the butter until soft. Chop the ham with the steel blade, and spread ham and leeks on the bottom of the partially baked shell. Beat eggs and cream with the steel blade, and pour over the leek-ham mixture. Dot with butter. Bake in the preheated oven for 30 to 40 minutes. Serves 6.

## ZUCCHINI QUICHE

4 small zucchini
½ cup cut-up provolone
2 shallots
1 garlic clove
2 Tbsp. butter
2 Tbsp. oil
1 deep quiche shell, or
    9 inch pan
3 eggs
1 cup light cream
¼ cup grated Parmesan
    cheese
salt and pepper

Preheat oven to 375°F. Slice zucchini with the slicing disc; set aside. Grate provolone with the steel blade; set aside. Mince shallots and garlic with the steel blade along with the butter, and sauté the mixture. Add the oil and zucchini slices and cook until crisp-tender. Spoon the shallot-zucchini mixture into the partially baked shell. Blend the eggs, cream, Parmesan cheese and seasoning to taste with the steel blade, and pour mixture over the vegetables. Top with the grated provolone. Bake in the preheated oven for 25 minutes, or until nicely browned and set. Serves 6.

## MUSHROOM QUICHE

1 lb. mushrooms
½ lb. Gruyère cheese, cut
    up
3 eggs
1 cup light cream
salt and pepper
5 Tbsp. butter
1 deep quiche shell, or
    9 inch pan

Preheat oven to 375°F. Slice the mushrooms with the slicing disc; set aside. Grate the cheese with the slicing blade, set aside. Blend the eggs, cream, and salt and pepper to taste with the steel blade. Cook the mushrooms in the butter until soft but not overbrowned. Place a layer of the mushrooms in the partially baked shell; sprinkle with cheese. Repeat a layer of mushrooms and another layer of cheese. Pour the egg mixture over the top. Bake in the preheated oven until set. Serves 6.

## CHEESE CROQUETTES

3 Tbsp. butter
⅓ cup flour
1½ cups cut-up Cheddar
  cheese, or Cheddar
  mixed with ½ cup
  grated Parmesan
⅔ cup hot milk or chicken
  stock
2 egg yolks
½ tsp. salt
½ tsp. dry mustard
2 whole eggs
2 Tbsp. water
2 cups dried bread
  crumbs

Blend the butter, flour and cut-up cheese in the container with the steel blade until crumbly. With the motor running, pour the hot liquid through the tube and blend again. Cook the mixture, stirring constantly, until thickened. Remove from heat and return to the container with the steel blade. Add the egg yolks and seasonings. Spread the cheese mixture on a buttered plate and chill thoroughly. Shape mixture into croquettes. Beat whole eggs and water. Roll each croquette in bread crumbs, then dip into the egg and water mixture, and again into bread crumbs. Let dry for 2 hours. Fry croquettes, a few at a time, in deep fat heated to 375°F. Drain on paper towels and place on a heated dish. Serve with Mushroom Sauce (see Index). Serves 4.

## CHEESE FONDUE

1 garlic clove, halved
½ lb. Emmental cheese
½ lb. Gruyère cheese
1 cup dry white wine
1 tsp. cornstarch
3 Tbsp. kirsch
¼ tsp. grated nutmeg
salt and pepper

Rub a heavy ovenproof casserole with the garlic. Cut the cheeses into pieces and place in the container with the steel blade. Add wine, cornstarch, kirsch, nutmeg, and salt and pepper to taste. Process until all is homogenized. Transfer the mixture to a fondue casserole and heat, stirring constantly. When hot, place the casserole over an alcohol lamp, or put the mixture in a chafing dish and keep warm. Serve with French or Italian bread, cut into 1-inch squares, for dunking. Serves 6.

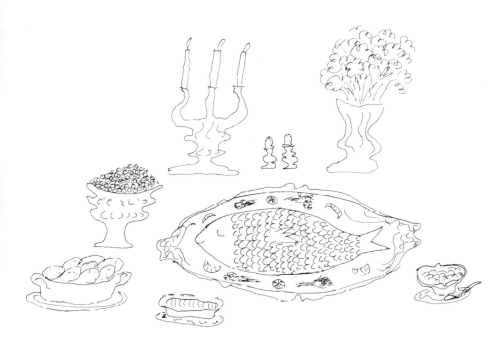

# FISH AND SHELLFISH

Quenelles, mousses, fish puddings, medallions, brandades and
seafood fillings, hitherto time-consuming and tedious in their
preparation, are fantastically easy when made in the Food
Processor, and with superb results to boot.

# QUENELLES

Quenelles are feather-light dumplings made with fish or meat forcemeat. There are many types. Mousseline quenelles are made only with seafood, cream, eggs and seasonings; these are very special. Quenelle forcemeat (also called mousseline of fish, etc.) can be baked in a large buttered dish like a mousse, or can be used as a filling for rolled-up fillets, or for stuffings.

## FISH OR SHELLFISH QUENELLES

*1 lb. fresh raw fish or shellfish (halibut, pike, shrimps, or part shrimps and part scallops), cut up*
*1 egg*
*6 drops of Tabasco*
*¼ tsp. grated nutmeg*
*1 tsp. salt*
*1½ cups heavy cream*
*2 to 3 cups sauce (for baking)*

Put fish or cleaned shellfish and cream along with the processor bowl and steel blade in the freezer compartment, and chill for 15 minutes. Cut fish into pieces and put them in the bowl with the steel blade. Process for about 1 minute, scraping down the sides, when necessary. Add the egg and seasonings and blend briefly. With the machine running, pour the cream through the tube. Process until smooth, or until the mixture will just hold its shape when dropped from a spoon. Chill. Heavily butter a large cold pan. Dip 2 teaspoons or tablespoons into hot water and use spoons to form oval shapes of the mixture. Place ovals in the cold pan. When the bottom of the pan is covered with quenelles, carefully pour in enough salted boiling water to make the quenelles float. Keeping the water just at the simmering point, poach the quenelles for 10 minutes; turn them after 5 minutes. Drain the quenelles on paper towels. Start afresh and repeat the process for each batch. (At this point, they may be frozen.) Place them in a single layer in a buttered flat baking dish. Spoon a generous amount of Sauce Nantua, Fish Béchamel, or Mushroom Sauce (see Index for pages) over the quenelles, and bake them in a preheated 425° F. oven for about 20 minutes, until the sauce bubbles. They almost double in size. Serves 5 or 6.

# TURBAN OF SOLE

8 large raw fillets of sole
1½ lb. raw haddock, cut
  up
¼ lb. butter (1 stick),
  melted
chopped parsley
salt and pepper
4 eggs, separated
3 Tbsp. flour
1 cup milk
1 cup heavy cream

Preheat oven to 375°F. Heavily butter an 8-cup ring mold. Season the raw fillets and score the edges to prevent curling. Line the mold with fillets, crosswise, leaving enough excess at the outside edge and center edge to fold back over the stuffing. Cut the haddock into pieces and place these in the container with the steel blade, along with the melted butter, and parsley and seasonings to taste. Blend to a paste, scraping down the sides when necessary. Add the egg yolks and the flour, and process until blended. Scrape down again. With the machine running, add the milk through the tube. If mixture curdles add 2 more teaspoons melted butter and continue to blend. Transfer the mixture to a bowl. Put the cream in the container with the plastic blade, and whip until quite stiff. Beat egg whites to the soft peak stage. Fold whipped cream into the fish mixture, then fold in beaten egg whites. Place all in the center of the prepared mold and fold the ends of the sole fillets over the filling. Cover with buttered wax paper, buttered side down. Set mold in a pan of hot water, and bake in the preheated oven for about 30 minutes. Unmold onto a warm platter and garnish with parsley. Serve with Sauce Aurore (see Index). Serves 6 to 8.

## HOT SEAFOOD MOUSSE

2 lb. raw seafood, boned
  and skinned (fresh
  salmon, lobster,
  halibut, sole or shelled
  shrimps), cut up
1 tsp. salt
½ tsp. white pepper
⅛ tsp. grated nutmeg
3 cups heavy cream
2 eggs

Preheat oven to 375°F. Process half the recipe at a time. Place the fish with the seasonings in the container with the steel knife; blend. With the motor running, add the cream through the tube. Turn off the motor and add eggs. Blend again. Spoon the mousse into a buttered mold, and cover mold with buttered wax paper, buttered side down. Set in a pan of boiling water, and bake in the preheated oven for 1 hour, or until a knife inserted in the mousse comes out clean. Unmold and serve with Sauce Nantua (see Index) or any creamy fish sauce. Serves 4 to 6.

## COLD SEAFOOD MOUSSE

2 envelopes unflavored
  gelatin
½ cup clam juice
1 cup vegetable stock or
  water, hot
1¼ cups cooked or
  canned fish, cut up or
  flaked
1 lemon, juice and rind
½ cup snipped chives
6 stuffed olives, halved
1 celery rib, roughly cut
½ cup white wine
salt and pepper
1 cup heavy cream
2 cucumbers, sliced
6 radishes, sliced

Soak the gelatin in ½ cup clam juice in the container with the steel blade for 10 minutes. Pour in the hot stock or water and blend to dissolve the gelatin. Add the cut-up or flaked fish and blend with the lemon juice, chives, olives and celery. Scrape down. Add the wine, season to taste, and set aside. Whip the cream in the bowl with the plastic blade, and fold it into the cooled gelatin mixture. Pour into a wet mold and chill until set. Garnish with cucumber and radish slices, cut with the slicing blade. Serve with Ravigote Dressing (see Index). Serves 4 or 5.

## COLD SHRIMP MOUSSE

2 lb. shelled deveined
   shrimps
1 bay leaf
1 lemon, sliced
2 envelopes unflavored
   gelatin
½ cup cold water
½ cup chopped scallions
2 cucumbers, peeled and
   seeded
½ cup sour cream
¾ cup Mayonnaise (see
   Index)
1 tsp. salt
½ tsp. white pepper
6 drops of Tabasco
hard-cooked eggs

Cook the shrimps with the bay leaf and lemon in water to cover. Drain, and save 2 cups of the cooking liquid. Soak gelatin in ½ cup cold water in the processor bowl with the steel blade for 10 minutes. Pour in 1 cup of strained hot shrimp cooking liquid and blend until gelatin is dissolved. Put in half of the shrimps and blend. Set aside. Process the other half of the shrimps with the scallions and remaining strained cooking liquid. Combine the shrimp mixtures and set aside. Shred the cucumbers with the shredding disc, and drain. Fold the cucumbers into the shrimp gelatin with the sour cream, mayonnaise and seasonings. Put in a wet mold and chill for at least 3 hours. Unmold and garnish with hard-cooked eggs. Serve with Cold Cucumber Sauce (see Index). Serves 4 or 5.

## SCANDINAVIAN FISH PUDDING

1½ lb. fresh haddock, or
   1½ lb. frozen fish
   fillets, thawed, cut up
½ cup milk
2 Tbsp. fresh bread
   crumbs
2 Tbsp. cornstarch
2 Tbsp. water
3 eggs
¼ tsp. grated nutmeg
1 Tbsp. butter
1 cup heavy cream

Preheat oven to 325°F. Put half of the cut-up fish into the container with the steel blade. Add milk and bread crumbs and purée; set aside. Mix cornstarch with water, and add to the remaining fish, eggs, nutmeg and butter; blend. With the machine running, add the cream through the tube. Mix all of this with the first fish mixture and stir. Spoon into a buttered 6-cup baking dish and set in a pan of hot water. Bake in the preheated oven for 1 hour, or until a knife comes out clean. Serve with Hollandaise or Dill Sauce (see Index). Serves 4 or 5.

## JANSSON'S TEMPTATION

*6 medium-size potatoes,*
  *peeled*
*4 medium-size onions*
*16 to 20 anchovy fillets*
  *and their oil*
*butter*
*1½ cups light cream*

Preheat oven to 350°F. Julienne or slice potatoes with the slicing disc. Place potato pieces in cold water to prevent discoloring. Slice the onions. Butter a shallow baking dish and layer the bottom with half of the drained potatoes. Cover the potatoes with a layer of sliced onions. Place the anchovy fillets on top of the onions, and remaining potatoes over all. Dot with butter. Scald the cream and pour over the potatoes. Bake in the preheated oven for 45 minutes, or until the liquid is nearly absorbed. Serves 6.

## BAKED POTATOES STUFFED WITH CODFISH

*½ cup cut-up Gruyère*
  *cheese*
*½ lb. salt cod*
*4 large baking potatoes*
*2 garlic cloves*
*¼ cup parsley*
*½ cup sour cream*
*½ cup snipped chives*
*1 tsp. pepper*
*¼ lb. butter (1 stick)*
*¼ cup dried bread crumbs*

Grate the cheese with the steel blade. Soak the cod for 8 to 12 hours, changing the water 3 times. Poach the fish in water to cover for 20 minutes; drain, and flake. Bake the potatoes for 45 minutes to 1 hour, or until done. Cut a thin lengthwise slice from each potato. Scoop out the insides of potatoes and set the shells aside. Put the scooped-out potato and flaked cod in the container with the steel blade, along with the garlic, parsley, half of the cheese, the sour cream, chives, pepper and 4 tablespoons butter. Blend well. Fill the potato shells with the mixture. Top with the rest of the cheese and the bread crumbs, and dot with remaining butter. Bake in a 400° oven for 15 minutes. Serves 4.

# BRANDADE DE MORUE

A Provençale specialty

*1½ lb. salt cod*
*1 large potato, ½ lb.*
*2 bay leaves*
*6 peppercorns*
*2 or 3 garlic cloves*
*⅔ cup heavy cream,*
  *scalded*
*1 cup olive oil, heated*
*1 tsp. white pepper*

Soak the cod for 8 to 12 hours, changing the water 3 times. Bake the potato for 45 minutes, or until soft. Poach the cod, covered with water, with the bay leaves and peppercorns until tender. Drain the cod and cut into 1-inch pieces. Scoop out the potato and place the pulp in the container with the garlic. Process for 5 seconds. Add the cod pieces and again process, scraping down the sides. With the motor running, add half of the scalded cream and half of the hot oil in small amounts, alternating until both are incorporated. Transfer the mixture to a bowl, season with pepper, and slowly beat in the rest of the cream and oil with a whisk. Continue to beat until the mixture has the consistency of fluffy mashed potatoes. To serve, heat the *brandade* in the top part of a double boiler over simmering water, and mound on a hot platter. Garnish with a border of ripe olives, and accompany with buttered or sautéed toast triangles. *Brandade de morue* may also be heated in a prebaked tart shell or served cold as a spread, with crusty bread. Serves 6.

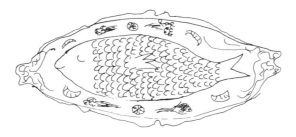

## SEAFOOD MEDALLIONS, POJARSKI

5½ cups soft bread
  crumbs
¼ lb. raw shrimps
1¼ lb. raw fillet of sole
¼ lb. sea or bay scallops
2½ tsp. salt
¼ tsp. Tabasco
1 tsp. freshly grated
  nutmeg
1½ cups milk
2 cups heavy cream
½ lb. butter (2 sticks)

Make the bread crumbs with the steel blade; reserve 1 cup for breading and set the rest aside. Shell and devein the shrimps. Cut all the seafood into small pieces. Process half of the seafood, the seasonings, half of the milk and half of the cream with the steel blade for 15 seconds. Transfer to a large bowl. Process the second batch in the same way, and combine the two mixtures. Correct seasoning. Add 4½ cups of the bread crumbs to the seafood mixture. If time permits, refrigerate the batter for 2 to 12 hours. Place reserved 1 cup of bread crumbs on a large plate. To shape the medallions scoop up about ⅓ cup of the batter with a large spoon. Drop the medallion into the crumbs, gently rolling it on all sides until well breaded. Transfer it to another plate and carefully pat it into a flat oval, ½ inch thick. Continue this procedure until all the batter has been used. Place a frying pan over medium-low heat and add 1 teaspoon butter for each medallion. When the butter is sizzling, add the medallions, leaving ample space between them. In 2 or 3 minutes they should be brown on the bottom. Again add 1 teaspoon butter per medallion and brown the other side. They are done when browned and springy to the touch. They may be served at once, or they can be cooled and refrigerated for a day. To reheat, place them on a cookie sheet and bake them in a 375°F. oven for about 20 minutes. Serve with very thin slices of lemon. They may also be served with a thin Sauce Béchamel (see Index) with a lemon accent.

To freeze, place the cooked medallions in a single layer on a cookie sheet. When they are frozen, package them in plastic bags. Frozen medallions should be removed from the freezer the night before you plan to serve them. Let them defrost in the refrigerator. Serves 6.

# COULIBIAC

This elegant Russian dish is a fish pie, usually made with salmon, baked in a brioche wrapping or alternatively in puff paste.

*Brioche Crust (see Index)*
*½ lb. mushrooms, sliced,*
*  or 1 cup Duxelles (see*
*  Index)*
*1 cup cut-up scallions*
*½ cup parsley*
*4 Tbsp. butter*
*½ cup Madeira wine*
*1 tsp. white pepper*
*¼ tsp. ground allspice*
*¼ tsp. ground cinnamon*
*¼ tsp. ground cloves*
*¼ tsp. grated nutmeg*
*1½ lb. cooked fresh or*
*  canned salmon, drained*
*  and flaked*
*2 cups cooked rice*
*2 cups thick Sauce*
*  Béchamel (see Index)*
*3 hard-cooked eggs,*
*  sliced*
*1 raw egg*
*1 tsp. milk*

Make the brioche dough and refrigerate after the first rising. Prepare the mushrooms by slicing, or make duxelles. Put scallions and parsley in the container with the steel blade and chop. Sauté scallions and parsley in the butter until limp. Add Madeira, mushrooms and spices, and simmer for 6 minutes. Gently stir in the flaked salmon and cook for a few minutes to mingle the flavors; cool.

Take brioche dough from refrigerator and roll it out on a large floured pastry cloth or a sheet of wax paper large enough so that the filled pastry can be lifted up and rolled over, with the seam side down, onto the baking sheet. Roll the dough ¼ inch thick to a rectangle 18 x 16 inches. Spread a layer of rice on the dough, leaving a 4-inch margin from the edge of the dough on all sides. Spoon a thick layer of béchamel over the rice and add a layer of the salmon mixture. Top with a layer of sliced eggs and moisten with another layer of béchamel; repeat the layering until all filling is used. Fold the dough over the filling, pinching the dough to seal the top and ends. Gently roll the dough over onto a cookie sheet. Make a small hole in the top of the dough to allow steam to escape. Beat raw egg and milk together. Glaze pastry with the egg mixture. Bake in a preheated 425°F. oven for 25 minutes, or until the dough is golden. Serve hot with melted lemon butter, or eat as a cold dish. Serves 8 to 10.

# CROQUETTES

Croquettes can be made of freshly cooked ingredients or from minced leftovers, bound with eggs or a cream sauce; they are then breaded and deep-fried.

## SHRIMP, CRAB OR LOBSTER CROQUETTES

*1 cup thick Sauce*
 *Béchamel (see Index)*
*2 Tbsp. sherry*
*1 egg yolk, beaten*
*2 cups cooked or canned*
 *shellfish*
*4 parsley sprigs*
*1 tsp. salt*
*½ tsp. white pepper*
*¼ tsp. grated nutmeg*
*2 whole eggs*
*4 Tbsp. water*
*1½ cups cracker crumbs*
 *(14 saltines)*

Prepare Sauce Béchamel. Remove sauce from heat and add the sherry and beaten egg yolk. Put cooked shellfish and parsley in the container and process with the steel blade until coarsely ground, about 3 seconds. *Do not overblend.* Add seasonings, and fold the mixture into the béchamel. Spread on a buttered large plate and refrigerate for 1 to 2 hours.

Form mixture into croquettes, small rolls or cakes. Beat whole eggs with water. Roll croquettes in cracker crumbs, then dip into the egg wash and again into the crumbs. Refrigerate for 1 hour for a crispier croquette. Fry in deep fat heated to 375°F. until golden brown. Serve with Sauce Tartare (see Index) and French fried parsley. Serves 4 to 6.

## CODFISH CAKES

*½ lb. salt cod*
*3 large raw potatoes*
*1 egg, beaten*
*¼ tsp. pepper*
*2 medium-size onions, cut*
 *up*
*4 Tbsp. butter*
*2 Tbsp. oil*

Soak the cod for 8 to 12 hours, changing the water 3 times. Peel the potatoes and slice in the processor with the slicing disc. Cut up the cod into big chunks and poach with the potatoes in water to cover until potatoes are soft; drain. Place the mixture in the container with the steel blade and add the egg, pepper and onions. Blend 1 cup at a time, until thoroughly combined. Form into cakes or balls and fry in the butter and oil until crunchy. Serve with a tomato-flavored sauce. Serves 4 to 6.

## CANNED FISH CAKES (SALMON OR TUNA)

*1½ cups golden bread*
*crumbs*
*1 lb. canned salmon or*
*tuna*
*rind of ½ lemon*
*1 tsp. dried dill*
*3 eggs*
*salt and pepper*
*3 Tbsp. butter*
*3 Tbsp. vegetable oil*

Prepare bread crumbs. Set aside. Put fish, lemon rind, dill, eggs, and seasonings to taste in the container, and process with the steel blade. With the machine running, pour the bread crumbs through the tube until the mixture is thick enough to form into cakes. Shape into cakes. Sauté in butter and oil until crisp on the outside. Serve with lemon butter and capers. Serves 4 to 6.

## BAKED FISH LOAF

*2 cups corn-bread crumbs*
*or soft bread crumbs*
*2 lb. cooked halibut,*
*haddock or turbot*
*1 tsp. salt*
*½ tsp. white pepper*
*¼ tsp. ground ginger*
*¼ tsp. grated mace*
*3 raw eggs, separated*
*2 cups light cream*
*3 hard-cooked eggs,*
*chopped*
*1 cup Sauce Béchamel*
*(see Index)*

Preheat oven to 350°F. Prepare bread crumbs; set aside. Cut fish into pieces. Process half of the ingredients using the steel blade, and turning the motor on and immediately off; set aside. Process the rest of the ingredients. Combine both of the processed fish mixtures in a large bowl, and fold in the egg whites, beaten stiff. Spoon into a buttered 8-cup loaf pan, and set in a pan of hot water. Bake in the preheated oven for 1¼ hours. Serve with egg sauce, made by adding the chopped hard-cooked eggs to the béchamel. Serves 6.

## FISH PÂTÉ

*1 lb. raw fillet of flounder*
*¼ cup milk*
*½ lb. butter (2 sticks),*
*softened and cut up*
*1 cup fresh bread*
*crumbs*
*1 cup quartered*
*mushrooms*

Preheat oven to 350°F. Place in the container, with the steel blade, the flounder, which has been cut into pieces, the milk, softened butter, bread crumbs, mushrooms, egg yolk and seasonings to taste. Blend until smooth. Remove the skin and bones from the salmon steak and cut fish into narrow strips. Put a ½-inch layer of the flounder mixture on the bottom of a buttered 6-cup mold

1 egg yolk
¼ tsp. grated mace
dash of cayenne
salt and pepper
1 lb. raw salmon steak
2 tsp. dried tarragon
3 Tbsp. butter
2 tsp. chopped parsley

and pack down. Place a layer of the salmon strips over the mixture. Sprinkle with the tarragon, and salt and pepper to taste. Continue layering the fish mousse and the salmon strips until the dish is tightly packed. Dot the top layer with butter, and cover with a lid or foil held tightly in place. Bake in the preheated oven for 2½ hours. Do not uncover until cold. Garnish with parsley. Serve with Melba toast. Serves 6 to 8.

# STUFFINGS FOR FISH

## NUT-MUSHROOM STUFFING

½ cup dry bread crumbs
½ cup toasted almonds
1 lb. mushrooms,
    quartered
3 shallots or scallions,
    cut up
1 tsp. dried thyme
½ tsp. salt
¼ tsp. pepper
3 Tbsp. butter
3 Tbsp. chicken stock
1 egg yolk
2 Tbsp. minced parsley

Process the bread crumbs and almonds together with the steel blade; set aside. Place the mushrooms, shallots or scallions, and seasonings in the container and chop fine. Sauté the mixture in the butter. Moisten almond-crumb mixture with stock. Combine the crumbs and mushroom-shallot mixture with egg yolk and parsley, and stir lightly. Makes enough stuffing for 5- to 7-pound fish.

## SEAFOOD STUFFING

2 cups soft bread crumbs
4 scallions, cut up
1 lb. cooked shrimps or
    crab meat
2 eggs
½ cup chopped parsley
1 tsp. sweet marjoram
¼ lb. butter (1 stick)

Prepare the bread crumbs with the steel blade. Put scallions in the container and chop. Add shrimps or crab meat, eggs and herbs. Process for 3 to 5 seconds, so that the mixture is not too fine. Toss mixture with bread crumbs and sauté in the butter until well blended. Makes enough stuffing for 5- to 7-pound fish.

# POULTRY AND STUFFINGS

Special dishes, stuffings, sauces, all manner of poultry delights are achieved with alacrity using the Cuisinart™ Food Processor—creamy mousses, chicken in pastry, chicken in cold shapes, poultry leftovers. The many variations for poultry are an exciting part of Food Processor Magic.

# CHICKEN BREASTS SUPRÊME

1½ cups golden bread
  crumbs
2 tsp. dried tarragon
2 Tbsp. walnuts
4 whole chicken breasts,
  boned and skinned
½ lb. Gruyère cheese, cut
  up
¼ lb. salami, cut up
4 scallions, cut up
1 egg yolk
2 Tbsp. water
8 strips of bacon

Preheat oven to 350°F. Prepare the bread crumbs with the tarragon and walnuts, using the steel blade, and set aside. Halve the chicken breasts. Place each half between 2 sheets of wax paper, and flatten until thin. With the shredding disc, process the cheese, salami and scallions. Spoon 4 tablespoons of this filling on each half breast, and fold over, securing with a small skewer or food pick. Beat egg yolk with water to make egg wash, and brush each breast with the mixture. Bread with the crumb mixture. Place one layer deep in a buttered large baking dish. Lay a bacon strip over each chicken piece. Bake in the preheated oven for 35 to 40 minutes. Reheat in Paprika Sauce or Sauce Suprême (see Index). Serves 4 to 6.

# CHICKEN CROQUETTES

2 cups cut-up cooked
  chicken
1 celery rib, cut up
4 eggs
2 Tbsp. cream
1 cup fresh bread crumbs
½ cup toasted almonds
1 tsp. salt
¼ tsp. pepper
2 Tbsp. water
1 cup golden bread
  crumbs
fat for deep-frying
chopped parsley

Put chicken and celery in the container with the steel blade and chop for 3 to 5 seconds. Add 2 eggs and the cream and process until just blended. Prepare fresh crumbs and process with the almonds, using the steel blade. Add crumb mixture to chicken mixture, and season to taste. Spread on a greased shallow dish, and refrigerate for at least 2 hours. Shape the mixture into croquettes. Mix remaining 2 eggs with water to make egg wash. Roll croquettes in the golden crumbs, then dip into the egg wash and roll again in the crumbs. Let dry for 2 hours. Fry a few at a time in deep fat heated to 375°F. Drain. Serve with Mushroom Sauce or Sauce Allemande (see Index), and dress with lots of chopped parsley. Serves 4.

## POULTRY MOUSSE WITH PECANS

*4 cups cut-up cooked*
*poultry*
*¼ lb. pecans*
*3 hard-cooked eggs, cut*
*up*
*2 cups Sauce Béchamel*
*(see Index)*
*2 tsp. dried tarragon*
*salt and pepper*

Preheat oven to 350°F. Grind the poultry with the pecans 2 cups at a time, using the steel blade, and set aside. Chop the cut-up eggs by turning the motor on and off quickly. Stir poultry and eggs into the béchamel. Season with tarragon and salt and pepper to taste. Put in a buttered 5- or 6-cup ring mold and set in a pan of hot water. Bake in the preheated oven for 30 minutes, or until a knife comes out clean. Serve with Sauce Suprème (see Index). Serves 4 to 6.

## CHICKEN QUENELLES

For a description of quenelles and their mode of preparation, see Fish Quenelles. Chicken and meat quenelles are not as airy as their seafood mousseline counterparts due to the nature of the meat, but they are very satisfactory and party pretty.

*1 lb. raw chicken (boned*
*breasts), cut up*
*1½ cups heavy cream*
*2 egg whites*
*1 tsp. dried rosemary*
*salt and white pepper*
*4 cups Chicken Stock (see*
*Index), hot*
*3 cups Mushroom or*
*Poulette Sauce (see*
*Index)*

Chill the chicken and cream, along with the processor bowl and blade, in a freezing compartment for 15 minutes. Put the chicken, egg whites, rosemary and seasonings to taste in the container with the steel blade, and process until smooth. With the motor running, slowly pour in 1 cup of the chilled cream. Stop the motor and check the consistency of the paste, scraping down the sides. It should not be too stiff but firm enough to drop from a spoon into a mounded oval. Should the addition of more cream be necessary, start the motor and add a little more cream; test again. Refrigerate the mixture for 1 hour.

Preheat oven to 350°F. Heavily butter a cold large pan. Slip the formed quenelles into the pan in a single layer. Gently add the hot stock, enough to allow the quenelles to float. Simmer for 10 minutes. *Do not let the stock boil.* Remove the "dumplings" with a slotted spoon and drain on paper towels. Quenelles may be prepared in advance up to this point. Before serving, place quenelles in a buttered shallow baking dish. Cover with Mushroom Sauce or Poulette Sauce, and bake in the preheated oven for 15 minutes, or until bubbly. Unsauced quenelles freeze beautifully, before baking. Serves 6.

## VOLAILLE MORNAY

6 cups cut-up cooked
  poultry
salt and white pepper
¼ tsp. grated nutmeg
pinch of cayenne
2 cups Duxelles (see
  Index)
4 cups Sauce Mornay (see
  Index)
½ cup sherry
½ cup cut-up Parmesan
  cheese
butter

Preheat oven to 350°F. Using the steel blade, put the poultry 2 cups at a time and seasonings to taste in the bowl and chop for 3 seconds. Combine poultry, duxelles and 3 cups of the Sauce Mornay in a 2-quart ovenproof serving dish. Drizzle with sherry and pour remaining sauce over the top. Grate the cheese with the steel blade. Sprinkle cheese over the sauce and dot with butter. Bake in the preheated oven for 20 minutes, or until thoroughly heated. Brown under the broiler. Serves 6 to 8.

## CHICKEN TARTS WITH EGGS

8 tart shells, or 1 large
  shell
2 cups cut-up poached or
  steamed chicken breasts
¼ cup dry vermouth
2 cups Sauce Béchamel
  (see Index)
8 eggs
1 cup Hollandaise (see
  Index)

Bake pie shell or tart shells until golden. (See Chapter 2 for directions.) Chop chicken in the bowl with the steel blade for 3 to 5 seconds. Combine chicken with vermouth and béchamel. Fill the shells or shell with chicken mixture. Poach the eggs, trim the edges, and place 1 egg in each tart, or arrange them in a circle over the big tart. Spoon the hollandaise over the eggs. Puff under the broiler for a few seconds. Serves 8.

## CHICKEN CUTLETS À LA RUSSE

*4 whole chicken breasts,*
*boned and cut up*
*1 Tbsp. butter*
*3 slices of white bread,*
*trimmed*
*3 eggs, separated*
*½ cup heavy cream*
*salt and white pepper*
*2 cups fresh bread crumb*
*10 Tbsp. clarified butter*

Grind 2 chicken breasts with the tablespoon of butter using the steel blade, set aside. Then process the remaining breasts adding the broken-up pieces of trimmed bread, egg yolks, cream, and seasonings to taste. Process until just blended. Combine chicken mixture. Beat egg whites until stiff but not dry. Stir in a quarter of the egg whites to lighten the base, then fold in the remainder. Form into oval patties about 1½ inches thick. Coat with fresh bread crumbs. Sauté in the clarified butter for about 6 minutes on each side, until crispy. Serve with more clarified butter, or with Sauce Béchamel (see Index) fortified with the addition of 2 teaspoons paprika, 2 teaspoons lemon juice, ½ cup sour cream and 1 tablespoon brandy. Serves 6.

## CHICKEN PATTIES SURPRISE

*1 cup blanched and*
*toasted almonds*
*3 cups cut-up cooked*
*chicken*
*salt and pepper*
*dash of grated nutmeg*
*1½ cups Mayonnaise (see*
*Index)*
*1 cup deviled ham, or*
*Duxelles (see Index), or*
*chopped cooked chicken*
*livers*
*6 Tbsp. clarified butter*
*½ cup toasted slivered*
*almonds*

Grind the nuts with the steel blade. Chop the chicken with the steel blade a cup at a time, processing for 3 to 5 seconds. Remove chicken from machine and mix in seasonings to taste. Fold in just enough mayonnaise to be able to form firm patties. Make thin patties from half of the chicken mixture, and top each with a dollop of the chosen filling—ham, duxelles, chicken livers. Cover with the rest of the chicken, pinching the edges together to seal. Coat with the almond crumbs and sauté in clarified butter. Top with slivered almonds. Serve with hot mayonnaise. Serves 6.

# KOTOPITA

*2 lb. cooked poultry, cut up*
*4 pkg. (10 oz. each) frozen chopped spinach*
*½ lemon, cut up and seeded*
*2 anchovy fillets*
*1 lb. Feta cheese, crumbled*
*5 eggs, separated*
*4 Tbsp. butter, softened*
*½ tsp. dried orégano*
*16 phyllo leaves, or 12 frozen patty shells*
*¼ lb. butter (1 stick), melted*

Preheat oven to 350°F. Grind the poultry a cup at a time with the steel blade for 5 to 8 seconds. Cook the spinach, drain, and press dry. Purée the spinach, lemon, and anchovy fillets with the steel blade, and set aside. Place in the Processor with the steel blade the Feta cheese, egg yolks, 4 tablespoons *softened* butter and orégano. Blend until smooth. Beat egg whites until stiff. Combine cheese mixture with poultry, and gently fold in the egg whites. Butter a shallow baking dish, 13 × 9 inches, and line with a leaf of phyllo pastry. Keep remaining leaves covered with a damp towel until they are used. Let the edges of the pastry extend over the sides. Brush pastry with some of the *melted* butter. Add another phyllo leaf, and brush with butter. Cover with 6 more leaves, brushing each one with melted butter. Spread on the spinach mixture, then top with the cheese and poultry mixture. Cover with 8 more sheets of phyllo, brushing each one with butter. Pinch the excess phyllo leaves together to make a rim. Bake in the preheated oven for 1 hour.

If frozen patty shells, made of puff paste, are used, defrost them and pat them together. You will need 6 for the bottom crust and 6 for the top. Roll out as thin as possible. Line the pan with half of the dough and cover the pie with the remainder. Bake as for the phyllo pie. Serves 8.

## CHICKEN LIVERS WITH PASTA

*1 lb. chicken livers*
*1 lb. mushrooms*
*1 cup parsley*
*1 garlic clove*
*6 Tbsp. olive or salad oil*
*1 lb. fettuccini, cooked*
*½ cup melted butter*

Pour boiling water over the chicken livers and drain. Trim mushrooms. With the steel blade, chop the livers, parsley and garlic together. Cook in 3 tablespoons of the oil until livers lose their color. Slice the mushrooms with the slicing disc. Push the livers aside, add the rest of the oil, and cook the mushrooms. Drain the cooked pasta and toss with melted butter, then with the liver and mushrooms. Serves 4 to 6.

## JELLIED POULTRY CLAM MOLD

*2 cups Chicken Stock,*
  *clarified (see Index)*
*3 envelopes unflavored*
  *gelatin*
*2 cups cut-up cooked*
  *poultry*
*1 Tbsp. lemon juice*
*2 scallions, cut up*
*salt and pepper*
*dash of cayenne*
*1 cup dry white wine*
*1 can (7 oz.) minced*
  *clams, drained*
*1½ cups heavy cream*
*1½ cups Mayonnaise (see*
  *Index)*

Put ½ cup of *cold* clarified chicken stock in the container with the steel blade. Sprinkle gelatin over the stock and let soak for 10 minutes. Add 1 cup of *hot* chicken stock and blend until gelatin is dissolved. Add the cut-up poultry, lemon juice, scallions, salt and pepper to taste and a dash of cayenne. Purée with the steel blade. Place the mixture in a bowl and add remaining ½ cup of cold chicken stock and the wine. Mix in the drained clams. Chill until mixture is syrupy. Fold in the whipped cream (whipped with the plastic blade), and the mayonnaise. Place in an 8-cup mold and chill. Unmold and serve with a sauce of yogurt and drained grated cucumber. Serves 6 to 8.

# RED, WHITE AND GREEN MOLD

## RED LAYER

*1 small onion, cut up*
*2 scallions, cut up*
*3 cups tomato juice*
*2 envelopes unflavored*
  *gelatin*
*salt and pepper*
*6 drops of Tabasco*
*2 Tbsp. lemon juice*
*½ tsp. dried thyme*
*½ tsp. dried basil*
*½ green pepper, cut up*
*¼ cup water chestnuts,*
  *cut up*
*2 cucumbers, seeded and*
  *cut up*

Chop the onion and scallions with the steel blade, and set aside. Place ½ cup *cold* tomato juice in the container with the steel blade, sprinkle the gelatin over, and let soak for 10 minutes. Add 2½ cups *boiling* tomato juice and blend until gelatin is dissolved. Add the scallions and onion, and season with salt and pepper and add Tabasco, lemon juice and herbs. Blend for 7 seconds. Chill until mixture becomes syrupy. Place green pepper, water chestnuts and cucumbers in the container, and chop with the steel blade for 3 to 5 seconds. Fold green pepper, water chestnuts and cucumbers into the tomato mixture. Pour into an 8-cup mold and chill until almost firm.

## WHITE LAYER

Prepare 2 cups chicken or seafood salad bound with Chaud-froid (see Index) or with 1 cup Mayonnaise (see Index) combined with 1 envelope unflavored gelatin dissolved in ¼ cup hot tarragon vinegar. Chill the salad. Place on top of the Red Layer when it is almost firm, and chill until set.

## GREEN LAYER

*1 cup water*
*2 envelopes unflavored*
  *gelatin*
*1 large avocado, cut up (1*
  *cup)*
*2 Tbsp. lemon juice*
*½ cup sour cream*
*½ cup Mayonnaise (see*
  *Index)*

Place ½ cup *cold* water in the container with the steel blade. Sprinkle gelatin over the water and let soak for 10 minutes. Add ½ cup *boiling* water and blend until gelatin is dissolved. Chill until mixture becomes syrupy. Put remaining ingredients in the container and blend. Fold them into the gelatin mixture. Spoon over chicken-salad layer and chill until firm. Unmold, and serve with Emerald Mayonnaise (see Index). Serves 6 to 8.

# POULTRY STUFFINGS

Stuffing, very often based on bread, may be varied by changing the kind of bread used, but there are also many flavorful fillings to be made with potatoes, rice, fruits and vegetables. If you are making an unusually delicious stuffing, why not make a double recipe? Bake the extra stuffing in a buttered casserole and serve instead of potatoes.

## APPLE AND RAISIN STUFFING

*3 cups fresh bread crumbs*
*(7 slices of bread)*
*1 onion, cut up*
*4 celery ribs, cut up*
*½ cup parsley*
*6 Tbsp. butter*
*¾ cup white raisins*
*1 cup dry white wine, hot*
*4 large apples*
*salt and pepper*

Make the bread crumbs and set aside. Put the onion, celery and parsley in the container, and process with the steel blade. Sauté the vegetables in the butter for 5 minutes. Steep raisins in the hot wine to plump. Core unpeeled apples and cut each one into 8 pieces. Process 1 cup at a time, using the steel blade, for 3 to 5 seconds. Be careful not to overchop. Set aside. Remove the raisins from wine with a slotted spoon; save the wine. Mix all ingredients together, and moisten with some of the wine. Season to taste. Makes enough stuffing for 6- to 7-pound bird.

## APRICOT-PRUNE STUFFING

*¼ lb. dried apricots*
*¼ lb. dried prunes*
*2 cups cooked barley or*
*  rice*
*½ cup melted butter*
*½ tsp. ground cinnamon*
*¼ tsp. ground coriander*
*  (optional)*

Cook the prunes and apricots in water to cover until soft; save cooking liquid. There should be ¾ cup of each cooked fruit. Put drained fruits in the container with the steel blade, and chop coarsely for 3 to 5 seconds. Combine with cooked barley or rice, melted butter and spices, and moisten with the fruit liquid. Makes enough stuffing for 6- to 7-pound bird.

# SWEET POTATO AND WALNUT STUFFING

1 cup walnuts
6 sweet potatoes
2 Tbsp. butter
4 Tbsp. heavy cream
2 egg yolks
1 tsp. ground ginger
3 cups corn-bread crumbs
  or prepared corn-bread
  stuffing
salt and pepper
sherry or stock

Chop walnuts with the steel blade; set aside. Boil sweet potatoes, peel, and quarter them. Put half of potatoes (2 cups) with the butter and cream in the container with the steel blade, and process. Place in a bowl. Process remaining potatoes with the egg yolks and ginger. Combine potato mixtures with corn-bread crumbs, and fold in the walnuts. Season to taste. Moisten, if necessary, with sherry or stock. Makes enough stuffing for 10-pound turkey or goose.

# CHESTNUT STUFFING

4 lb. fresh chestnuts, or
  2 lb. dried chestnuts
  soaked overnight
6 cups Chicken Stock (see
  Index)
2 celery ribs, cut up
4 Tbsp. melted butter
1 cup cracker crumbs
  (7 saltines)
1 cup heavy cream

To prepare fresh chestnuts, slit each one on the flat side. Cover with water and boil for 5 minutes. Drain, and remove shells and inner skins. Simmer chestnuts in the chicken stock for 30 minutes, or until tender. Drain; save stock for a future soup or sauce. Put chestnuts a cup at a time in the container with the steel blade, and process; set aside. Chop the celery with the steel blade, and sauté in the butter. Combine chestnuts, celery, cracker crumbs and cream, and mix lightly. Makes enough stuffing for 6- to 7-pound bird.

This becomes an excellent side dish with beef or turkey when baked in a casserole and dotted with butter.

## GREEN STUFFING

½ cup pecans
6 cups fresh bread crumbs
½ tsp. each of dried
  tarragon, salt and
  pepper
2 celery ribs, cut up
½ cup parsley
½ cup watercress
4 scallions with tops, cut
  up
1 egg
½ cup melted butter
salt and pepper

Chop pecans with the steel blade; set aside. Make the bread crumbs, and flavor with tarragon, salt and pepper; remove from container. Place all the vegetables in the container with the steel blade; add the egg and process. Mix vegetables with bread crumbs, melted butter and pecans. Season to taste. Makes enough stuffing for 6- to 7-pound bird.

## BRAZIL-NUT STUFFING

4 cups fresh bread crumbs
¼ lb. shelled Brazil nuts
giblets from 2 chickens,
  cut up
¼ lb. butter (1 stick)
1 medium-size onion, cut
  up
4 celery ribs with leaves,
  cut up
1 tsp. dried thyme
salt and pepper
chicken stock

Make the crumbs and set aside. Place Brazil nuts in the container with the steel blade and coarsely chop; set aside. Sauté cut-up giblets in the butter; remove with a slotted spoon, leaving butter in the pan. Chop the giblets with the steel blade; remove and set aside. Process onion and celery. Sauté Brazil nuts, onion and celery in the butter in the pan. Add this mixture to the bread crumbs along with the giblets and seasonings to taste. Moisten with chicken stock. Makes enough stuffing for two 5-pound birds.

# HAM AND OLIVE STUFFING

½ cup dry roasted
  peanuts
4 cups fresh bread crumbs
1½ cups cubed cooked
  ham
1 cup stuffed olives
1 medium-size onion, cut
  up
½ cup vermouth
½ cup Chicken Stock (see
  Index)
1 egg

Place peanuts in the container with the steel blade, and chop coarsely; set aside. Prepare the bread crumbs, and set aside. Chop ham, olives and onion together with the steel blade. Mix all ingredients together. Makes enough stuffing for 6- or 7-pound bird.

# MEATS

—◆—

## GROUND MEATS

Ground meats are used in every cuisine. Their variety and combinations are endless, changing in shape from patties to loaves, meatballs to terrines; in taste from bland to spicy; in texture from firm to crumbly. The processor makes them rapidly with style.

Here are a few suggestions for chopped meat dishes, using both raw and cooked meats. (In Chapter 4 there are recipes for meatballs; any of those can be expanded for main-course serving.) Let your imagination take giant leaps, the Cuisinart™ Food Processor will make the exact kind of chopped meat dish you wish.

Always begin with the steel blade in place, and have the meat cut into cubes no larger than 1 inch. Put no more than 1 cup of meat in the processor at one time. Process for 10 to 12 seconds. Stop the motor and check the texture. For a fine texture process longer. Textures may be mingled—part coarse, part fine. Seasonings and additions to the meat—vegetables, nuts, bread crumbs—can be processed along with the meat or can be added later.

When using cooked meat, a range of textures can be achieved by the time allowed for processing, from 3 to 10 seconds. Chop other ingredients with the meat if you wish a real marriage of flavors.

# BEEFBURGERS

Use 1 pound ground beef, sirloin, round or chuck, to make 4 patties. Broil, charcoal-broil or dry-fry in a very hot skillet that has been generously covered with plain or seasoned salt. Top with a compound butter (see Chapter 3).

## BEEFBURGER ENHANCEMENTS

Process any of the following together with the meat.

*Smoked Beefburgers*—Use hickory salt, ½ cup cut-up onions, 4 strips of raw bacon, cut up, ¼ cup smoked almonds.

*Tia Juana*—Use 2 garlic cloves, 2 cut-up scallions, and 2 small chilies or chili powder to taste.

*Orientale*—Use ½ cup teriyaki sauce and 4 to 8 water chestnuts. Before serving, sprinkle burgers with toasted sesame seeds and pass more teriyaki sauce.

*Tuscan*—Use rind of 2 lemons, 2 teaspoons dried orégano, 3 garlic cloves and ¼ teaspoon grated nutmeg. Sauté the patties in olive oil and serve with grated Parmesan cheese and a tomato-flavored sauce.

*Bombay*—Use ½ cup dry roasted peanuts, ¼ cup chopped chutney, ½ teaspoon turmeric, ½ teaspoon ground ginger and 1 small onion, cut up. Serve with Curry Sauce (see Index).

*Burgundy*—Use ½ cup red wine, 2 tablespoons shallots, 1 cup soft French-bread crumbs and ½ teaspoon dried marjoram. Serve with Cress Sauce (see Index).

*Mushroom*—Use ¾ pound fresh mushrooms, cut up, and 2 tablespoons chives. Serve with Mushroom Sauce (see Index).

## OTHER MEAT PATTIES

*Lamb Patties*—Process 1 pound lean raw lamb, cubed, with 3 tablespoons fresh mint or 1½ teaspoons dried mint, 1 garlic clove, 1 tablespoon grated lemon rind and ¼ cup dry vermouth. Serve with minted yogurt.

*Indian Patties*—Chop 1 pound lean raw lamb, cubed, with 1 small cut-up onion, a dash of cayenne, and 2 teaspoons curry powder. Serve with chutney.

*Veal Patties*—Cube 1 pound raw veal and ¼ pound raw pork. Chop meats fine. Add ¼ pound mushrooms, cut up, and 2 shallots, and blend again with the steel blade. Mix in ¾ cup cracker crumbs (7 saltines). Sauté in butter until cooked through. Serve with Caper Sauce (see Index).

## CHOPPED BEEF ROULADES

*3 lb. raw beef (sirloin or top round), cubed*
*1 cup cheese bits (blue, Stilton or Cheddar)*
*2 eggs, beaten*
*1 Tbsp. parsley flakes*
*1 Tbsp. chives*
*salt and pepper*
*½ cup clarified butter*

Put the cubed meat, 1 cup at a time, in the container with the steel blade and grind medium-fine. Divide the meat into halves. Roll or pat out one part and make 6 to 8 thin rectangles. Using the steel blade, blend remaining meat with the cheese, eggs, herbs, and seasonings to taste. Form the cheese mixture into little logs. Lay one log on each rectangle. Fold the plain meat around the cheese mixture and pinch to seal. Sauté roulades in clarified butter in a very hot pan for a few minutes; keep turning and cook until the outside is crisp but the inside rare. Serve roulades with pan butter mixed with a little red wine. Other meats may be so treated and the flavorings varied to taste. Serves 6 to 8.

## PICADILLO (CUBAN GROUND BEEF)

*1 cup raisins*
*4 garlic cloves*
*1 green pepper, cut up*
*1 large onion, cut up*
*4 Tbsp. olive or salad oil*
*3 lb. raw lean beef, cubed*
*2 tsp. salt*
*1 tsp. black pepper*
*2 cups tomato purée*
*1 cup Italian salad olives
    and juice (condité)*

Plump raisins in hot water. Process vegetables with the steel blade, and sauté in the oil in a large kettle. Grind the meat a cup at a time and add it to the vegetables, tossing with a spoon until the meat loses its color. Season. Add the tomato purée, raisins and olives. Simmer for 1 hour. This dish benefits by being made in advance so that the flavorings are well blended. Serve with black beans and rice (see Cuban Black-Bean Soup). This dish freezes very well. Serves 5 or 6.

## SAUERKRAUT BALLS

*½ lb. cooked ham, cubed*
*½ lb. cooked corned beef,
    cubed*
*½ lb. raw lean pork,
    cubed*
*1 large onion, cut up*
*2 Tbsp. parsley*
*4 Tbsp. bacon fat*
*1 cup thick Sauce
    Béchamel (see Index)*
*1 lb. prepared sauerkraut*
*flour*
*2 eggs, beaten*
*2 Tbsp. water*
*2 cups dried bread
    crumbs*

Grind the meats, onion and parsley together with the steel blade, 2 cups at a time. Sauté in the bacon fat until lightly browned. Add béchamel to the meats, and set aside. Simmer the sauerkraut for 15 minutes. Drain and wring dry in a towel. Add sauerkraut to the meat mixture and blend all together in the machine, 1 cup at a time; cool. Form into small balls. Dip each ball into flour, shaking off the excess, then dip into the eggs, which have been mixed with the 2 tablespoons water, and finally into the bread crumbs. Fry a few at a time until crisp. Drain on paper towels and place in a moderate oven to keep warm. Serve with Beer Sauce (recipe follows). Serves 4 to 6.

BEER SAUCE

*¾ cup brown sugar*
*1½ cups ketchup*
*½ cup beer*

Mix all ingredients together, being sure sugar is dissolved. Makes about 2½ cups.

# SAUSAGE AND SAUSAGE DISHES

Don't be afraid to make your own sausage meat. Season it to suit the individual palate, mild to very hot. Use your homemade sausage meat in main dishes. Experiment!

## SAUSAGE MEAT

*1½ lb. raw lean pork,*
*cubed*
*½ lb. pork fat*
*2 tsp. ground sage*
*1 tsp. dried thyme*
*1 tsp. ground coriander*

With the steel blade process all the ingredients together, 2 cups at a time. For a coarser-grain sausage, process the meat and the pork fat separately. Wrap sausage tightly in a piece of muslin or several layers of plastic bags and refrigerate overnight.

## CHARLESTON LAMB BREAKFAST SAUSAGE

*1 lb. lean raw lamb,*
*cubed*
*¼ tsp. each of ground*
*marjoram, thyme and*
*sage*
*salt and pepper*
*butter*

Grind the lamb with the steel blade and mix with herbs and seasoning to taste. Cover with foil and place in the refrigerator overnight. Shape into patties and cook in butter until brown on both sides. Reduce heat and cook for 10 minutes, or until patties are cooked through and crisp.

## SCRAPPLE

*1½ lb. raw pork*
*shoulder, cut up*
*½ lb. pork liver, cut up*
*⅛ tsp. ground cloves*
*1 tsp. ground sage*
*1 cup cornmeal*
*1 tsp. salt*
*1 cup water*
*flour*
*butter*

Simmer pork shoulder and liver in water to cover for 1 hour. Drain, saving the cooking broth. Process the pork, liver, cloves and sage in the container with the steel blade, and chop a cup at a time. Place cornmeal, salt, 1 cup water and 2 cups of the cooking broth in a saucepan, and cook until mixture thickens. Add meat and liver mixture and simmer for 1 hour. Press the scrapple into a 6-cup loaf pan. Refrigerate for at least 3 hours. Remove from pan and slice. Dip into flour, and sauté in butter. Serves 4 to 6.

## BUBBLE AND SQUEAK

*1 lb. sausage meat,*
  *cooked*
*2 cups chopped cabbage*
*1 cup dried bread crumbs*
*2 cups Sauce Béchamel*
  *(see Index)*

Cook the sausage; drain. Cook cabbage until just tender; drain. Prepare bread crumbs. Layer sausage and cabbage in a greased baking dish. Cover with béchamel, and sprinkle with bread crumbs. Bake in a 350°F. oven for 30 minutes. Serves 6.

------

# MEAT LOAVES

Meat loaves are good hot or cold. They can be made with fresh or cooked ingredients, to be served sauced or plain. They can be layered with fillings—vegetables, bread stuffings, fruit, cheese, eggs. Meat loaves may be baked in large containers or in popover pans for small individual servings.

## BASIC MEAT LOAF

*2 lb. raw beef, cubed*
*½ lb. boned raw pork,*
  *cubed*
*1 small onion, cut up*
*4 parsley sprigs*
*4 celery ribs, cut up*
*1 tsp. dry mustard*
*½ tsp. ground sage*
*2 tsp. salt*
*½ tsp. pepper*
*1 egg*
*½ cup water*

Preheat oven to 350°F. With the steel blade process half of the beef, pork, onion, parsley, celery and seasonings, for 8 to 10 seconds. Add egg and water to the second batch and process for 8 to 10 seconds. Mix all together and pack into a loaf pan. Bake in the preheated oven for 1 hour. Serve with a variation of brown sauce, Bordelaise perhaps. Serves 6.

### MEAT LOAF VARIATIONS

Fold into the meat loaf mixture any of the following combinations, omitting the ground sage.

*Curried Loaf*—Add 1 cup chopped apples, ½ cup plumped raisins and 1 tablespoon curry powder.

*Munich Loaf*—Add 1 cup pumpernickel crumbs, ½ cup beer in place of water, ½ cup sauerkraut or canned red cabbage.

*Sauerbraten Loaf*—Add ½ cup wine vinegar and 1 cup thin gingersnap crumbs.

*Chinese Loaf*—Add 1 cup cooked rice, 4 tablespoons soy sauce and 1 cup sliced water chestnuts.

*Mexican Loaf*—Add ½ cup crumbled corn chips, ½ cup taco sauce, 1 cup canned refried beans, and chili powder to taste.

## CORNED BEEF LOAF

*1½ lb. cooked corned beef, cubed*
*¾ cup rye bread crumbs*
*1 Tbsp. prepared horseradish*
*1 tsp. ground sage*
*1 onion*
*1 raw egg yolk*
*salt and pepper*
*3 hard-cooked eggs*
*brown sugar*
*ketchup*

Process with the steel blade all the ingredients except the hard-cooked eggs, brown sugar and ketchup. Season to taste. Place half of the mixture in a greased 4-cup loaf pan which has been spread with brown sugar and ketchup. Arrange the hard-cooked eggs lengthwise down the middle of the loaf. Pat the rest of the meat around and over the eggs. Bake in a 350°F. oven for 45 to 60 minutes, or until the sides shrink from the pan. Serves 4.

## CRANBERRY MEAT LOAF

*¾ cup cracker crumbs (7 saltines)*
*1 cup brown sugar*
*1 cup cranberries*
*1 lb. raw beef, cubed*
*½ onion, cut up*
*1 lb. Sausage Meat (see Index)*
*½ cup Applejack*
*¾ cup milk*
*salt and pepper*

Prepare the cracker crumbs with the steel blade; set aside. Spread ¼ cup brown sugar over the bottom of a greased 8-cup loaf pan. Purée the cranberries with remaining brown sugar, and place in the loaf pan. Process the beef and onion, 1 cup at a time, and mix with the sausage. Pour in the Applejack and milk, and add cracker crumbs and seasoning to taste; toss together with 2 forks. Spoon on top of cranberries. Bake in a 350°F. oven for 1½ hours. Remove excess fat with a baster. Unmold, and serve with Applejack-spiked cranberry sauce. Serves 4 to 6.

## HAM UPSIDE-DOWN CAKE

*1 cup dried bread crumbs*
*2 lb. cooked ham, cubed*
*2 eggs*
*8½ oz. canned crushed*
*pineapple with syrup*
*½ tsp. minced dill*
*½ cup brown sugar*
*¼ tsp. ground cloves*
*½ tsp. dry mustard*
*6 slices of canned*
*pineapple, drained,*
*saving the syrup*

Preheat oven to 350°F. Make the bread crumbs; set aside. Grind the ham with the steel blade for 10 seconds, and blend in the eggs, bread crumbs, crushed pineapple and dill for about 5 seconds. Butter the bottom of an 8-inch springform pan or iron skillet and spread with a layer of brown sugar mixed with the cloves and mustard. Lay the pineapple slices over this. Pack ham mixture on top of pineapple slices; pressing down firmly. Bake in the preheated oven for 1 hour. Invert on a hot plate, and serve with Pineapple-Currant Sauce (recipe follows). Serves 6.

### PINEAPPLE-CURRANT SAUCE

*1 tsp. cornstarch*
*2 tsp. vinegar*
*6 oz. currant jelly*
*1 tsp. ground ginger*
*½ tsp. dry mustard*
*syrup from canned sliced*
*pineapple*

Moisten the cornstarch with the vinegar. Heat all the ingredients together, using just enough of the pineapple syrup to give desired texture and sweetness. Makes about 1 cup.

---

# MEAT-FILLED VEGETABLES

## STUFFED EGGPLANT

*1 large eggplant, or 2 me-*
*dium-size, or 6 indi-*
*vidual eggplants*
*2 lb. raw beef or lamb,*
*cubed*
*2 onions, cut up*
*3 garlic cloves*

Preheat oven to 350°F. Cut off stem end of eggplant and cut lengthwise into halves, but do not peel. Brush cut side with olive oil. Lay cut side down in a baking dish or on a cookie sheet. Bake eggplant in the preheated oven until barely tender. Remove from oven and scoop out the pulp, leaving a shell firm enough to hold the filling. Chop

*1 Tbsp. grated lemon rind*
*¼ cup parsley*
*½ tsp. dried basil*
*½ tsp. ground cinnamon*
*salt and pepper*
*5 Tbsp. olive oil*
*2 eggs, beaten*

pulp by hand into small pieces. Chop the beef or lamb in the processor, using the steel blade, with onions, garlic, lemon rind, parsley, basil, cinnamon, and seasonings to taste. Combine eggplant pulp with meat mixture, and sauté in the olive oil until meat is crumbly. Fold in the beaten eggs. Pile mixture into eggplant shells. Before baking, shells may be topped with bacon strips, thin slices of cheese, or buttered seasoned bread crumbs. Bake in the preheated oven until heated through. Serve plain or with thin tomato sauce. The stuffing mixture is equally delicious as a stuffing for squash—yellow, acorn, or Turk's head. Serves 6.

## MEATBALLS IN CABBAGE

*1 large head of Savoy*
*cabbage*
*1 cup dried bread crumbs*
*1 lb. raw boneless loin of*
*pork, cubed*
*1 lb. raw beef, cubed*
*1 medium-size onion, cut*
*up*
*2 eggs*
*¼ tsp. grated mace*
*salad oil or bacon fat*
*1½ cups Sauce Béchamel*
*(see Index)*
*2 Tbsp. paprika*
*1 tsp. caraway seeds*

Preheat oven to 350°F. Peel off tough outer leaves of cabbage. Cut out stalk end of the head, leaving a 1½-inch shell. Cook the shell in boiling salted water, uncovered, until barely tender; drain upside down. Fit the cabbage into a buttered casserole that is just large enough to accommodate it. Prepare the bread crumbs. Grind the meats together with the steel blade. Quickly incorporate the onion, eggs, mace and bread crumbs into the meats by turning the machine on and immediately off. Form the mixture into small meatballs. Brown meatballs in salad oil or bacon fat. Fill the cabbage with the little meatballs. Mix béchamel with paprika, and spoon over cabbage. Sprinkle top with caraway seeds. Bake in the preheated oven for 25 minutes. Serve with a tomato-flavored sauce. Serves 4 or 5.

Instead of meatballs, cabbage can be filled with the sautéed meats.

## FILLED ZUCCHINI

½ cup cut-up Gruyère
cheese
1 pkg. (10 oz.) frozen
chopped spinach
8 medium-size zucchini,
or 1 big one, halved
3 cups cubed cooked ham
or tongue
1 cup thick Sauce
Béchamel (see Index)
½ tsp. dry mustard
½ cup Madeira wine

Preheat oven to 350°F. Grate the cheese with the shredding blade; set aside. Cook spinach and press dry. Parboil zucchini. Cut zucchini lengthwise into halves, and scoop out seeds. With the steel blade, grind the ham or tongue. Combine meat with spinach, and blend for 5 seconds. Make the béchamel and season with dry mustard. Combine sauce and meat mixture, and add Madeira. Fill zucchini boats, and top with Gruyère cheese. Bake in the preheated oven until bubbly. Serves 6.

## STUFFED PEPPERS

6 large green peppers,
seeded
2 cups cubed smoked meat
1 small onion, cut up
1 cup thick Sauce
Béchamel (see Index)
3 eggs, separated
1 tsp. dry mustard
2 cups whole-kernel corn
salt and pepper
1 cup consommé

Preheat oven to 350°F. Parboil peppers until barely tender. Cut lengthwise into halves, seed, and remove ribs. In the processor grind smoked meat and onion together with the steel blade; set aside. Make béchamel, and blend in egg yolks and mustard. Combine smoked meat, drained corn and sauce. Adjust seasoning. Beat egg whites stiff but not dry, and fold them into the smoked-meat mixture. Fill the pepper shells with the corn soufflé. Place peppers in a baking dish with the consommé. Bake in the preheated oven for 30 minutes, or until puffy. Serves 6.

# MEAT-FILLED MEATS

## BEEF OR VEAL BIRDS

*1 cup fresh bread crumbs*
*2 lb. top round of beef, ¼ inch thick, or 2 lb. veal scallops*
*1 lb. mushrooms, quartered*
*1 can (2 oz.) anchovy fillets*
*1 can (8 oz.) pitted ripe olives*
*1 garlic clove, cut up*
*1 large onion, cut up*
*6 Tbsp. olive or vegetable oil*
*3 hard-cooked eggs, chopped*
*1 raw egg, beaten*
*1 cup Marsala wine*
*1 cup Beef Stock (see Index)*
*¼ tsp. dried thyme*
*2 Tbsp. tomato paste*
*1 Tbsp. flour*
*1 Tbsp. meat glaze*
*salt and pepper*

Make the bread crumbs, and set aside. Pound the meat between 2 sheets of wax paper to ⅛-inch thickness. Cut into rectangles 3 x 5 inches. Process mushrooms, anchovies and olives with the steel blade; set aside. Chop garlic and onion, and cook in 2 tablespoons of the oil. Mix mushroom and onion mixtures with the bread crumbs, hard-cooked eggs and beaten egg. Spread some of this filling over each rectangle of meat. Roll up and secure the "birds" with small skewers or wooden picks. Brown them, a few at a time, in the remaining oil in a large skillet; set aside. Pour the Marsala, beef stock and thyme into the skillet, and bring to a boil. Return beef rolls to the pan and simmer for 45 minutes to 1 hour. Baste from time to time. Remove birds to a heated platter. Pour the liquid from the skillet into the container with the steel blade, and add tomato paste, flour and meat glaze. Blend quickly and cook until thickened. Season to taste. Pour sauce over the meat. Serves 4 to 6.

## ROLLED STUFFED BREAST OF VEAL

*1 breast of veal*
*½ lb. smoked ham, cubed*
*1 lb. raw veal, cubed*
*2 Tbsp. chopped parsley*
*½ tsp. dried rosemary*
*1 Tbsp. chives*

Preheat oven to 350°F. Have your butcher bone a breast of veal, saving the bones. Grind the ham and the extra veal with the steel blade, along with the herbs, cream, and seasonings to taste, 1 cup at a time. Combine the filling mixtures. Flatten out the breast and spread the filling evenly over the

½ tsp. dried orégano
1 cup light cream
salt and pepper
2 pkg. (10 oz. each)
  frozen chopped spinach
1 egg, beaten
oil
1 cup white wine
2 cups Chicken or Veal
  Stock (see Index)

surface. Cook the spinach and press dry. Add beaten egg to spinach, and spoon this over the meat filling. Roll up the veal breast and tie with string. Brush a shallow baking pan with oil and place the meat in it, along with the bones. Roast in the preheated oven for 1½ hours. When the meat begins to brown, add the wine and stock and baste frequently. Thicken the pan juices for the sauce. Serves 6.

## BREAST OF LAMB WITH VEAL QUENELLE FILLING

2 breasts of lamb
2 eggs, separated
½ cup flour
6 Tbsp. butter
salt and pepper
½ cup milk, scalded
1 lb. raw lean veal, cut up
2 cups heavy cream
1 cup parsley
1 cup watercress
2 oz. brandy
1½ cups red wine
1½ cups water

Have your butcher bone the lamb breasts. Combine egg yolks, flour, butter, and seasonings to taste in the container with the steel blade. Add the scalded milk and process all together. Place this *panade* in the top part of a double boiler over barely simmering water, or over low heat, and stir until the mixture leaves the side of the pan. Place *panade* in the freezer, along with the cut-up veal, the cream and the container of the processor with the blade, for 15 minutes. (It is important that these items be cold.) Chop parsley and watercress, press dry, and put in the refrigerator. When well chilled, place the veal in the cold container with the steel blade, and process until a paste forms. Scrape down the sides. With the motor running, add *panade,* watercress and parsley, a little at a time, and blend after each addition. Add the egg whites and blend. With the motor running, pour 1 cup of the chilled cream in a stream through the tube. Stop the machine and check the consistency. The mixture should be firm enough for you to be able to drop it from a spoon into a mounded oval. Scrape down and continue to pour in cream until the right consistency is reached.

Preheat oven to 350°F. Brush the breasts of lamb with brandy on both sides and sprinkle them with salt and pepper. Spread the breasts with the quenelles (forcemeat mixture). Roll up the breasts and tie securely. Put half of the wine and water in a roasting pan with a rack. Bake the lamb in the preheated oven for 1 hour, basting frequently; add more wine and water as needed. Serve with Herb Sauce (see Index). Serves 6.

A shoulder or breast of lamb is excellent with an Apricot-Prune Stuffing (see Index) also.

------

# COLD MEAT DISHES

## VITELLO TONNATO

4 lb. veal, cut from the
  leg
6 anchovy fillets
1 small onion, cut up
1 small carrot, cut up
1 celery rib, cut up
2 parsley sprigs
½ tsp. salt
2 cloves
white stock or water

TUNA SAUCE

4 oz. canned tuna
2 Tbsp. capers
½ cup olive oil
4 anchovy fillets
2 Tbsp. lemon juice
white pepper
1½ cups Mayonnaise (see
  Index)

Have the butcher remove the bones and fat from the veal and tie the meat into a roll. With a sharp knife make slits in the veal and insert small pieces of anchovy. Put onion, carrot, celery, parsley and salt in the container with the steel blade, and chop. Place the veal roll in a deep saucepan with the chopped vegetables and cloves. Cover with white stock or water. Bring to a boil and simmer the meat, covered, for 1½ hours, or until tender. Remove from heat and let the meat cool in the broth.

Process all sauce ingredients except mayonnaise with the steel blade. Remove mixture from the machine and fold gently and thoroughly into the mayonnaise. Slice the cooled meat very thin and arrange slices in a single layer on a platter. Spoon tuna sauce over the meat. Refrigerate overnight, or for a minimum of 12 hours. Serves 6 to 8.

## TONGUE MOLD

½ cup port wine
1 Tbsp. lemon juice
2 envelopes unflavored
  gelatin
1½ cups consommé, hot
3 to 4 pounds cooked
  smoked tongue
½ cup pitted green olives
3 celery ribs, cut up
½ green pepper, cut up
1 Tbsp. Dijon-type
  mustard
salt and pepper
½ cup Mayonnaise (see
  Index)
4 hard-cooked eggs
parsley sprigs

Lightly oil a ring mold. Pour port wine and lemon juice into the container with the steel blade. Sprinkle gelatin over the wine and let soften for 10 minutes. Add hot consommé, and blend until gelatin dissolves. Pour only enough of the gelatin into the ring mold to cover the bottom; refrigerate.

Cut the center portion of the tongue into thin slices, 12 to 14, enough to go around the ring mold; set aside. Chop 2 cups of remaining tongue with gelatin remaining in the processor; set aside. Chop olives, celery and green pepper, with mustard and seasonings to taste, in the processor with the steel blade for 7 seconds. Fold these into the tongue-gelatin mixture. Fold in the mayonnaise.

When the first layer of gelatin in the ring mold is almost set, lay the tongue slices, evenly spaced, across the mold. Spoon in the ground tongue mixture; chill. Unmold and fill the center with potato balls dressed with oil and vinegar, or marinated asparagus tips. Surround the ring with quartered eggs and parsley. Serves 8.

## VEAL AND LIVER LOAF IN JELLY

*1 cup walnuts*
*1½ lb. beef liver*
*1½ lb. raw lean veal*
*3 shallots, crushed*
*1 bay leaf*
*¼ tsp. dried thyme*
*6 peppercorns*
*1 tsp. salt*
*½ cup sherry*
*2 envelopes unflavored*
*  gelatin*
*¼ tsp. grated nutmeg*
*¼ tsp. ground cloves*

Process the walnuts coarsely with the steel blade, and set aside. Cover liver and veal with 1 quart of boiling water, adding crushed shallots, the bay leaf, thyme and peppercorns tied in cheesecloth, and the salt, and simmer for 30 minutes. Remove meats from heat, drain, and save the cooking liquid. Remove skin and membranes from liver. Cut liver and veal into small chunks. Place sherry in the container with the steel blade, and sprinkle the gelatin on top; soak for 10 minutes. Add half of the hot cooking liquid, and process until gelatin is dissolved. Process 1 cup of the meats with the spices in the gelatin mixture, using the steel blade; set aside. Process the rest of the meat, and fold into the meat-gelatin mixture. Add walnuts, and pour into an oiled 8-cup loaf pan; chill. Unmold and serve with Melba toast. Serves 8 to 10.

# PÂTÉS

Some pâtés are uncooked—easy to whip up (see Chicken-Liver Pâté). Some are baked. They may be dressed *en croûte* or served simply with crusty bread. Heavy pâtés, like terrines, are good for a luncheon, or for a summer dinner or supper main dish. Accompany such a main dish with a green salad dressed with vinaigrette.

## NOELLE'S PÂTÉ

1 slice of bread, crumbled
2 Tbsp. milk
⅓ lb. raw lean pork,
  cubed
2 raw chicken breasts
⅓ lb. hot sausage
1 egg
4 chicken livers
¼ cup parsley
½ tsp. pepper
½ tsp. grated nutmeg
½ cup whiskey or red
  wine
6 slices of raw thick
  bacon, diced by hand

Preheat oven to 350°F. Soak the bread in the milk. Place the pork in the container with the steel blade, and process for 8 to 10 seconds. Set aside in a big bowl. Cut up the chicken and chop coarsely with the steel blade for 5 to 8 seconds; add to the pork in the bowl. Process the sausage, egg, chicken livers and parsley, together with the soaked bread and seasonings, using the steel blade. Add to the pork and chicken. Pour in whiskey or wine, and mix all the ingredients together by hand. Place half of the diced bacon in a 6-cup loaf pan and pack the pâté on top of the bacon. Pat remaining bacon on top. Bake in the preheated oven for 2 hours. Pour off the excess fat and chill well. Serves 8 to 10.

## PÂTÉ DE CAMPAGNE BLEU RIEUMAILHOL

½ lb. sweet Italian
  sausage
¾ lb. chicken livers
4 scallions, cut up
6 slices (1 inch thick)
  French bread, crumbled
¼ cup parsley
½ tsp. dried tarragon
salt and pepper
¾ cup champagne or dry
  vermouth
1 Tbsp. brandy

Preheat oven to 350°F. Place the first 3 ingredients in the container, and blend with the steel blade for 15 seconds. Transfer to a bowl. Process remaining ingredients for 5 seconds. Combine all together. Put the mixture in a 4-cup loaf pan, cover with aluminum foil, and bake in the preheated oven for 1½ hours. Drain if necessary. Decorate with hearts of palm or cornichons. Serves 6 to 8.

## PÂTÉ MAISON MIDDLETON

*1½ lb. calf's liver, cut up*
*½ lb. raw bacon, cut up*
*10 anchovy fillets*
*1 garlic clove, cut up*
*salt and pepper*
*1½ cups heavy cream*
*4 eggs*
*1 Tbsp. brandy*

Preheat oven to 300°F. Process liver, bacon, anchovies and garlic with salt and pepper to taste, using the steel blade. Blend until a paste forms. Whisk the cream, eggs and brandy together. With the motor running, add them through the tube to the paste. Pour mixture into a baking dish, and cover with foil. Set baking dish in a pan of hot water. Bake in the preheated oven for 2 hours. Let cool with weights on top. Drain if necessary. Serve with Melba toast. Serves 10 to 12.

# MEAT FRILLS AND FANCIES

## APRICOT FINISH FOR BAKED HAM

*1 lb. dried apricots*
*¼ cup brown sugar*
*2 tsp. ground cloves*
*2 tsp. dry mustard*
*2 tsp. ground ginger*
*2 tsp. ground cinnamon*
*1 Tbsp. corn syrup*

Soak apricots overnight. Simmer until tender. Drain. Place all ingredients in the processor and homogenize. During the last 30 minutes of baking a ham, spread the paste over the skinned ham.

## BASTING SAUCE FOR PORK OR CHICKEN

*1 can (6 oz.) frozen*
  *orange juice*
*3 garlic cloves*
*½ cup soy sauce*
*1-inch piece of peeled*
  *fresh gingerroot, or 1*
  *tsp. ground ginger*

Blend all together in the processor with the steel blade. Baste pork and chicken with this, and let it be the pan sauce to accompany the dish.

## ESSENCE OF CAPER SAUCE

Blend 2 jars (2 ounces each) capers with their juice to make a delicious dressing for lamb steaks, sautéed veal, scallops or poached white fish.

## COATING FOR ROASTED MEAT

*1 cup dried bread crumbs*
*½ cup parsley*
*3 shallots*
*6 Tbsp. butter*

Blend all together in the processor with the steel blade. Spread over the meat for the last 30 minutes of roasting. Use for leg of lamb, or roast veal or pork.

## MARINADE AND BASTING SAUCE FOR LAMB

*1 cup French-style*
  *mustard*
*3 Tbsp. soy sauce*
*1 tsp. dried rosemary*
*½ tsp. ground ginger, or*
  *1-inch piece of peeled*
  *fresh gingerroot*
*2 garlic cloves*
*3 Tbsp. salad oil*
*½ cup red wine*

Blend all ingredients together in the processor with the steel blade. Brush on meat, and use as a basting sauce when roasting or broiling butterfly lamb, lamb steaks, chops. Good for barbecued chicken too.

# VEGETABLES

Sauces for vegetables can raise a plain dish to culinary heights. For suggestions, see the chapter on sauces. Compound butters, also in Chapter 3, add zest too. The shape and cut of vegetables heightens their interest, and the Food Processor shreds, chops, slices, juliennes and purées perfectly in seconds.

## BEETS À LA FRANÇAISE

*8 medium-size raw beets,*
  *peeled*
*4 Tbsp. butter*
*1 cup Chicken Stock (see*
  *Index)*
*6 large lettuce leaves*
*salt and pepper*

Place the slicing blade in the container and slice the beets. Melt the butter in a heavy skillet, and toss the beets in it until they are coated. Pour in the stock, and cover beets with wet lettuce leaves. Steam until fork tender, adding more stock if necessary. Season to taste. Serves 6.

## BEETS IN SOUR-CREAM SAUCE

*3 lb. medium-size beets*
*2 Tbsp. sugar*
*2 Tbsp. flour*
*2 Tbsp. butter*
*8 Tbsp. hot vinegar*
*1 cup sour cream*
*chives (optional)*

Wash and scrub the beets. Place them in a baking dish with a tight-fitting cover, and bake in a 350°F. oven until tender, about 1 hour. Peel the beets when cool. Place the shredding disc in the container and shred the beets. Remove beets to a saucepan and sprinkle with the sugar. Place flour, butter and vinegar in the container with the steel blade; blend. Cook the mixture in a saucepan until it thickens. Add it to the beets, toss, and heat. When ready to serve, stir in the sour cream and heat through. Dust with chopped chives. Serves 5 or 6.

## CABBAGE AND APPLES

*1 red cabbage, 4 lb.*
*2 apples, unpeeled*
*3 Tbsp. bacon fat*
*salt and pepper*
*1 tsp. grated nutmeg*
*½ cup red wine*

Core the cabbage and remove the outer leaves. Cut cabbage into chunks that will fit in the tube. Place the slicing disc in the container and slice the cabbage. Set cabbage aside in a large bowl. Pour boiling water over cabbage and let stand for a few minutes; drain. Quarter the apples, place them in the tube, and slice. Sauté cabbage in bacon fat for 2 or 3 minutes, until it is just done, stirring constantly. Add seasonings to taste, nutmeg, wine and apples, and simmer, covered, for 10 minutes. Add more wine if necessary. Correct seasonings. Serves 5 or 6.

## RED AND GREEN CABBAGE WITH CHESTNUTS

*1 small Savoy cabbage*
*1 small red cabbage*
*2 cups cooked chestnuts,*
*    fresh, canned or dried*
*4 cups Chicken Stock (see*
*    Index)*
*4 Tbsp. butter*
*3 Tbsp. flour*
*¼ tsp. ground ginger*
*salt and pepper*

Core cabbages carefully, saving the cores. Place slicing blade in the container and slice the cores. Quarter the heads, then slice the leaves; set aside. Place the steel blade in the container and chop the chestnuts, scraping down the sides. Cook cabbage leaves and cores in the stock, uncovered, until barely tender. Drain and save the stock. Mix cabbage and chopped chestnuts. Put the butter, flour and ginger in the container and blend. Pour 2 cups of the reserved hot stock through the tube, and blend. Add to remaining hot stock and cook until thickened. Season to taste. Pour over the cabbage and chestnuts. Serves 8 to 10.

## CARROTS CRÉCY

*2 lb. carrots*
*½ cup raw rice*
*3 Tbsp. butter*
*1 tsp. ground ginger*
*salt and pepper*

Cover carrots with water and cook until tender; drain. Cook the rice. In the container with the steel blade, purée carrots and rice with the butter. Add seasonings to taste. Place in a buttered baking dish, and reheat in a 350°F. oven. Serves 6.

## CARROT RING

Prepare the recipe for Carrots Crécy and add 3 beaten eggs. Pour into a buttered ring mold and set it in a pan of hot water. Bake in a 350°F. oven for 25 minutes. Unmold and fill with peas. Serves 6 to 8.

## CELERIAC STUFFED WITH PEAS

½ cup cut-up Gruyère
    cheese
6 medium-size celeriacs
    (celery root)
4 scallions, cut up
2 cups cooked peas
butter
1 cup Chicken Stock (see
    Index)

Grate the cheese with the steel blade; set aside. Peel the celeriacs and boil them until tender. Cut a slice from the top of each celeriac and scoop out the centers, leaving a firm shell. Place scallions, cooked peas and celeriac pulp in the container with the steel blade, and blend. Refill celeriac shells with the mixture. Sprinkle with cheese, dot with butter, and place in a deep pan with the chicken stock. Cover. Reheat in a 400°F. oven. Serves 6.

## CREAMED CUCUMBERS AND RADISHES

3 small cucumbers, peeled
    and seeded
2 bunches of radishes
3 Tbsp. butter
2 cups Sauce Béchamel
    (see Index)
1 Tbsp. lemon juice
salt and pepper

Place the slicing blade in the container and slice the cucumbers and the radishes. Sauté them in the butter and add to the béchamel. Add lemon juice, and season to taste. Reheat. These are excellent in the center of a lima-bean purée ring.

## EGGPLANT WITH MUSHROOMS

1 large eggplant
1 medium-size onion,
    quartered
3 scallions, roughly cut
2 garlic cloves
1 lb. mushrooms, cut up
½ cup parsley
4 Tbsp. olive oil
salt and pepper
1 cup dried bread crumbs
3 Tbsp. butter

Parboil the eggplant. Cut lengthwise into halves and scoop out the pulp, leaving a firm shell. Chop the pulp by hand. Chop onion, scallions, garlic, mushrooms and parsley with the steel blade; scrape down. Add to the eggplant pulp. Sauté in the olive oil. Season to taste. Pile into the eggplant shells, top with bread crumbs, and dot with butter. Bake in a 350°F. oven for 20 minutes. Serves 6 to 8.

## STUFFED ONIONS

6 large onions
½ lb. mushrooms,
   quartered
3 Tbsp. butter
½ cup fresh bread crumbs
salt and pepper
1 cup Sauce Béchamel
   (see Index)
1 cup cracker crumbs (7
   saltines)
butter

Make a cross in the stem end of each onion to keep them from separating while cooking. Cook them in salted boiling water until nearly tender. Drain and cool. Place quartered mushrooms in the container with the steel blade, and chop. Sauté mushrooms in the butter. Carefully remove the center part of the onions, leaving a firm shell, and chop the centers with the steel blade. Add the mushrooms, bread crumbs, seasonings to taste and béchamel sauce to the chopped onion pulp. Stuff the onion cases with the mixture and place in a buttered baking dish. Sprinkle the tops with cracker crumbs and dot with more butter. Bake in a 350°F. oven for 20 minutes. Serves 6.

Puréed spinach, peas or squash also make good fillings. Spiced cranberry sauce is tasty, too, when serving these with roast poultry.

## PARSNIPS WITH SHERRY

2 lb. parsnips
4 Tbsp. butter, melted
4 oz. sherry
1 tsp. sugar
salt and pepper
6 lettuce leaves

Pare parsnips and julienne with the shredder. Place them in a pan with the melted butter, sherry, sugar and seasonings to taste. Toss to coat. Cover parsnips with the wet lettuce leaves. Cover and steam until tender. Serves 6.

## POTATOES DAUPHINOISE

*1 lb. potatoes, peeled*
*1½ cups milk, scalded*
*2 eggs, beaten*
*1 garlic clove, cut up*
*⅛ tsp. grated nutmeg*
*½ tsp. salt*
*¼ tsp. pepper*
*¼ lb. Swiss cheese,*
  *cut up*
*2 Tbsp. butter*

Slice the potatoes in the container with the slicing blade; set them aside in a large bowl and cover with cold water. Slowly add the scalded milk to the beaten eggs, stirring constantly. Drain potatoes and pat dry. Place potatoes in a baking dish that has been rubbed with the cut garlic clove and buttered. Pour the egg-milk mixture over the potatoes and add the nutmeg and seasonings. Grate the cheese with the slicing disc and sprinkle over the potatoes. Dot with butter. Bake in a 350°F. oven for 45 minutes. Serves 4.

## POTATOES À LA NORMANDE

*1 lb. potatoes, peeled*
*3 leeks, white part only*
*1 to 2 cups Brown Stock*
  *(see Index)*
*3 Tbsp. parsley*

Place the slicing blade in the container and slice the potatoes. Cover potatoes with cold salted water until needed. Place the shredding disc in the container and process the leeks. Wash leeks well. Drain potatoes and put them in a buttered baking dish with the leeks. Cover the mixture with brown stock, and bring to a boil on top of the stove. Transfer to a 350°F. oven and bake for 25 minutes, or until the potatoes are tender. Garnish with parsley. Serves 4 or 5.

## POTATOES ANNA

*8 potatoes, peeled*
*½ cup parsley*
*1 cup melted butter*
*salt and pepper*

Preheat oven to 400°F. Place the slicing blade in the container and slice the potatoes; there should be 6 cups. Place potatoes in salted cold water until ready to use. Put the parsley in the container with the steel blade and chop. Generously butter a round mold or pie plate. Dry the potatoes and arrange them neatly in the dish, with the rounds overlapping. Pour melted butter over each layer and season with salt and pepper. Repeat the layers until the dish is full. Press down. Cook in the preheated oven for 40 to 50 minutes, or until potatoes are crusty and brown. Invert on a serving dish and garnish with parsley. Serves 8.

## POTATOES ANNETTE

Prepare in the same way as Potatoes Anna, but instead of slicing the potatoes, julienne them.

## POTATOES VOISIN

Prepare in the same way as Potatoes Anna, then sprinkle each layer with grated cheese.

## POTATOES GALETTE

To the recipe for Potatoes Anna, add a layer of sautéed sliced onions or a layer of sautéed sliced mushrooms or any sautéed, thinly sliced vegetables in between the potato layers.

## POTATO QUENELLES

¼ lb. Cheddar cheese,
  cut up
1 lb. potatoes
1 egg
¼ cup flour
¼ tsp. grated nutmeg
⅛ tsp. salt
¼ tsp. pepper
¼ cup melted butter

Grate the cheese with the steel blade and set aside. Peel the potatoes, quarter, and cook in boiling salted water. Drain, and dry over high heat. Place potatoes in the container with the steel blade and purée, scraping down from time to time. Add the egg, ¼ cup flour, the nutmeg, salt and pepper; blend and scrape down. With 2 wet tablespoons, form oval shapes from the mixture, and drop the quenelles into simmering salted water. Poach for 8 to 10 minutes. Drain on paper towels and place in a buttered baking dish that has been sprinkled with grated cheese. Sprinkle quenelles with more cheese and drizzle melted butter over them. Brown in a 450°F. oven. Finish with one of the compound butters—Bovril Butter, Green Butter made with chives, etc. (see Index). Serves 4 to 6.

# POTATO CASSEROLE

8 potatoes, peeled
¼ lb. butter (1 stick)
3 carrots
1 onion
1 sweet red pepper
1 cup pitted olives
2 cups Sauce Béchamel
  (see Index)
salt and pepper
1 lb. cottage cheese
½ cup snipped chives
1 egg

With the slicing disc, slice the potatoes. Dry them, and sauté lightly in butter until just soft. Cut the carrots, onion and red pepper into manageable chunks, and chop with the steel blade. Add the olives and chop for 2 seconds more. Add vegetables to the seasoned Sauce Béchamel. Blend the cottage cheese with the chives and egg. Place a layer of potatoes in a greased baking dish. Spread chive and cottage-cheese mixture over this. Spoon on 1 cup of vegetable sauce, then top with more potatoes and more sauce. Bake in a 350°F. oven for 35 minutes. Serves 8.

# RUTABAGA SOUFFLÉ

1 or 2 rutabagas, peeled,
  cut into 1-inch pieces
¾ cup sugar
3 eggs, separated
3 Tbsp. melted butter
1 tsp. baking powder
1 tsp. salt
1 tsp. pepper
½ tsp. grated nutmeg
2 cups sour cream
½ cup dried bread crumbs
3 Tbsp. butter

Cook cubed rutabagas with sugar in water to cover. Drain and place in the container with the steel blade; purée. Add egg yolks, 3 tablespoons melted butter, the baking powder and seasonings; blend. Put the mixture in a large bowl, and stir in the sour cream. Fold in beaten egg whites. Pour into a 6-cup soufflé dish, and dust with bread crumbs; dot with remaining butter. Bake in a preheated 350°F. oven for 20 to 25 minutes. Serves 6 to 8.

## SWEET-POTATO AND ALMOND CROQUETTES

¼ lb. blanched almonds
6 medium-size sweet
   potatoes
2 Tbsp. butter
1 egg
2 cups dried bread
   crumbs
2 to 3 Tbsp. cream
2 Tbsp. chopped parsley
½ cup milk

Put almonds in the container with the steel blade and chop; set aside. Boil the sweet potatoes, and peel, and place them in the bowl with the steel blade 1 cup at a time; process. Add the other ingredients except 1 cup of the crumbs and milk; blend. Spread the mixture on a buttered dish and refrigerate for 2 hours. Form into croquettes. Dip each one into remaining bread crumbs, then into the milk, and roll again in crumbs. Fry the croquettes, a few at a time, in deep fat heated to 375°F. Drain on paper towels. Serves 6 to 8.

## SPINACH NIÇOISE

6 pkg. (10 oz. each)
   frozen spinach
2 cans (3¾ oz. each)
   sardines
1 lemon, grated rind and
   juice
1 cup light cream
1 cup dried bread crumbs
4 Tbsp. butter
salt and pepper
2 hard-cooked eggs

Cook the spinach, drain, and press dry. Place it in the container with the steel blade, and add the sardines, saving 6 sardines for garnish; add lemon rind and juice, and cream. Process until smooth, about 5 seconds. Sauté the bread crumbs in the butter and add to the spinach. Whir for 3 seconds. Season to taste. Reheat the mixture and mound on a hot serving platter. Garnish with slices of eggs and the reserved sardines. Serves 6.

## SPINACH BALLS

2 lb. spinach, cooked,
    chopped and drained
2 Tbsp. flour
½ tsp. sugar
1 Tbsp. cream
2 eggs
⅛ tsp. grated mace
2 cups sauce

Place all ingredients except sauce in the container with the steel blade, and blend. Cook the mixture for 5 minutes, stirring constantly. Butter a tablespoon and fill it with the spinach mixture. Drop in mounds into a saucepan of simmering water; do not let water boil. Poach for 4 or 5 minutes, until firm. Drain on paper towels. Prepare Mushroom Sauce or Sauce Mornay (see Index). Place the spinach balls in a single layer in a shallow baking dish and cover with the sauce. Reheat in a 350°F. oven. Serves 4.

## SPINACH GNOCCHI

2 pkg. (10 oz. each)
    frozen chopped
    spinach, or 1 lb. fresh
    spinach
1 cup grated Parmesan
    cheese
1 cup ricotta cheese
¼ tsp. grated nutmeg
2 tsp. salt
1 tsp. white pepper
2 lb. potatoes
2 eggs
3 cups flour
3 Tbsp. butter, melted

Cook spinach, drain, and press dry. Place spinach in the container with the steel blade and add ½ cup of the Parmesan and all the ricotta cheese, as well as nutmeg, salt and white pepper. Blend until smooth, and set aside in the refrigerator. Peel the potatoes. Place the slicing disc in the processor and slice potatoes. Cook potatoes in boiling salted water until tender, drain them well, and dry over low heat by shaking in a pan. Purée the potatoes in the machine with the steel blade; scrape down. Add eggs and blend. Add 1 cup of the flour and blend. Turn mixture out on a floured board and knead in 1¾ cups more flour, or enough to make a soft dough. Roll out on a lightly floured pastry cloth into a 14-inch square. Spread the dough with spinach filling, and roll up like a jelly roll. Cut into 1-inch-thick slices with a wet knife. Place in a buttered baking dish. Drizzle with melted butter, and sprinkle with the rest of the Parmesan cheese, grated with the steel blade. Bake in a 400°F. oven for 25 minutes, or until brown. Serve with a tomato-flavored sauce. Serves 6 to 8.

# VEGETABLE AND POTATO PURÉES

Mashed potatoes, although good in themselves, are very interesting when combined with other vegetables. To 1 cup of mashed potatoes add 2 cups of puréed vegetables and finish off with cream, butter, salt and pepper to taste. Baked potatoes can be filled with a blend of the puréed scooped-out potato mixed with puréed vegetables. Enrich the purées with 2 egg yolks, fold in 3 beaten egg whites, and return to the oven to puff and brown. Watercress, celeriac, onions, leeks, green beans and carrots have an admirable affinity for potato purées.

## SOUFFLÉED VEGETABLES, BASIC RECIPE

*2 cups cooked vegetables*
*¼ cup light cream*
*3 eggs, separated*
*salt and pepper*
*¼ cup chives*
*¼ cup parsley*
*⅛ tsp. grated nutmeg*

Preheat oven to 350°F. Place the vegetables in the container with the steel blade, and purée them with the cream, egg yolks, seasonings to taste, herbs and nutmeg. Fold in the stiffly beaten egg whites. Pour into a buttered baking dish and set in a pan of hot water. Bake in the preheated oven for 25 minutes. Serve alone or with an herb-flavored Sauce Béchamel. Serves 4.

*Suggested vegetables*—asparagus, lima beans, green snap beans, celery, cauliflower, corn, eggplant, leeks, onions, peas, potatoes, sweet potatoes, mushrooms, watercress. Purées enriched with cream and butter may be served without souffléing them.

## VEGETABLE-STUFFED TOMATOES

7 zwieback biscuits,
  broken up
6 firm tomatoes
salt
1 small onion, quartered
1 lb. mushrooms,
  quartered
3 celery ribs, cut up
2 strips of raw bacon, cut
  into 1-inch pieces
pepper
3 Tbsp. butter

Place the pieces of zwieback in the container with the steel blade and process to make 1 cup crumbs; set crumbs aside. Scoop out the tomatoes, sprinkle them with salt, and turn them upside down to drain. Place the quartered onion and mushrooms in the container and chop with the steel blade; set aside. Blend the cut-up celery and bacon for 3 to 5 seconds. Sauté bacon and celery together. Add mushroom mixture and zwieback crumbs and cook for about 5 minutes. Season with salt and pepper to taste. Fill the tomato shells and dot with butter. Bake in a 350°F. oven for 15 to 20 minutes. Serves 6.

Duxelles (see Index) make a good filling too. Dress with Hollandaise (see Index).

## ZUCCHINI AND SOUR-CREAM CASSEROLE

1 cup dried bread crumbs
1 large onion, quartered
6 Tbsp. melted butter
2 lb. zucchini
½ cup sour cream
salt and pepper

Preheat oven to 350°F. Make the bread crumbs and set aside. Place the onion in the container with the steel blade and chop for 3 seconds. Sauté ½ cup of crumbs and the chopped onion in 4 tablespoons of the butter until golden. Place the shredding blade in the container and shred the zucchini; drain. Fold zucchini into onion mixture with sour cream; season with salt and pepper to taste. Spoon into a casserole and top with the rest of the bread crumbs. Drizzle the rest of the butter over the top. Bake in the preheated oven for 25 minutes, or until the casserole begins to bubble. Place under the broiler until the crumbs are brown. Serves 4.

## ZUCCHINI STUFFED WITH PEAS

*6 medium-size zucchini*
*2 pkg. (10 oz. each)*
  *frozen peas*
*2 Tbsp. butter*
*3 Tbsp. light cream*
*salt and pepper*
*dried bread crumbs*
*butter for topping*

Boil the zucchini until just tender; drain. Cut them lengthwise into halves and scoop out the seeds. Place zucchini halves in a baking dish. Cook peas until tender. Place drained peas in the container with the steel blade. Add the butter, cream, and salt and pepper to taste; purée. Fill zucchini halves with the pea purée, top with bread crumbs, and dot with butter. Bake in a 350°F. oven for 20 minutes. Serves 6.

Yellow summer squash may be stuffed with pea or lima-bean purée in the same fashion.

## ZUCCHINI AND SWISS-CHARD CASSEROLE

*1 cup dried bread crumbs*
*3 lb. Swiss chard or*
  *spinach*
*4 scallions, cut up*
*4 parsley sprigs*
*4 eggs*
*½ cup light cream*
*⅛ tsp. dried thyme*
*1 tsp. salt*
*½ tsp. pepper*
*6 zucchini*
*4 Tbsp. olive oil*

Preheat oven to 350°F. Make the bread crumbs, and set aside. Remove the white midribs from the chard and chop with the steel blade. Steam the chard leaves until limp, then simmer the chopped midribs until tender. Combine the ribs with the leaves and press dry. Place scallions and parsley in the container with the steel blade, and chop. Add Swiss chard, eggs, bread crumbs and cream, 1 cup at a time, and blend. Add thyme and seasoning; set aside. Slice the zucchini with the slicing disc, and cook in the olive oil until barely tender. Fold the zucchini carefully into the chard mixture; correct seasoning. Put in a buttered baking dish. Bake in the preheated oven for 45 minutes, or until a knife inserted in the middle comes out clean. Spinach may be substituted for the chard. Serves 4 to 6.

# WINTER SQUASH CASSEROLE

4 cups cooked winter
    squash
8 Tbsp. light cream
salt and pepper
½ cup walnuts
2 Tbsp. butter
2½ Tbsp. brown sugar
⅛ tsp. ground cloves

Place cooked squash and cream in the container with the steel blade, and purée; season to taste. Put in a buttered casserole. Chop the walnuts with the steel blade for 3 to 5 seconds. Melt the butter and add brown sugar and cloves. Coat the walnuts evenly with the butter-sugar mixture by shaking them back and forth in the pan. Spoon the nuts on top of the squash. Bake in a 350°F. oven until squash is heated through. Serves 4.

# MEDITERRANEAN CASSEROLE

6 medium-size zucchini
1 medium-size eggplant
½ Tbsp. salt
2 green peppers, cut up
1 medium-size onion,
    quartered
2 garlic cloves
1 cup oil
¼ tsp. dried thyme
salt and pepper
4 cups chopped tomatoes,
    canned or fresh, well
    drained
½ lb. mozzarella cheese

Put the slicing blade in the container and slice the zucchini; set aside. Cut the unpeeled eggplant by hand into rather thick slices. Sprinkle with salt; set aside to drain. Put pieces of green pepper upright in the tube and slice. Slice onion and garlic. Cook zucchini and eggplant slices in the oil until wilted and somewhat browned. Remove the mixture with a slotted spoon and set aside. Cook the garlic, onion, thyme and green pepper in the oil remaining in the pan until they take on color. Return eggplant and zucchini mixture to the pan and simmer until the flavors are blended. Season to taste. Layer the bottom of a baking dish with 2 cups of the drained tomatoes. Add a drained layer of the zucchini and eggplant. Add remaining tomatoes. Shred the cheese with the shredding disc, and sprinkle on top of the vegetables. Bake in a 400°F. oven until the cheese is melted. Serves 6.

# SALADS

One of the fascinating things about making salads in the food processor is that cutting into slices, julienne or shreds is so easy, and so many interesting textures can be achieved. Molded salads, from the gelatin preparation to the incorporation of most of the ingredients, can be prepared with a minimum of fuss. Chef's salads are simple to prepare when the cheese and meats are cut into strips in the processor.

## PALE PINK CLAM AND TOMATO ASPIC

4 cups tomato juice
1 medium-size onion, cut
  up
2 bay leaves
4 peppercorns
6 cardamom seeds
2½ envelopes unflavored
  gelatin
1 cup clam juice
6 oz. cream cheese
salt and pepper
1 cup heavy cream

Simmer 3½ cups of the tomato juice with onion, bay leaves, peppercorns and cardamom for 15 minutes. Strain. Pour ½ cup *cold* tomato juice into the container with the steel blade. Sprinkle the gelatin over the tomato juice and soak for 10 minutes. Heat the clam juice; pour it into the container and process until gelatin has dissolved. Add cream cheese to the gelatin mixture and blend. Stir this into the strained tomato juice. Taste, and season to taste. Put the plastic blade in the container and whip the cream. Fold cream into the tomato mixture, pour into a wet 2-quart mold, and refrigerate until set. This is good served with chicken salad. Serves 8.

## AVOCADO MOLD

½ cup cold water
1 envelope unflavored
  gelatin
1 cup grapefruit juice, hot
1 large or 2 small
  avocados
6 drops of Tabasco
1 Tbsp. lemon juice
salt and pepper

Pour the cold water into the container with the steel blade. Sprinkle gelatin over the water and soak for 10 minutes. Pour in hot grapefruit juice and blend until gelatin has dissolved. Peel avocado and cut into pieces. Add pieces to the container with the Tabasco and lemon juice and blend. Season to taste. Fill a wet ring mold with the mixture and refrigerate until set. Fill the center with melon balls or grapefruit sections and serve with Avocado Sauce (see Index).

## CUCUMBER RADISH MOLD

6 medium-size cucumbers,
   seeded and peeled
1 cup radishes, washed
1¾ cups Chicken Stock
   (see Index)
2 envelopes unflavored
   gelatin
1 bunch of watercress, cut
   up
¼ cup chives
1 cup sour cream
salt and pepper
watercress for garnish

Place the shredding blade in the container and shred cucumbers; drain and set aside. Slice the radishes with the slicing disc; set aside. Pour ¾ cup of the chicken stock into the container with the steel blade. Sprinkle gelatin on the stock and let soak for 10 minutes. Heat remaining chicken stock and add to the container; blend until gelatin has dissolved. Add watercress, chives and sour cream, and process. Fold in shredded cucumbers and sliced radishes. Season to taste. Pour into a wet mold and refrigerate until set. Garnish with additional watercress. Serves 6 to 8.

## CRANBERRY-WINE RING

½ cup walnuts
2 cups raw cranberries
½ tsp. grated lemon rind
¾ cup sugar
½ cup cold water
2 envelopes unflavored
   gelatin
1 cup red wine, hot
2 Tbsp. lemon juice
½ cup Mayonnaise (see
   Index)

Place walnuts in the container with the steel blade and chop; set aside. Add cranberries, lemon rind and sugar, and chop; set aside. Pour the cold water into the container. Sprinkle gelatin on the water and soak for 10 minutes. Add hot wine and process until gelatin has dissolved. Mix all ingredients together, pour into a wet mold, and refrigerate until set. Serves 6 to 8.

## POTATO ASPIC

4 cups raw potatoes,
  peeled
½ cup cooked spinach
½ cup ripe olives
4 scallions, roughly cut
¼ cup parsley
¼ cup chives
½ green pepper, cut up
½ cup white vinegar
2 envelopes unflavored
  gelatin
1 cup hot water
1 cup Mayonnaise (see
  Index)
¼ cup lemon juice
½ tsp. tarragon vinegar
½ tsp. dry mustard
½ tsp. dried tarragon
½ tsp. dried thyme

Place the slicing disc in the container and slice the potatoes. Cook them in salted water until just tender. Drain and shake dry over high heat. Put the steel blade in the container and chop the spinach, olives, scallions, parsley, chives and green pepper; set aside. Pour the vinegar into the container. Sprinkle gelatin over the vinegar and soak for 10 minutes. Add the hot water and blend until gelatin has dissolved. Add mayonnaise, lemon juice, tarragon vinegar, mustard and herbs, and blend. Mix all ingredients together, pour into a wet 2-quart mold, and refrigerate. Serves 6 to 8

## CURRY RING

½ cup cold water
2 envelopes unflavored
  gelatin
⅔ cup vinegar, hot
4 eggs
½ cup sugar
1 Tbsp. curry powder
½ cup chutney
1 cup heavy cream
salt and pepper

Pour the water into the container with the steel blade. Sprinkle gelatin over the water and let soak for 10 minutes. Add the hot vinegar and blend until gelatin has dissolved. Add remaining ingredients and blend. Pour into a wet 4-cup ring mold and refrigerate until set. Serves 4 to 6.

# ASPARAGUS MOUSSE

3 pkg. (10 oz. each)
frozen asparagus
spears
5 oz. canned water
chestnuts
½ cup cold water
2 envelopes unflavored
gelatin
1 cup Consommé
Madrilène (see Index),
hot
1 cup Mayonnaise (see
Index)
1 Tbsp. lemon juice
2 Tbsp. minced fresh
thyme, or 1 tsp. dried
2 hard-cooked eggs,
sliced

Cook the asparagus, and drain. Purée with the steel blade; set aside. If asparagus should be stringy, force through a sieve with a wooden spoon. Place the slicing disc in the container and slice the water chestnuts; set aside. Put the steel blade in the container and pour in the cold water. Sprinkle gelatin over the water and soak for 10 minutes. Pour in the hot Madrilène and process until gelatin has dissolved. Add puréed asparagus to the gelatin mixture and process for 3 to 5 seconds. Fold in water chestnuts, mayonnaise, lemon juice and thyme. Pour into a wet mold, and refrigerate until set. Garnish with sliced eggs, and serve with Emerald Mayonnaise (see Index). Serves 4 to 6.

# JELLIED PEPPER RINGS

½ cup tarragon or garlic
vinegar
1 envelope unflavored
gelatin
1 cup Vegetable Stock
(see Index), hot
4 scallions, cut up
2 celery ribs, cut up
2 carrots, cut up
1 pimiento
8 oz. cream cheese
3 Tbsp. ketchup
4 peppers, seeded

Pour vinegar into the container with the steel blade. Sprinkle gelatin over it and soak for 10 minutes. Add hot vegetable stock and process until gelatin has dissolved. Add remaining ingredients except peppers, and process. Remove the tops and seeds from the peppers. Set peppers in muffin tins to keep them upright, and fill them with the gelatin mixture. Chill until set. Cut peppers into rings with a sharp knife, and serve on tomato slices or a bed of spinach. Serves 8.

# CREAM-CHEESE AND HAM MOLD

½ lb. cooked ham
6 hard-cooked eggs
½ cup cold water
1 envelope unflavored
   gelatin
1 cup orange juice, hot
6 small gherkins
8 oz. cream cheese, cubed
¼ cup parsley
1 Tbsp. prepared mustard
1 Tbsp. chives
salt and pepper

Cut the meat into pieces, place in the container with the steel blade, and chop; set aside. Chop eggs by turning the motor on and off; set eggs aside. Pour the cold water into the container. Sprinkle gelatin over the water, and soak for 10 minutes. Add hot orange juice and process until gelatin has dissolved. Add remaining ingredients and blend. Season to taste. Fold into the meat and egg mixture. Pour into a wet mold and refrigerate until set. Dress with Mayonnaise (see Index). Serves 4 to 6.

# GROUND COLESLAW

1 large white cabbage
1 cup Mustard
   Mayonnaise (see Index)
1 Tbsp. dill seeds
salt and pepper

Core cabbage and cut into wedges. Place the steel blade in the container and chop the cabbage, 1 wedge at a time. Remove from the container and mix with mustard mayonnaise, dill seeds, and seasonings to taste. Tomatoes filled with this mixture are very good. Grinding the cabbage instead of shredding it gives another dimension to the usual coleslaw. Serves 8.

# CELERIAC (CELERY ROOT) RÉMOULADE

4 celeriacs
1 Tbsp. lemon juice
salt and pepper

Peel the celeriacs and cut into julienne. Parboil with the lemon juice for 10 minutes; drain. Dress with Sauce Rémoulade or with Avocado Sauce (see Index). Serves 8.

## CELERIAC (CELERY ROOT) SALAD WITH MUSTARD CREAM DRESSING

*4 celeriacs*
*2 Tbsp. lemon juice*
*2 Tbsp. oil*
*1 Tbsp. vinegar*
*½ tsp. salt*
*¼ tsp. white pepper*
*Mustard Cream Dressing*
  *(see Index)*

Peel the celeriacs and slice with the slicing disc. Marinate in lemon juice, oil, vinegar, salt and pepper overnight. Drain, and dress with mustard cream dressing. (Grated parsnips or white turnips may be substituted for the celeriacs.) Serves 8.

## PUNGENT CARROT SALAD

*2 lb. raw carrots, peeled*
  *and cut up*
*2 garlic cloves*
*½ cup salad oil*
*¼ cup lemon juice*
*salt and pepper*
*Bibb lettuce leaves*

Place the shredding disc in the container and shred the carrots. Place them in ice water and refrigerate for at least 2 hours. Mash garlic and simmer in oil for 10 minutes. Remove garlic and cool the oil. Drain carrots and shake dry. Toss the carrots in the lemon juice and garlic-flavored oil. Season to taste. Serve in Bibb lettuce cups. Sliced raw mushrooms may be combined with the carrots for added interest. Serves 8 to 10.

## TABBOULEH

*1 cup bulgur (cracked*
  *wheat)*
*1½ cups parsley*
*1 cup fresh mint*
*4 scallions, cut up*
*1 onion, cut up*
*½ cup lemon juice*
*¾ cup olive oil*
*salt and black pepper*
*2 tomatoes, peeled,*
  *chopped by hand*
*cherry tomatoes*
*mint leaves*

Cover the cracked wheat with water and soak for 2 hours. Drain and squeeze dry in a towel. Place the steel blade in the container and chop parsley, mint, scallions and onion. Fold vegetables into the cracked wheat. Mix in lemon juice and oil, and season with salt and black pepper to taste. Toss, then gently stir in chopped tomatoes. Chill. Garnish with whole cherry tomatoes and mint leaves alternating around the serving bowl. Serves 4 to 6.

## CRISP-CRISP SALAD

*1 cup peeled white turnip
  or Jerusalem artichokes
1 cup celery
4 scallions, using green
  part
6 radishes
1 medium-size head of
  Chinese cabbage
½ tsp. basil
1 tsp. sugar
2 Tbsp. soy sauce
¼ cup salad oil
juice of 1 lemon
salt and pepper*

In the container with the slicing disc slice all the vegetables, which have been cut into pieces to fit the tube. Empty the container from time to time. Place vegetables in the refrigerator to crisp. Put remaining ingredients in the container and blend. Season to taste. Toss dressing with the vegetable mixture just before serving. Serves 6 to 8.

## RAW VEGETABLE SALAD

*beets
carrots
cabbage
zucchini
lettuce cups*

Place the shredding disc in the container and grate each kind of vegetable separately, processing enough to have 1 cup of each kind grated. Place each kind of vegetable in single lettuce cups and arrange them attractively on a platter. Refrigerate. Moisten each lettuce cup with an oil and vinegar dressing (see Index) before serving. Serves 8 to 12.

# BREADS

—◆—

## BISCUITS

Biscuits are part of the American tradition. They can be varied to suit any kind of a meal. The trick is to have any shortening and liquid at room temperature before mixing, and then to knead them as gently and as little as possible.

# BAKING POWDER BISCUITS

2 cups flour
3 tsp. double-acting
  baking powder
½ tsp. salt
½ tsp. cream of tartar
¼ lb. butter (1 stick)
½ cup milk
1 Tbsp. sugar

Preheat oven to 450°F. Sift the dry ingredients except sugar. Cut butter into pieces. Place cut-up butter in the processor and process with the steel blade very quickly, about 5 seconds. With the motor running, add dry ingredients little by little, until the mixture resembles cornmeal. Scrape down the sides of the bowl. Still with the motor running, slowly pour the milk and sugar through the tube. The dough will be spongy. With floured hands remove the dough to a floured board or wax paper and gently knead, making no more than 10 folds. Roll out with a floured rolling pin to ½-inch thickness. Cut with a floured biscuit cutter, using a straight downward motion, being careful not to twist the cutter. Let biscuits rest for 15 minutes before baking; they can be glazed with milk or melted butter if you like. Bake in the preheated oven for 10 to 12 minutes. Makes about 24 biscuits, 1-inch size.

## DROP BISCUITS

To make drop biscuits, follow the recipe for Baking Powder Biscuits, but increase the milk to 1 cup. Spoon batter into buttered muffin tins, filling them two-thirds full; or drop them by spoonfuls onto a buttered baking sheet. Bake in the preheated oven until golden.

### BISCUIT ADDITIONS

Orange—Add grated rind of 1 orange to the dough. Press 1 cube of dot sugar, which has been dipped into orange juice, into the top of each biscuit before baking.

Cheese—Blend in ½ cup grated American cheese, 1 tablespoon chopped pimiento and 2 tablespoons chopped green pepper before adding milk.

*Herb*—Incorporate 2 tablespoons chopped chives, ¼ teaspoon dried sage and
1¼ teaspoons caraway seeds into the dough.

*Bacon*—Mix in 4 strips of bacon, cooked and crumbled.

*Ham and Onion*—Combine 3 tablespoons chopped ham and 4 tablespoons sautéed chopped onion with the batter.

*Blue Cheese*—Crumble in ⅓ cup blue cheese and ½ cup chopped nuts.

*Curry*—Fold in ½ teaspoon curry powder and ¼ cup ground peanuts.

*Pinwheels*—Roll the dough ¼ inch thick and spread with filling. Roll up in
jelly-roll fashion, and cut into ½-inch slices. Bake on an oiled cookie
sheet. Fillings may be deviled ham; butter, cinnamon and sugar; chopped
nuts, raisins and brown sugar; chopped meat, cheese, Duxelles (see Index),
etc. Bake in the preheated oven.

------

# MUFFINS

It's great to use the processor for muffins because flavoring
ingredients, sugar, liquids and shortenings are so readily combined.
However, the processed ingredients must be quickly stirred *by hand*
into the dry mixture in another bowl to get the lumpy batter that is es-
sential for a good muffin.

## APPLE MUFFINS

2 cups cake flour
¾ tsp. salt
2 tsp. double-acting
  baking powder
½ tsp. ground ginger
1 or 2 cooking apples
2 eggs
¾ cup milk
4 Tbsp. butter, melted
¼ cup sugar
cinnamon sugar

Preheat oven to 400°F. Sift together dry ingredients except the sugar into a mixing bowl. Peel
and quarter the apples, and drop pieces into the
container with the steel blade; chop; there should
be 1 cup. Add eggs, milk, melted butter and plain
sugar; blend for 4 or 5 seconds. Stir liquid mixture by hand into the dry ingredients until just
moistened. Spoon into buttered muffin tins, filling them two-thirds full. Sprinkle with cinnamon
sugar. Bake in the preheated oven for 20 to 25
minutes. Makes about 12 muffins.

## CHEESE MUFFINS

2 cups cake flour
1 Tbsp. double-acting
  baking powder
½ tsp. dry mustard
½ cup cut-up Swiss cheese
1 egg
⅓ cup cooking oil
¾ cup milk

Preheat oven to 400°F. Sift dry ingredients together into a bowl. Grate the cheese with the steel blade, then add egg, oil and milk to the container and process for 5 seconds. By hand, stir the cheese and liquid into the dry ingredients until just moistened. Bake in the preheated oven for 20 to 25 minutes. Makes about 12 muffins.

## GINGER BANANA MUFFINS

2 cups cake flour
¾ tsp. salt
2 tsp. double-acting
  baking powder
2 bananas, cut up
1 egg
4 Tbsp. butter, melted
¼ cup sugar
2 Tbsp. cut-up crystallized
  gingerroot

Preheat oven to 400°F. Sift dry ingredients except sugar together into a bowl. Put cut-up peeled bananas into the container with the steel blade. Add the egg, melted butter, sugar and gingerroot; blend. Scrape down, and blend until smooth. With a spoon stir the liquid into the dry ingredients until just moistened. Spoon into buttered muffin tins, filling them two-thirds full. Bake in the preheated oven for 20 to 25 minutes. Makes about 24 muffins, 2-inch size.

## CRANBERRY ORANGE MUFFINS

2 cups cake flour
¾ tsp. salt
2 tsp. double-acting
  baking powder
1 cup cranberries
½ orange, seeded and cut
  into pieces
1 egg
¾ cup milk
⅓ cup melted butter
½ cup sugar

Preheat oven to 400°F. Sift dry ingredients except the sugar together into a bowl. Put cranberries and orange in the container with the steel blade, and chop. Scrape down. Add egg, milk, melted butter and sugar. Blend for 5 seconds. By hand, stir the liquid mixture into the dry ingredients until just moistened. Spoon into buttered muffin tins, filling them two-thirds full. Bake in the preheated oven for 20 to 25 minutes. Makes about 12 muffins.

# QUICK BREADS

A recipe based on 2 cups of flour will fill a loaf tin 9 by 5 inches or 2 small loaf pans. Fill the pan and let stand for 20 minutes before baking. These breads freeze well.

## FRUIT BREAD

5½ Tbsp. butter, cut up
⅔ cup sugar
2 eggs
3 Tbsp. cream
1 cup fruit
2 cups flour
2 tsp. double-acting
   baking powder
½ tsp. salt
½ cup chopped nuts
   (optional)

Preheat oven to 350°F. Place cut-up butter in the container with the steel blade. With the motor running slowly, add sugar through the tube. Scrape down the sides. Add eggs, one at a time; blend for 15 seconds for each egg. Add the cream and fruit; blend for 3 seconds. Sift dry ingredients together, and pour them onto the butter-egg mixture. Blend, turning the motor on and off until the flour disappears, about 3 times. Fold in the nuts (chopped with the steel blade). Place in a greased loaf pan. Let stand for 20 minutes before baking. Bake in the preheated oven for 50 minutes to 1 hour, or until a straw inserted in the center comes out clean.

## SUGGESTED FRUIT FOR FRUIT BREAD

*Applesauce*—Add 1 cup applesauce, ¼ teaspoon ground cloves and ¼ teaspoon ground cinnamon. Substitute brown sugar for white.

*Apricot-Orange*—Add 1 cup cut-up dried apricots, ¾ cup orange juice and 1 tablespoon grated orange rind.

*Banana-Nut*—Add 1 cup mashed bananas and ½ cup chopped pecans.

*Prune*—Add 1 cup plumped drained prunes, cut up, ¾ cup prune juice and 2 teaspoons grated lemon rind.

## ZUCCHINI BREAD

2 cups zucchini
3 eggs
¾ cup salad oil
1½ cups sugar
1 tsp. grated lemon rind
2½ cups flour
1 tsp. salt
½ tsp. grated nutmeg
¼ tsp. ground ginger
1 tsp. baking soda
2 tsp. double-acting
   baking powder
½ cup nut pieces

Preheat oven to 350°F. Shred zucchini with the shredding blade; drain and set aside. Place eggs, oil, sugar and lemon rind in the container with the steel blade; blend. Sift dry ingredients together and add, 1 cup at a time, to the egg-oil mixture. Blend only until the flour disappears. Remove from container, and fold in zucchini shreds and nut pieces. Spoon into greased small loaf pans, and bake in the preheated oven for 1 hour. Let cool in the pan.

## LEMON BREAD

rind of 1½ lemons
6 Tbsp. butter
1 cup granulated sugar
2 eggs
1½ cups flour, sifted
½ Tbsp. double-acting
   baking powder
½ tsp. salt
½ cup milk
¾ cup white raisins,
   floured

Preheat oven to 350°F. Grate lemon rind with the steel blade. Add butter and granulated sugar to lemon rind and blend until smooth. Add the eggs; blend for 15 seconds. Then add the flour, sifted with baking powder and salt, and whir until flour is just incorporated. Pour in the milk and blend for 3 seconds. Fold raisins into the batter. Spoon into a buttered loaf pan, and bake in the preheated oven for 1 hour.

Mix confectioners' sugar, water and lemon juice to make a glaze. Brush over the bread when it has cooled.

LEMON GLAZE

½ cup sifted
   confectioners' sugar
½ Tbsp. warm water
½ tsp. lemon juice

Mix confectioners' sugar, water and lemon juice to make a glaze. Brush over the bread when it has cooled.

## POPOVERS

*1 cup flour, sifted*
*½ tsp. salt*
*2 eggs*
*1 cup milk*
*1 Tbsp. melted butter*

Preheat oven to 425°F. Place all ingredients in the container with the steel blade. Blend until just smooth, not more than 2 or 3 seconds. Pour into greased deep muffin cups, filling them three-quarters full. Bake in the preheated oven for 35 to 40 minutes, until golden brown. Five minutes before they are finished, prick the sides to permit steam to escape. Makes 6 to 8 large popovers.

*Yorkshire Pudding*—Preheat oven to 450°F. Make the popover batter and pour into a shallow ovenproof dish, 11 by 14 inches, well coated with hot beef drippings or butter or oil. Bake in the preheated oven for 10 minutes. Reduce heat to 375° and bake for 20 minutes longer.

*Cheese Popovers*—Add ¼ pound grated cheese to basic popover batter. Additional cheese may be sprinkled on the top before baking.

—————

# YEAST BREADS

The processor is very handy for making small amounts of raised doughs, and it takes a lot of the labor out of such things as *brioche*. To make raised doughs in quantity, process 1 recipe at a time.

## WHITE BREAD

*1 pkg. dry yeast*
*¼ cup warm water*
*3 cups flour*
*2 tsp. sugar*
*2½ tsp. salt*
*2 Tbsp. butter*
*1 cup cold water*
*melted butter*
*1 egg*
*2 Tbsp. cream*

Proof the yeast in the warm water (115°F.) with a pinch of sugar. Put flour, sugar and salt in the container with the steel blade. Add the butter, turn on motor, and immediately turn it off. Add yeast mixture and again turn on the motor and immediately turn it off. Add ⅓ cup cold water and quickly blend it in. Let the dough rest. With the machine running, add more water until a ball forms. Let the ball rotate for about 1 minute. Place the balled dough in a greased bowl and brush with melted butter. Cover and set aside in a warm, draftfree spot. Let dough rise until it doubles in bulk. Punch down and knead until the dough is elastic. Place the dough in a greased pan (9 by 5 inches) and let rise again. Mix the egg in with the cream and use to glaze the bread. Or glaze with the white of an egg. Place in the oven which has been preheated to 400°F. Immediately reduce heat to 325°, and bake for 40 minutes, or until bread is golden brown.

When mixing the dough, do not be concerned if the motor slows down or even shuts off. Just turn the processor off and let it rest for a few minutes. Makes 1 loaf.

## SWEET BREAD

1 pkg. dry yeast
¼ cup warm water
1¼ cups heavy cream
3 egg yolks
3 to 4 cups flour
¼ cup sugar
¼ lb. butter (1 stick),
   cut up
1 tsp. salt
2 Tbsp. soft butter

Proof the yeast in the warm water (115°F.) with a pinch of sugar. When dissolved, mix with the cream and egg yolks. Place 3 cups of the flour, the sugar, ¼ pound of butter and the salt in the container with the steel blade. Turn on the motor and immediately turn it off. Add the yeast-egg mixture and blend by turning the motor on and immediately off. Turn out on a floured board. If the dough seems too sticky, add a little more flour by kneading it in. Form dough into a ball, place in a buttered bowl, and cover the dough with a film of softened butter. Cover bowl with plastic and refrigerate overnight.

When ready to use, let the dough sit for a few minutes. Knead it and form into the desired shape—bun, braid, ring, etc. Let rise again for about 1 hour. Bake in a preheated 350°F. oven until golden brown. For the best effect brush the dough with an egg glaze (see White Bread) before baking.

# BRIOCHE

*1 pkg. dry yeast*
*¼ cup warm water*
*2⅓ cups flour*
*⅓ cup sugar*
*⅜ pound butter (1½ sticks), very cold*
*3 eggs*
*1 egg yolk*
*2 Tbsp. water*

Proof the yeast in the water (115°F.) with a pinch of sugar; make sure yeast is completely dissolved. Place the flour, sugar and cold butter, cut into pieces, in the container, and blend until mixture resembles cornmeal. Add yeast and water, and blend by turning the machine on and immediately off. Put the 3 whole eggs on top of the mixture and let the motor run for 1½ minutes; if the motor stops, consider the dough ready. Remove the spongy dough and drop it into a floured bowl. Cover with plastic wrap, then with a towel. Let dough rise in a warm place (75° to 80°F.). When tripled in bulk, punch down and let rise again, covered, in the refrigerator for 6 hours or overnight. Take two thirds of the dough and form into balls to fit *brioche* tins or muffin pans. Cut a deep cross in the center of each ball. With the remaining dough, form small pear-shaped knobs; fit the pointed ends of the little knobs into the crosses, tamping them firmly in place. Let *brioches* rise uncovered in a warm spot until the dough has doubled. Glaze with the egg yolk beaten with 2 tablespoons water. Bake in a preheated 375°F. oven for 20 minutes, or until nicely browned. If *brioches* brown too rapidly, cover the tops loosely with foil. Makes about 10 *brioches*.

The whole batch of dough can be baked in a ring mold if you prefer.

# BRIOCHE CRUST

Brioche wrapping is excellent for *coulibiac,* for sausage rolls, for some *croûtes,* for all manner of fillings.

Follow directions for Brioche. When the dough is removed from the refrigerator, immediately place it between 2 sheets of wax paper and roll out ¼ inch thick in the shape desired for filling. After filling, paint with an egg glaze, made with 1 egg yolk beaten into 2 tablespoons of milk or cream, before baking.

## BROTHER BERNARD'S LITTLE BUTTER BISCUITS

½ pkg. dry yeast
2 Tbsp. warm milk
1 tsp. plus 4 Tbsp. sugar
1 Tbsp. sour cream
1 egg
¼ tsp. salt
1⅓ cups flour
5⅓ Tbsp. cold sweet
   butter, cut up
1 egg, beaten
1 Tbsp. water

Proof the yeast in the warm milk (115°F.) with 1 teaspoon sugar. Let sit for 10 minutes. Add sour cream, 1 egg and the salt. Put the flour, 4 tablespoons sugar and cut-up butter in the machine with the steel blade. Process until mixture looks like cornmeal. Pour yeast mixture over this and process until a ball forms. Roll out dough on a floured board and let it rest for 30 minutes. Roll out a second time and again let it rest for 30 minutes. Roll out the dough again to about ½ inch thick, and cut out biscuits with a 1½-inch cutter. Brush the tops with the beaten egg mixed with 1 tablespoon water. Place biscuits on a greased cookie sheet. Bake in a preheated 350°F. oven for 15 minutes. Makes about 12 biscuits.

# CRÊPES,
# PANCAKES,
# WAFFLES

## CRÊPES

Crêpes, those feather-light, thin, thin pancakes, are one of the great cooking discoveries—easy to make, easy to freeze, easy to keep, unsurpassed for turning out all kinds of delicacies from appetizers, to main courses, to desserts. They can be rolled, folded or stacked. They can all be prepared in advance and heated or chilled before serving, depending on their nature.

Be sure that you have a special pan for making the crêpes, a pan that is never washed but only wiped out. Crêpe batter should rest for at least 1 to 2 hours before using. The first 1 or 2 crêpes are to test the batter and heat of the pan, and they are usually "iffy."

For dessert crêpes, add 1 tablespoon sugar to the batter. Crêpe batter can be stored in the refrigerator for 2 days, but must be covered, and should be stirred each time before using.

# ENTRÉE CRÊPES

*3 eggs*
*1 cup flour*
*1 tsp. salt*
*¾ cup water*
*3 Tbsp. melted butter*
*¾ cup milk*
*2 Tbsp. brandy*
*vegetable oil*

Place all the ingredients except the oil in the processor with the steel blade, and blend until smooth. Scrape down the sides and blend again. The batter should have the consistency of heavy cream. Let the batter rest for 1 hour before using.

Put crêpe pan over medium high heat and brush with 1 teaspoon vegetable oil. (Do not oil the pan again unless you have a problem with sticking.) Heat the pan until a drop of water forms a ball, or until the pan is just beginning to smoke. Pour 2 tablespoons of batter into the pan, at the same time swirling the pan so that the batter spreads evenly over the bottom. Any surplus batter should be poured back. The first crêpe is a trial one to test the batter and the pan. Cook the batter for about 1 minute, then loosen the edge with a spatula, turn the crêpe over, and cook for about 20 seconds longer. The underside of the crêpe will be spotty brown, but no matter because this is the side that will be filled or folded. Continue to make the crêpes, and stack them on a plate. If they are to be frozen, place a piece of wax paper between each two. Makes 18 to 24 crêpes, 6-inch size.

Stock or cooking liquid may be used instead of water for a stronger-flavored crêpe; for example, shrimp broth, chicken stock, mushroom juice from *duxelles,* etc. A mixture of ½ cup buckwheat flour with ½ cup all-purpose flour makes a lovely crêpe for a caviar and sour-cream or ratatouille filling.

## FILLED ENTRÉE CRÊPES

Crêpes provide a marvelous way of disguising leftovers and bringing them up to party standard. The fillings may consist of anything that tempts the appetite and is suitable for the meal to be served. Cold filled crêpes are great for picnics, small crêpes for cocktail parties.

*2 cups diced or ground cooked poultry, meat, seafood or vegetables*
*1 ½ cups thick Sauce Béchamel (see Index)*
*1 recipe Entrée Crêpes*
*½ cup grated Parmesan or Swiss cheese (optional)*
*butter*

Season the filling and combine with ¾ cup of the Sauce Béchamel. Put some of the mixture on each crêpe and roll up. Place crêpes in a baking dish. Thin remaining filling with remaining Sauce Béchamel. Pour this sauce over the crêpes. Sprinkle with grated Parmesan or Swiss cheese, and dot with butter. At this point, the dish may be covered and refrigerated. To reheat, place in a 375°F. oven and bake for 20 minutes. Serves 6.

## SUGGESTED FILLINGS FOR CRÊPES

Many mixtures and fillings in previous chapters are delicious used with crêpes. The poultry and Feta-cheese mixture from Kotopita, Duxelles, cooked Sausage Meat—all these are good (see Index for pages). The fillings may also be spread on layers of big crêpes, arranged like a layer cake. Cut into wedges to serve.

*Coulibiac Filling* (see Index)—Omit rice; serve crêpes with melted butter.
*Seafood Stuffing* (see Index)—Serve with Fish Béchamel Sauce or Shrimp Hollandaise (see Index).
*Poultry Mousse Mixture* (see Index)—Bake filled crêpes, and sauce with a Béchamel (see Index) to which ½ cup ground ham or tongue has been added.
*Stuffing for Zucchini* (see Index)—Use only the stuffing. Fill crêpes with stuffing and cover with Sauce Mornay (see Index).

## APPLE AND SAUSAGE FILLING

*2 lb. cooking apples*
*2 Tbsp. butter*
*1 cup cooked Sausage*
    *Meat (see Index)*

Core the apples and cut into thin slices with the slicing disc. Cook apples in butter until just browned. Spread a layer of apples on each crêpe, and spoon some sausage meat on top. Roll up, and heat. Serve with maple syrup on the side. Buckwheat batter is very good with this filling.

## DESSERT CRÊPES I

Add 4 tablespoons confectioners' sugar to the batter for Entrée Crêpes.

## DESSERT CRÊPES II

*1 ¾ cups milk*
*1 ½ cups flour*
*2 eggs, separated*
*2 Tbsp. sugar*
*¼ lb. butter (1 stick),*
    *melted*

Blend milk and flour with the steel blade. With the motor running, add egg yolks and sugar. Scrape down the sides and, again with the motor running, add melted butter. Let batter rest for 2 hours. Fold in the beaten egg whites before using the batter. Cook as for Entrée Crêpes. Makes 18 to 24 crêpes, 6-inch size.

## CRÊPES GRAND MARNIER

*1 lb. cream cheese*
*¾ cup honey*
*¼ cup Grand Marnier*

Blend cream cheese, honey and liqueur, using the steel blade. Fill Dessert Crêpes I or II, and serve with thawed frozen raspberries.

## CRÊPES SOUFFLÉ

*1 recipe Dessert Soufflé
batter, any flavor (see
Index)*
*sweet butter, melted*
*sugar or whipped cream*

Preheat oven to 400°F. Make Dessert Crêpes II. Butter a shallow baking dish. Put 2 tablespoons of the soufflé mixture on half of each crêpe. Fold over. Place folded crêpes in the baking dish, and brush them with melted butter. Bake in the preheated oven for 15 minutes, or until the soufflé filling is puffed up. Sprinkle with sugar, or serve with whipped cream. Serve at once. Praline (see Index) is a very special flavoring for these.

## NUT FRUIT CRÊPES

*2 cups walnuts*
*½ cup brown sugar*
*½ cup milk*
*¼ cup rum*
*⅓ cup dried apricots, cut
up*
*grated rind of 1 lemon*
*butter*

Make Dessert Crêpes I or II. Grind the walnuts and brown sugar in the container with the steel blade. With the motor running, add the milk and rum through the tube, and blend. Add apricots and lemon rind. Blend to a paste. Spread the crêpes with the mixture and fold them envelope-fashion. Sauté crêpes in butter until lightly browned. Serve with Hard Sauce (see Index).

## COTTAGE CHEESE CRÊPES

*½ cup raisins*
*sherry*
*1 lb. cottage cheese*
*1 cup sour cream*
*1 egg yolk*
*¼ cup slivered almonds,
toasted*

Make Dessert Crêpes I or II. Plump the raisins in hot sherry. Mix cottage cheese, sour cream and egg yolk with the steel blade. Fold in the raisins. Fill the crêpes. Cover crêpes with foil, and bake in a preheated 450°F. oven for 15 minutes. Sprinkle with almonds.

## MANDARIN CRÊPES

¾ *cup heavy cream*
*1 cup Crème Pâtissière*
 *(see Index)*
¼ *cup Triple Sec or*
 *Curaçao*
¾ *cup mandarin oranges,*
 *drained*
*sugar*
*brandy*

Make Dessert Crêpes II. Whip the cream in the processor with the plastic blade. Blend in the Crème Pâtissière and the liqueur. Fold in the oranges. Fill the crêpes and fold over. Sprinkle the crêpes with sugar and brown rapidly under the broiler. Serve hot, and flame with warmed brandy. Serve with Whipped-Cream Sauce (see Index). Other fruits may be used with this.

## CHOCOLATE CRÊPES

*1 oz. unsweetened*
 *chocolate*
*2 eggs*
¼ *cup sugar*
*1 tsp. salt*
*1 cup water*
½ *cup light cream*
¾ *cup flour*
*1 to 1½ pints ice cream,*
 *softened*

Melt chocolate over hot water. Beat the eggs in the container with the steel blade. With the motor running, slowly add sugar and salt, then melted chocolate. Combine the water and light cream. With the motor running, alternately add the flour and the cream and water mixture through the tube. Cook the crêpes, following the basic recipe. Fill with softened ice cream, roll up tightly, and place in the freezer. When ready to serve, remove from freezer and serve with hot May's Chocolate Sauce (see Index).

A flavored whipped cream can be used to fill the crêpes; in that case do not freeze them but refrigerate. Makes about 20 crêpes.

## PANCAKES

*2 cups flour, sifted*
*2 Tbsp. sugar*
*1 Tbsp. baking powder*
*1 tsp. salt*
*2 eggs*
*1½ cups milk*
¼ *cup melted butter or oil*

Combine all ingredients in the container with the steel blade, and blend. Cook on a hot griddle. Makes about 12 pancakes.

## VARIATIONS

Blend any of the following into the batter.

*Bacon*—Substitute 3 tablespoons fat for the butter, and add 4 slices of bacon, cooked and crumbled.

*Orange*—Grate 2 tablespoons orange rind with the steel blade. Substitute ½ cup orange juice for ½ cup of the milk.

*Western*—Place 1 cup cut-up ham, ½ green pepper and ½ onion, both cut up, in the container with the steel blade, and chop. Fold into the batter.

*Apple*—Peel and cut up 2 large apples. Chop the apples with the steel blade, 1 apple at a time, for 3 seconds. Add 1 teaspoon ground cinnamon, and mix with the batter.

*Pecan*—Chop ¼ pound shelled pecans with the steel blade. Add ¼ teaspoon grated nutmeg, and mix with the batter.

## COTTAGE CHEESE PANCAKES

*1 cup cottage cheese*
*1 tsp. baking powder*
*3 eggs*
*2 Tbsp. melted butter*
*2 tsp. sugar*
*½ cup flour, sifted*
*⅔ cup milk*

Place all ingredients in the container with the steel blade, and blend for 8 to 10 seconds. Use 1 tablespoon of batter for each pancake, and cook on a greased griddle. Makes about 12 pancakes.

## PFANNKUCHEN

*6 eggs*
*1½ cups flour, sifted*
*¼ tsp. salt*
*1 Tbsp. sugar*
*2 cups milk*
*½ lb. butter (2 sticks)*
*powdered sugar*
*kirsch or rum*

Place the eggs in the container with the steel blade, and blend by turning machine on and off. Add the flour, salt and sugar. With the motor running, pour the milk through the tube and blend until the batter is smooth. Butter the bottom and sides of a large skillet with melted butter, and heat. When hot add 4 to 5 tablespoons of batter. Tilt the pan so that the batter spreads evenly over the bottom. Cook until bubbles form in the batter. Turn over and cook the other side. Sprinkle with powdered sugar or lace with kirsch or rum. Makes 4 to 6 large pancakes.

# WAFFLES

Waffles are different from pancakes mainly in the amount of shortening used. They are crisper when the egg whites are folded in separately.

2 cups flour
2 tsp. baking powder
2 Tbsp. sugar
½ tsp. salt
2 eggs, separated
6 Tbsp. butter, melted
2 cups milk

Sift the flour, and resift with baking powder, sugar and salt. Place the flour mixture and egg yolks in the container with the steel blade, and blend quickly. With the motor running, add melted butter and milk through the tube, and blend very quickly by turning the motor on and off. Fold the stiffly beaten egg whites into the batter. Bake in a waffle iron. Makes 6 waffles.

To vary waffles, follow any of the variations suggested for pancakes.

# CAKES

—•◆•—

The Cusinart™ Food Processor is a natural for making nut tortes, fruited cakes and crumb-based cakes. The usual shortening and baking-powder cakes may be made in the food processor, too, if certain precautions are taken. Emulsified shortenings may be used in place of butter. However, very high fluffy cakes are not the forte of the processor.

---

## METHOD

All ingredients should be at room temperature. Sift the flour and measure. Then sift twice all of the dry ingredients except the sugar into a mixing bowl. Put sugar, flavoring and shortening in the container with the steel blade, and process for 30 seconds. Add the eggs, one by one, processing 15 seconds for each egg. Add the milk, and process for 3 seconds. Carefully pour the sifted dry ingredients over the liquid ingredients in the container and blend, turning the machine on and off three times, or until the flour is just incorporated. *Don't overbeat.*

### YELLOW CAKE

2½ cups cake flour, sifted
1 Tbsp. double-acting
   baking powder
1 tsp. salt
½ cup shortening
1½ cups sugar
1 tsp. vanilla extract
2 eggs
1 cup milk

Preheat oven to 350°F. Sift and measure the flour. Resift all dry ingredients except the sugar together twice. Blend shortening, sugar and flavoring in the container with the steel blade. Scrape down and process for 30 seconds. Add the eggs, one by one, processing 15 seconds for each egg. Add the milk, and process for 3 seconds. Pour the sifted ingredients over this and process until the flour just disappears. Pour batter into the cake pans. Bake in the preheated oven for 30 to 35 minutes for 8-inch layers, or for 40 to 45 minutes for a 9-inch-square cake. Grated lemon or orange rind, floured nuts or fruit may be added to enhance the cakes. Makes two 8-inch layers or one 9-inch square cake.

# WHITE CAKE

Follow the instruction for the Yellow Cake, but substitute 4 egg whites for the 2 whole eggs.

# CHOCOLATE CAKE

*1 ¾ cups sifted cake flour*
*1 tsp. baking powder*
*½ tsp. baking soda*
*1 tsp. salt*
*½ cup shortening, or*
  *¼ lb. butter (1 stick),*
  *cut up*
*1 ½ cups sugar*
*1 tsp. vanilla extract*
*2 eggs*
*1 cup milk*
*2 oz. baking chocolate,*
  *melted*

Preheat oven to 350°F. Follow the method for Yellow Cake, blending the melted chocolate with the milk.

# COCOA CAKE

*1 ½ cups flour*
*¼ tsp. double-acting*
  *baking powder*
*1 ½ tsp. baking soda*
*¾ tsp. salt*
*½ cup cocoa powder*
*½ cup shortening, or*
  *¼ lb. butter (1 stick),*
  *cut up*
*1 ⅓ cups sugar*
*1 tsp. vanilla extract*
*2 eggs*
*¾ cup water*

Preheat over to 350°F. Follow the method for Yellow Cake, sifting the cocoa with the flour

# FRESH APPLE CAKE

4 cups cut-up peeled apples

¼ lb. butter (1 stick), cut up

¾ cup sugar

2 eggs

1½ cups flour, sifted

2 tsp. baking soda

1 tsp. ground cinnamon

½ tsp. grated nutmeg

½ tsp. salt

1 cup bran flakes

Preheat oven to 350°F. Coarsely chop the apples, 1 cup at a time, with the steel blade; set aside. Put the butter and sugar in the container with the steel blade, and process until the mixture appears smooth. Add the eggs, one at a time, and process for 10 seconds after each addition. Sift together the flour, baking soda, spices and salt. Add to the mixture in the container and blend, turning the machine on and off three times, or until the flour is just incorporated. *Do not overbeat.* Stir bran flakes and chopped apples into the batter. Spoon into a greased pan 13 by 9 inches or in an 8-inch springform pan. Bake in the preheated oven for 45 minutes or until a tester comes out clean. Cool. Serve plain, or top with applesauce or whipped cream.

# NUT TORTE

These light nut confections substitute ground nuts and crumbs for flour. They can be served plain or iced, and they are particularly suited to the capacities of the food processor.

¼ lb. unblanched almonds, pecans or walnuts

½ cup dried bread crumbs

6 eggs, separated

1 cup sugar, sifted

1 lemon, grated rind and juice

Preheat oven to 350°F. Put the nuts in the container with the steel blade and grind fine to make 1 cup; set aside. Process bread crumbs, and set aside. Put egg yolks in the container; with the motor running, gradually add the sugar. Add lemon juice, the rind cut into chunks, nuts and bread crumbs. Process until smooth; scrape down. Beat the egg whites until stiff but not dry. Fold them into the nut mixture, and spoon batter into an ungreased 8-inch springform pan. Bake for about 40 minutes, or until a cake tester when inserted in the center of the torte comes out clean. Let cool in the pan. Do not be concerned if the torte falls a little as it cools. Invert on a serving plate. Serve plain, dusted with powdered sugar, or frost with a butter icing, or spread with custard filling, or finish with whipped cream.

## ZWIEBACK TORTE

*12 zwieback, crumbled*
*¼ lb. nuts*
*2½ tsp. double-acting baking powder*
*6 eggs, separated*
*2 cups sugar*
*½ cup orange juice*
*½ cup Triple Sec*
*2 cups heavy cream*

Preheat oven to 300°F. Place broken pieces of zwieback in the container with the steel blade, and process until well pulverized. Set aside in a large bowl. Chop the nuts coarsely to make 1 cup, and add them to zwieback with the baking powder. Place egg yolks in the container; with the motor running, slowly add the sugar through the tube; blend until smooth. Fold into the nut crumb mixture. Beat the egg whites until stiff but not dry, and fold into the egg-nut mixture. Spoon into 2 buttered and floured 9-inch cake pans. Bake in the preheated oven for 25 to 30 minutes.

Mix orange juice and Triple Sec and pour ½ cup of the mixed liquids over each baked layer. Whip the cream in the processor with the plastic blade, and spread some between the layers. Ice the cake with the rest of the cream. Refrigerate overnight.

## GRAHAM CRACKER CAKE

*1 lb. graham crackers, broken up*
*2 cups almonds, pecans or walnuts*
*½ lb. butter (2 sticks)*
*2¼ cups brown sugar*
*½ cup white sugar*
*6 eggs*
*1 tsp. vanilla extract*
*½ tsp. salt*
*1 Tbsp. baking powder*

Preheat oven to 350°F. Process the graham crackers, a little at a time, with the steel blade until crumbled fine; set aside in a large bowl. Process the nuts and add to the crumbs. Put the butter, cut into pieces, into the container; with the motor running, gradually add the sugars through the tube; blend until smooth. Add eggs, vanilla, salt and baking powder, scrape down, and blend for 5 seconds. Combine with the crumb-nut mixture. Spoon into a buttered and floured 9-inch springform pan. Bake in the preheated oven for 1 hour or until a tester comes out clean. Ice with a fruit frosting.

## CARROT CAKE

¾ lb. carrots, cut up
2 eggs
¾ cup vegetable oil
1 cup sugar
1 cup flour
1 tsp. baking soda
½ tsp. salt
1 tsp. ground cinnamon
1 cup raisins, floured

Preheat oven to 325°F. Place cut-up carrots in the container with the steel blade, and chop for 5 seconds; set aside. With the steel blade in the container, put in the eggs and oil and blend. With the motor running, add the sugar slowly through the tube. Sift flour with baking soda, salt and cinnamon, and pour onto the egg and oil mixture. Blend until the flour is just incorporated, a few seconds. Scrape down. Place the mixture in a bowl and fold in the carrots and raisins. Spoon into a buttered and floured loaf pan. Bake in the preheated oven for 1 hour.

## BANANA ORANGE CAKE

rind of 1 orange
½ cup raisins
¼ lb. butter (1 stick), cut up
1 cup sugar
2 eggs
3 bananas, peeled
¼ cup yogurt or buttermilk
2 cups sifted flour
1 tsp. baking soda
1 tsp. salt
1 tsp. orange extract (optional)

Preheat oven to 350°F. Cut orange rind into manageable pieces, and grind with the raisins, using the steel blade; set aside. Place butter in the container with the steel blade. With the motor running, slowly add the sugar through the tube. Continue to blend, add the eggs, and whir. Add bananas and blend until smooth; scrape down. Add yogurt or buttermilk; blend. Add the flour, which has been sifted with the baking soda and salt. Blend, turning the motor on and off three times, or until the flour just disappears. Stir in the orange-raisin mixture. Place the batter in buttered and floured 8-inch cake tins. Bake in the preheated oven for 30 minutes. Frost with a white icing.

## UNBAKED CHEESECAKE

1½ cups zwieback or graham-cracker crumbs
4 Tbsp. nuts
2 Tbsp. sugar
1 tsp. grated lemon rind
½ cup melted butter
3 eggs, separated
¾ cup sugar
½ tsp. salt
1 cup milk
2 envelopes unflavored gelatin
½ cup cold water
1 Tbsp. lemon juice
1 lb. cream cheese, cubed
1 cup heavy cream

Prepare the crust by processing the first 4 ingredients together with the steel blade. Stir in the butter. Pat the crumbs into a buttered 8-inch springform pan, reserving a quarter of the crumbs for the top. Bake in a 350°F. oven for 10 minutes. Let the crust cool.

Put egg yolks, ¾ cup sugar, salt and milk into the container with the steel blade, and blend. Pour into the top part of a double boiler and cook over simmering water until the custard is thickened. Soften the gelatin in ½ cup cold water, stir into the custard, and cool. Put lemon juice and cubed cheese in the container with the steel blade. Add the cooled custard and blend until smooth; put in a large bowl. Beat the egg whites until stiff, and fold into the custard. Beat the cream with the plastic blade, and fold into the cheese mixture. Turn into the crumb crust, and sprinkle remaining crumbs on the top. Chill until firm. Remove the sides from the pan, loosen the cake from the bottom, and slide onto a serving plate.

## BAKED CHEESECAKE

graham cracker crust (see Crumb Shells)
1 lb. cottage cheese
1 lb. cream cheese
1½ cups sugar
4 eggs
3 Tbsp. cornstarch
3 Tbsp. flour
1 Tbsp. cut-up orange peel
rinds of 2 lemons, cut up
1 tsp. vanilla extract
2 cups sour cream
½ cup melted butter

Preheat oven to 325°F. Prepare graham-cracker crust and press into a buttered 9-inch springform pan. Place the cheeses in the container with the steel blade and blend until smooth. With the motor running, gradually add the sugar through the tube. Add the eggs, cornstarch, flour, fruit rinds and vanilla; blend until smooth. Place in a large bowl, and beat in the sour cream and cooled melted butter. Spoon into the crust. Bake in the preheated oven for 1 hour and 15 minutes. Turn off the oven and let the cake cool in the oven for 3 hours. Chill. This cake looks very pretty when topped with a fruit glaze or preserves. Serves 8.

# MOCHA CHEESECAKE

1 chocolate wafer crust
  (see Crumb Shells)
1 cup sugar
3 eggs
1½ lb. cream cheese
6 oz. semisweet chocolate
  bits, melted
2 Tbsp. cocoa powder
1 Tbsp. instant coffee
  powder
2 Tbsp. rum
1 tsp. vanilla extract
3 cups sour cream
¼ cup melted butter
whipped cream

Preheat oven to 350°F. Make the crust and press the crumb mixture onto the bottom and sides of a 9-inch springform pan. Blend sugar and eggs with the steel blade. Add 1 pound of the cream cheese, cut into cubes, and blend until smooth. Put in a large bowl. Blend remaining cheese with the melted chocolate, cocoa powder, coffee powder dissolved in rum, the vanilla and sour cream, until smooth. Pour in the melted butter and combine by turning the machine on and immediately off. Whisk the cheese mixtures together. Bake in the preheated oven for 1 hour. The cake will be runny but it will become firm when it is chilled. Chill for at least 5 hours. Garnish with whipped cream.

# GENOA CAKE

½ lb. Almond Paste (see
  Index)
1 cup sugar
3 whole eggs
4 eggs, separated
⅔ cup melted butter
½ cup arrowroot
1 oz. kirsch

Preheat oven to 350°F. Butter and flour an 8-inch springform pan, and line with buttered parchment or brown paper. Put the almond paste, cut into bits, the sugar and 3 whole eggs in the container with the steel blade, and blend. Blend in the 4 separated egg yolks, then the melted butter, arrowroot and kirsch. Beat the 4 egg whites until stiff but not dry, and fold them into the mixture. Fill the pan two thirds full. Bake in the preheated oven for 30 minutes, or until the top is spongy and the cake leaves the sides of the pan. Sprinkle cake with powdered sugar, or ice with a white icing flavored with kirsch.

# PECAN ROLL

butter
⅜ lb. pecans
7 eggs, separated

Preheat oven to 350°F. Butter a jelly-roll pan generously. Cover with wax paper slightly larger than the pan so that it can be easily peeled off later.

*1 cup sugar*
*1 tsp. baking powder*
*¼ tsp. almond extract*
*1 cup heavy cream*
*1 tsp. vanilla extract*

Butter the wax paper. Place pecans in the container with the steel blade and grind fine to make 1½ cups crumbs; set aside. Put the egg yolks in the container. With the motor running, gradually add the sugar and blend until smooth. Add baking powder, almond extract and nut crumbs. Blend by turning the motor on and immediately off. Beat the egg whites until stiff but not dry. Fold them into the nut mixture. Spread batter evenly in the pan. Bake in the preheated oven for 18 to 20 minutes, or until a cake tester inserted in the roll comes out clean. Place a kitchen towel on the table and turn cake out onto it. Carefully remove wax paper, and cut off any crisp edges of the cake. Roll up cake in the towel and let cool. Whip the cream and vanilla with the plastic blade. Unroll the cake, spread with half of the cream, and roll up again. Place on a serving platter and frost with remaining cream. Pistachios, almonds or walnuts, may be substituted for the pecans.

---

# FROSTINGS

Uncooked icings can be made in the processor with no effort to give perfectly smooth results. However, some of these made with confectioners' sugar may have a slightly raw taste. To overcome this, let them sit over hot water for 10 to 15 minutes. Cool before spreading.

## BUTTER FROSTING

*3 cups confectioners'*
*  sugar, sifted*
*5½ Tbsp. butter*
*1 egg yolk*
*1½ tsp. flavoring*
*cream*

Blend first 4 ingredients in the processor with the steel blade. Add just enough cream to give the frosting the right consistency for spreading. If too thin, add more sugar. Makes enough for a 9-inch cake.

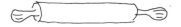

## SUGGESTED VARIATIONS

Add any of these to Butter Frosting.

*Chocolate*—Melt 3 ounces unsweetened chocolate, and blend.
*Mocha*—Make chocolate frosting, but substitute prepared strong black coffee for the cream.
*Citrus*—Do not use vanilla for flavoring. Substitute citrus juice for the cream, and add 1 tablespoon grated rind.
*Coffee*—Enrich with 1 tablespoon instant coffee powder dissolved in 2 tablespoons rum or brandy. Omit the cream.
*Wine*—Substitute wine for vanilla flavoring and cream.
*Cocoa*—Use 4 tablespoons cocoa powder mixed with 3 tablespoons hot water in place of the cream.

## FRUIT FROSTING

½ *cup fruit pulp*
2 *cups confectioners'*
  *sugar*
2 *Tbsp. butter*
1 *Tbsp. lemon juice*

Purée the fruit with the steel blade (bananas, cooked peaches, apricots, prunes, crushed pineapple, etc., drained). Add remaining ingredients and blend until smooth. If too thin, gradually add more sugar.

## CREAM-CHEESE FROSTING

8 *oz. cream cheese*
2 *cups confectioners'*
  *sugar*
1½ *tsp. flavoring*
*cream*

Blend the ingredients with the steel blade, adding cream if necessary to thin it. This is very good when it is flavored with rum and has raisins folded into it.

## ROYAL ICING

1 *lb. confectioners' sugar*
1 *Tbsp. lemon juice*
2 *or 3 egg whites*

Blend sugar, lemon juice and 2 egg whites with the steel blade. If icing seems too stiff, gradually blend in a little more egg white, which has been beaten until foamy, until you achieve the right consistency for smooth spreading. If icing becomes too thin, add more sugar.

# COOKIES

Cookies may be dropped, rolled and cut out, refrigerated, molded or pressed. The processor is very helpful in making many kinds of cookies.

# DROP COOKIES

## DROP COOKIE DOUGH I

¼ *lb. butter (1 stick), cut*
  *up*
½ *cup sugar*
*1 egg*
*1 tsp. vanilla extract*
*1 cup flour, sifted*
¼ *tsp. baking soda*
½ *tsp. salt*

Preheat oven to 375°F. Place the cut-up butter in the container with the steel blade. With the motor running, add the sugar slowly. Whisk the egg with the vanilla and add to the sugar mixture; blend quickly. Add the flour, which has been sifted with the baking soda and salt, and blend until just incorporated, about 3 seconds. Drop by teaspoons onto a lightly greased cookie sheet, placing mounds 2 inches apart. Bake in the preheated oven for 8 to 10 minutes. Cool cookies slightly before removing from cookie sheet. Makes about 48 wafers, 2¼-inch size.

### SUGGESTED VARIATIONS

Add any of these to Drop Cookie Dough I.

*Chocolate Chip*—Use ⅜ cup white sugar and ⅜ cup brown sugar in place of ½ cup white sugar. Fold in 6 ounces chocolate bits.
*Citrus*—Add 1½ teaspoons grated citrus rind and 1 teaspoon lemon or orange extract.
*Cinnamon-Nut*—Add 2 cups nuts, chopped, and 1 teaspoon ground cinnamon.
*Coffee*—Add 1 tablespoon instant coffee powder dissolved in 2 tablespoons hot water.

# DROP COOKIE DOUGH II

¼ *lb. butter (1 stick), cut up*
*3 oz. cream cheese*
½ *cup confectioners' sugar*
*1 egg*
*1 Tbsp. flavoring (vanilla, etc.)*
*1 cup sifted flour*

Preheat oven to 350°F. Blend butter and cream cheese with the steel blade. With the motor running add the sugar slowly through the tube. Add egg and liquid flavoring. Combine the flour and dry flavorings (if any), and add to the mixture in the container. Blend until flour is just incorporated. Drop the batter by spoonfuls onto a cookie sheet and bake in the preheated oven for 10 minutes. Makes about 48 cookies, 2¼-inch size.

## SUGGESTED VARIATIONS

Add any of these to Drop Cookie Dough II.

*Rum and White Raisin*—Add ½ cup white raisins and 1 tablespoon rum extract.
*Brandy Spice*—Add ½ teaspoon each of ground ginger, cloves, cinnamon and grated nutmeg, and 1 tablespoon brandy.
*Pistachio*—Add 1 cup pistachios, chopped, and ½ teaspoon almond extract.
*Maple Walnut*—Add 1 teaspoon each of maple flavoring and vanilla extract, and ½ cup walnuts, chopped.

# OATMEAL DROP COOKIES

¼ *lb. butter (1 stick), cut up*
1 ½ *cups firmly packed brown sugar*
*1 egg*
¼ *cup milk*
1 ½ *cups flour*
½ *tsp. baking soda*
½ *tsp. salt*
¼ *tsp. ground ginger*
1 ¾ *cups quick-cooking rolled oats*
*1 cup dried currants*

Preheat oven to 375°F. Cream the cut-up butter in the processor with the steel blade. With the motor running, slowly add the sugar through the tube. Add the egg and milk to the sugar mixture, and blend. Sift the dry ingredients and blend with the egg-milk mixture for 3 to 5 seconds. Fold in the oats and currants and drop by spoonfuls onto a greased cookie sheet, placing them 3 inches apart. Bake in the preheated oven for 20 minutes. Makes about 48 cookies, 2-inch size.

## LEMON DROP THINS

¼ lb. butter (1 stick), cut
   up
1 Tbsp. grated lemon rind
⅓ cup sugar
⅓ cup honey
1 egg
2 cups sifted flour
1 tsp. double-acting
   baking powder
1 tsp. salt

Preheat oven to 350°F. Cream the butter with the lemon rind, with the steel blade. With the motor running slowly add the sugar through the tube. Add the honey and egg to the sugar mixture and blend. Sift the flour, baking powder and salt. Add the dry ingredients to the container and blend for 3 to 5 seconds. Drop by teaspoons onto a greased baking sheet, and flatten with a fork. Bake in the preheated oven for 10 to 12 minutes. Makes about 48 cookies, 2-inch size.

## BUTTER THINS

¼ lb. butter (1 stick), cut
   up
1½ cups sugar
3 eggs
1¼ cups flour, sifted
⅛ tsp. grated nutmeg
1 Tbsp. grated orange
   rind

Preheat oven to 350°F. Cream the butter in the processor with the steel blade. With the motor running, slowly add the sugar through the tube. Add the eggs to the sugar mixture; blend. Pour in the flour sifted with nutmeg, and blend for 3 seconds. Drop ½ teaspoons of batter onto a foil-lined baking sheet, placing mounds at least 3 inches apart. Bake in the preheated oven for 5 to 7 minutes. Remove from cookie sheet while still warm. Makes about 36 thins.

## BRANDY SNAPS

4 Tbsp. butter, cut up
¼ cup sugar
2 Tbsp. corn syrup
¼ tsp. ground ginger
1 Tbsp. brandy
½ cup flour

Preheat oven to 350°F. Cream the butter in the processor with the steel blade. With the motor running, gradually pour in the sugar through the tube. Add remaining ingredients and blend until smooth. Drop by teaspoons onto a foil-lined cookie sheet, placing mounds 2 inches apart. Bake in the preheated oven for 10 minutes. Makes 12 to 16 snaps.

## BROWN SUGAR COOKIES

¼ lb. nuts
1 cup brown sugar
1½ Tbsp. flour
1 tsp. double-acting
  baking powder
1 egg
1 tsp. vanilla extract

Preheat oven to 375°F. Chop the nuts with the steel blade, then add all the other ingredients and process until nuts are incorporated into the batter. Drop by teaspoons onto a foil-lined cookie sheet, placing mounds 3 inches apart. Bake in the preheated oven for 10 to 12 minutes. Cool slightly. Remove with a broad spatula. Makes about 48 cookies, 3-inch size.

## ALMOND LACE COOKIES

1 cup blanched almonds
¼ lb. butter (1 stick), cut
  up
1 cup sugar
3 Tbsp. flour
2 Tbsp. milk

Preheat oven to 350°F. Place almonds in the container with the steel blade, and grind fine; set aside. Put the butter in the container; with the motor running, slowly add the sugar through the tube. Add the flour, the milk and ground almonds, and blend for 3 to 5 seconds. Heat the mixture until just hot. Cover a cookie sheet with foil and drop the warm mixture on it, using no more than ½ teaspoon per cookie and placing mounds 3 inches apart. Bake in the preheated oven until browned. Allow to cool *slightly,* then gently remove with a broad spatula. Makes about 48 cookies.

# ROLLED COOKIES

## SUGAR COOKIES

¼ lb. butter (1 stick), cut
   up
¾ cup sugar
1 Tbsp. cream
1 tsp. flavoring
1 egg
1¼ cups sifted flour
¼ tsp. double-acting
   baking powder
¼ tsp. salt
sugar

Preheat oven to 425°F. Cream the butter in the processor with the steel blade. With the motor running, slowly add the sugar through the tube. Add the cream, flavoring and egg, and blend. Sift together flour, baking powder and salt, and pour into the sugar mixture. Blend for 3 to 5 seconds. Chill the dough. Roll out dough very thin on a floured board, and cut into any desired shape. Place cookies on a lightly greased baking sheet, and sprinkle them with sugar. Bake in the preheated oven for 5 to 7 minutes. Makes about 48 cookies, 2-inch size.

## SUGGESTED VARIATIONS

Add any of these to sugar cookies.

*Chocolate Crisps*—Blend 2 ounces unsweetened chocolate, melted and cooled, into the dough.
*Jam Pinwheels*—Roll out the dough into a rectangle ¼ inch thick. Spread with jam and roll up tightly, beginning at the long side. Chill. Cut into ⅛-inch-thick slices and place on a lightly greased baking sheet. Bake in a 350°F. oven for 10 to 12 minutes. Try other fillings too—nuts, cinnamon, sugar.
*Butterscotch*—Substitute brown sugar for the white sugar.
*Maple*—Use maple sugar, crushed very fine in the processor, in place of white sugar.
*Liqueur*—Add 2 tablespoons of any liqueur to the dough.

# MOLDED COOKIES

## NUT COOKIES

½ lb. nuts
½ lb. sweet butter (2 sticks), cut up
½ cup confectioners' sugar
2 tsp. vanilla extract
2 cups flour
½ tsp. salt
granulated sugar

Preheat oven to 350°F. Grind the nuts with the steel blade. Add the cut-up butter, confectioners' sugar and vanilla to nuts. Process until well incorporated. Add flour and salt, and blend until the flour just disappears. Chill until the dough is easy to handle. Form 1-inch balls, and place them on a cookie sheet. Bake in the preheated oven for 25 minutes. Dust with granulated sugar while still warm. This dough can also be formed into triangles, rolls or crescents, or can be flattened into rounds. Makes about 60 cookies.

## SUGGESTED VARIATIONS

Add any of these to the dough for Nut Cookies before baking.

*Crystallized Fruit*—Dip dough balls into slightly beaten egg white and roll in chopped crystallized fruit (gingerroot, citron).

*Extra Nutty*—Dip dough balls into slightly beaten egg white and roll in chopped nuts.

*Tropical*—Roll dough balls in shredded coconut.

*Surprise*—Shape each dough ball around a toasted almond or a sugared pecan.

*Tender Rounds*—Add 2 teaspoons double-acting baking powder to the dough. Press these dough balls flat on the cookie sheet before baking. While still warm, glaze them with lemon juice and powdered sugar. Makes about 40 cookies.

*Butterscotch Chews*—Add 6 ounces butterscotch bits and grind with the nuts when making the dough.

## RUM BALLS

1½ cups pecans
3 cups vanilla wafers
1 cup confectioners' sugar
3 Tbsp. white corn syrup
3 Tbsp. cocoa powder
½ cup rum, or enough to
    bind the mixture
cocoa powder

Grind pecans and wafers together with the steel blade. Blend with the remaining ingredients, adding the rum a little at a time, so that the mixture just holds together. Form into small balls. Refrigerate overnight. Dust with more cocoa before serving. Makes about 45 balls, 1-inch size.

Bourbon can be used instead of rum, to make Bourbon Balls.

# ICEBOX COOKIES

## ICEBOX COOKIES I

½ lb. butter (2 sticks)
    or shortening
½ cup granulated sugar
½ cup brown sugar
2 eggs
1½ tsp. flavoring
2¾ cups flour, sifted
½ tsp. baking soda
1 tsp. salt

Cut butter or shortening into pieces and put in the container with the steel blade. With the motor running, add the sugars little by little, and blend in the eggs and flavoring. Sift dry ingredients together and blend into the butter mixture until the flour just disappears. Divide the dough into halves and form each portion into a roll about 2 inches in diameter. Wrap in wax paper and chill until stiff.

When ready to bake, cut roll into thin slices. Bake on an ungreased cookie sheet in a preheated 400°F. oven for 6 to 8 minutes. Makes about 72 cookies, 2-inch size.

### SUGGESTED VARIATIONS

Add any of these to the dough for Icebox Cookies I, and blend in.

Orange Pecan—Add 1 tablespoon grated orange rind and ½ cup pistachios or pecans, chopped.
Chocolate—Add 2 ounces unsweetened chocolate, melted and cooled.
Wine—Add 2 tablespoons sweet sherry or Madeira or brandy.

# ICEBOX COOKIES II

½ lb. butter (2 sticks)
1 cup sifted confectioners' sugar
1 tsp. flavoring
2½ cups flour, sifted
¼ tsp. salt

Cut the butter into pieces, place in the container with the sugar and the flavoring, and process with the steel blade until mealy. Add flour and salt, and blend together for 3 to 5 seconds. Form into 1 or 2 smooth rolls, about 2 inches in diameter. Wrap in wax paper, and chill until stiff but not crumbly.

Cut roll into very thin slices. Bake on an ungreased cookie sheet in a preheated 400°F. oven for about 8 minutes, or until lightly browned. Makes about 72 cookies.

## SUGGESTED VARIATIONS

Add any of these to the dough for Icebox Cookies II.

*Almond*—Use almond flavoring. Press a blanched almond in the center of each cookie before baking.

*Rose*—Use 1 teaspoon rosewater as the flavoring. Sprinkle cookies with vanilla sugar.

*Peppermint*—Use 1 teaspoon peppermint extract as the flavoring. Dust with pulverized peppermint candies.

## SPRITZ COOKIES OR PRESS COOKIES

The classic for butter cookie fancies.

5½ Tbsp. shortening
11 Tbsp. butter, cut up
¾ cup confectioners' sugar, sifted
2 egg yolks
1 egg white
1 tsp. vanilla extract
1 tsp. ground cardamom (optional)
2 cups flour, sifted
½ tsp. salt

Preheat oven to 375°F. Place all ingredients except flour and salt in the container with the steel blade, making sure the butter is cut into pieces. Blend well. Add the flour sifted with salt, and blend until smooth. Force the dough through a cookie press onto an ungreased cookie sheet. Bake in the preheated oven for 7 to 10 minutes, or until set, but not brown. Makes about 50 cookies.

These make marvelous Christmas cookies for they take to being decorated with colored sugars, shot, sprinkles and candied fruits, and they can be made in so many shapes. If the dough becomes too soft, chill until pliable.

## SHORTBREAD

½ lb. butter (2 sticks)
⅝ cup sugar
2½ cups flour, sifted
¼ tsp. double-acting
   baking powder
½ tsp. salt

Preheat oven to 325°F. Cut the butter into pieces and blend in the machine with the steel blade. With the machine running, gradually add the sugar through the tube. Sift dry ingredients and add them to butter and sugar mixture. Blend until flour is well incorporated. Chill the dough and roll out ½ to 1 inch thick. Cut into any desired shape. Prick the dough with a fork. Bake on an ungreased baking sheet in the preheated oven for 20 to 25 minutes.

## MACAROONS

½ lb. Almond Paste (see
   Index)
¾ cup confectioners'
   sugar
½ cup granulated sugar
3 egg whites
½ tsp. almond extract

Cut the almond paste into small pieces and place in the container with the steel blade along with the sugars, 2 egg whites and flavoring. Blend until smooth. The dough should be soft but not runny, and it should be able to hold its shape when dropped from a spoon or piped through a pastry tube. If the dough is too stiff, beat remaining egg white until foamy and add, a little at a time, turning the motor on and off until the right consistency is achieved. Line a cookie sheet with parchment paper or brown paper. Drop dough by spoonfuls, or squeeze through a pastry bag with a star or round tip. Let the cookies rest, covered, for 2 hours or overnight. Brush with water. Bake in a preheated 325°F. oven for 20 to 25 minutes or until lightly browned. Makes about 30 macaroons, 2-inch size.

# FLORENTINES

½ *cup heavy cream*
½ *cup sugar*
¼ *tsp. salt*
*1¼ cups blanched*
  *almonds or*
  *hazelnuts, chopped*
¼ *lb. candied orange*
  *peel, chopped*
¼ *cup flour*

Preheat oven to 325°F. Heat cream, sugar and salt together. Place nuts, candied peel and flour in the container with the steel blade, and chop coarsely, turning the machine on and off. Stir this into the hot ingredients and cook until the mixture thickens, about 2 minutes. Drop by teaspoons, 2 inches apart, on a well-greased cookie sheet. Bake for 12 minutes, or until brown around the edges. Let cool slightly on the cookie sheet. Then remove and let cool until crisp. Makes about 24 thin 3-inch cookies.

CHOCOLATE FILLING

*8 oz. semisweet*
  *chocolate, melted*
*3 Tbsp. butter*
*1 Tbsp. Grand Marnier*

Mix filling ingredients together. Spread the flat side of one cookie with filling and top with a second cookie. Be sure filling is firm and cookie "sandwiches" set before serving.

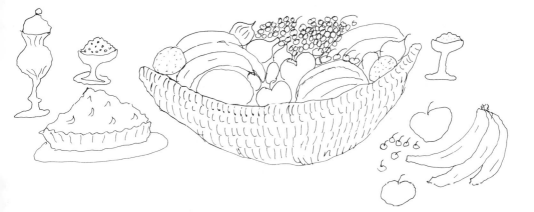

# DESSERTS AND DESSERT SAUCES

Formerly fussy desserts are easy as can be with the help of the food processor. New desserts can be invented. Combine this pastry with that filling and add still another topping. Create new soufflé combinations. Try different fruit whips. Concoct brand-new sauces. Use your imagination to invent and let the processor do the work.

# HOT DESSERT SOUFFLÉ I

3 Tbsp. butter
2 Tbsp. flour
1 cup milk, scalded
¼ tsp. salt
½ cup sugar
4 egg yolks
1 tsp. vanilla extract
5 egg whites

Preheat oven to 375°F. Butter and sugar a 1½-quart soufflé dish. Put butter and flour in the container with the steel blade, and blend until crumbly. With the motor running, add the hot milk through the tube. Add salt, sugar, egg yolks and flavoring. Cook this mixture over low heat, stirring constantly, until thickened. Cool. Beat egg whites until stiff but not dry, then fold into the cooled sauce. Pile into the prepared soufflé dish. Bake in the preheated oven for 30 minutes. Serve at once. Serves 4 to 6.

## SUGGESTED VARIATIONS FOR HOT DESSERT SOUFFLÉ I

When using a liqueur as a flavoring, add 1 extra egg yolk and egg white for every 2 tablespoons liqueur.

Chocolate—Melt ½ cup grated chocolate when scalding the milk.

Nut—Fold in ¾ cup ground nuts and substitute ½ teaspoon almond extract for the vanilla.

Coffee—Dissolve 2 tablespoons instant coffee powder in the scalded milk.

Lemon—Add grated rind of 1 lemon, ⅓ cup of lemon juice and ⅓ cup of cream, and increase sugar to 1 cup.

Orange—Add grated rind of 1 orange, ⅓ cup of orange juice and ⅓ cup of cream.

Rothschild—Fold in ½ cup chopped candied fruits which have been soaked in kirsch.

Maple—Substitute ¼ cup maple sugar for half of the granulated sugar, and use maple or rum flavoring.

Liqueur—Flavor with ½ cup liqueur (Grand Marnier, Apricot, Framboise, Triple Sec, B & B, etc.). Use 8 egg yolks and 10 egg whites. For extra panache, layer the bottom of the soufflé dish with split ladyfingers soaked with more of the liqueur, or sandwich ladyfingers in the middle.

## HOT DESSERT SOUFFLÉ II

This is an easy soufflé to prepare if you have leftover Crème Pâtissière.

*4 Tbsp. Crème Pâtissière*
*(see Index)*
*1 Tbsp. sugar*
*½ tsp. vanilla extract*
*5 egg yolks*
*5 egg whites*

Preheat oven to 350°F. Place Crème Pâtissière, sugar, vanilla and egg yolks in the container with the steel blade, and blend. Beat egg whites until stiff but not dry, and fold into the egg-yolk mixture. Spoon into a buttered and sugared 5-cup soufflé dish. Bake in the preheated oven for 25 to 30 minutes. Serves 4.

## COLD DESSERT SOUFFLÉ or MOUSSE

*¼ cup cold water*
*1 envelope unflavored*
*gelatin*
*½ cup juice or liqueur,*
*heated*
*1½ cups sugar*
*3 eggs, separated*
*1 tsp. vanilla extract*
*2 cups heavy cream*

Pour ¼ cup water into the container with the steel blade. Sprinkle gelatin over the water and soak for 10 minutes. With the motor running, add the heated juice or liqueur through the tube. Turn off the motor and add the sugar, egg yolks and vanilla. Blend, scraping down the sides, until well homogenized. Allow the mixture to cool until just starting to congeal. Whip the cream with the plastic blade, and fold into the egg-yolk mixture. Beat egg whites stiff but not dry, and fold into mixture. Pile into a serving dish, or into a soufflé dish with a collar. Chill. Remove the collar before serving. Serves 4 to 6.

### VARIATIONS ON THE COLD DESSERT SOUFFLÉ

*Macaroon*—Fold in 1 cup crumbled macaroons soaked in a liqueur. Dissolve the gelatin in 4 tablespoons of hot liqueur plus 4 tablespoons of hot water.

*Orange-Lemon-Grand Marnier*—Dissolve the gelatin in 4 tablespoons orange or lemon juice and 4 tablespoons Grand Marnier, heated; add the grated rind of ½ orange.

*Coffee*—Dissolve gelatin in 4 tablespoons prepared strong hot coffee and 4 tablespoons Crème de Cacao, heated.

*Daiquiri*—Dissolve the gelatin in ½ cup lime juice, heated. Add grated rind of 1 lime and 1 tablespoon rum extract.

*Ginger*—Add ⅓ cup chopped preserved gingerroot and use ½ cup hot milk for dissolving the gelatin.

*Apricot*—Dissolve the gelatin in ½ cup apricot juice, heated, and add ¼ cup chopped dried apricots and ¼ teaspoon almond extract.

## FROZEN FRUIT MOUSSE

*2 pkg. (10 oz. each)*
*frozen fruit*
*½ cup cold water*
*2 envelopes unflavored*
*gelatin*
*2 tsp. lemon juice*
*½ cup sugar*
*3 cups heavy cream*

Thaw the fruit and drain, saving the juice. If necessary, add enough water to the juice to make ½ cup. Pour the ½ cup cold water into the container with the steel blade, and sprinkle gelatin over it. Let it soak for 10 minutes. Heat the fruit juice. With the motor running, add the hot juice to the gelatin and blend until gelatin is dissolved. Add the lemon juice, fruit and sugar, and blend together; set aside. Beat the cream, 1½ cups at a time, with the plastic blade. Fold the fruit purée into the whipped cream, and spoon into a 10-cup mold. Freeze until firm. Serves 8.

## FROZEN FRUIT AND CHEESE MOUSSE

*½ small lemon, seeded*
*and cut into pieces*
*2 cups fruit purée*
*8 oz. cream cheese*
*1 cup light cream*
*¾ cup sugar*
*1 tsp. vanilla extract*

Put all ingredients in the container with the steel blade, and blend until smooth. Spread into 2 foil-lined ice trays with enough foil overhang to help in handling the mixture. Place the trays in the freezer for about 2 hours. Return the mousse mixture to the processor and blend by turning the motor on and immediately off, or until just smooth. Pour back into the trays and freeze until firm. Serves 4 to 6.

## GELATIN FRUIT CREAM

This light concoction is very well suited for making special desserts in molds lined with ladyfingers, cake, meringue, or macaroons.

*½ cup cold water*
*2 envelopes unflavored*
*gelatin*
*1½ cups milk or juice,*
*scalded*
*2 cups fruit purée*
*½ cup sugar*
*1 cup heavy cream*
*1½ tsp. vanilla extract*

Pour the water into the container with the steel blade. Sprinkle gelatin over the water and let soak for 10 minutes. With the motor running, add the scalded milk or juice through the tube. Add the fruit purée (canned, cooked fresh, or thawed frozen) and the sugar. Blend until well puréed, scraping down the sides. Let the mixture cool until just starting to set. Whip the cream and vanilla with the plastic blade, and fold into the mixture. Pour into a lined 8-cup mold. Unmold when set, and garnish with a ring of fruit. Serves 5 or 6.

## SUGGESTED WAYS OF SERVING GELATIN FRUIT CREAM

Hollow out an angel-food cake, leaving a 2-inch rim, and fill with any flavor. Let the filling set. Garnish with more fruit and whipped cream.

Line a charlotte mold or springform pan with split ladyfingers which have been brushed with melted butter or sherry. Fill the mold and chill.

Split a single round layer of white cake and fit one piece into the bottom of a springform pan. Cover with the gelatin cream and when the gelatin is firm place the other piece of cake on top. Unmold cake and frost with fruited whipped cream.

## PRUNE-APRICOT WHIP

*¾ cup dried apricots*
*¾ cup dried prunes*
*¾ cup sugar*
*1 cup Madeira wine*
*1 Tbsp. lemon juice*
*1 cup heavy cream*
*sugar*

Soak the fruit until plump and cook in water to cover with the sugar until tender; drain. Add Madeira and simmer for 10 minutes more. Drain the fruit, saving the wine. Place fruit in the container with the steel blade and add the lemon juice. Purée with a little of the wine. Fold into the cream which has been whipped with the plastic blade, and sweetened with sugar to taste. If desired, dollop with more whipped cream and sprinkle with chopped pistachios. Serves 4 to 6.

## BAKED FRUIT WHIP

*1 lb. dried fruit*
*½ cup sugar*
*1 tsp. grated lemon rind*
*5 egg whites*
*¼ tsp. salt*

Preheat oven to 350°F. Soak the dried fruit, and cook in water to cover. Drain the fruit and place it in the container with the steel blade. Add the sugar and lemon rind; purée. Beat the egg whites with the salt until stiff but not dry, and fold into the fruit purée. Butter and sugar a 2-quart soufflé dish and pile in the mixture. Set the dish in a pan of hot water and bake in the preheated oven for 1 hour. Serve hot with whipped cream. Serves 8.

## QUICK POTS DE CRÈME AU CHOCOLAT

*6 oz. chocolate bits*
*3 egg yolks*
*1 cup prepared strong*
*black coffee, hot*
*1 cup heavy cream*

Place chocolate bits and egg yolks in the container with the steel blade, and blend briefly. With the motor running, add the hot coffee through the tube, and process until thoroughly mixed. Pour into a serving dish or into individual dessert cups. Chill. Top with whipped cream which has been whipped in the processor with the plastic blade. Serves 6.

## COEUR À LA CRÈME I

*1 lb. cream cheese*
*2 Tbsp. sweet cream*
*1 cup sour cream*
*¼ tsp. salt*

Cut the cream cheese into cubes and place in the container with the steel blade, along with the sweet cream, sour cream and salt. Blend until smooth. Pack into traditional heart-shaped baskets lined with dampened cheesecloth, or into a sieve lined with dampened cheesecloth large enough to fold over the top. Set baskets or sieve on a rack over a pan; place in the refrigerator and let drain overnight. Unmold on a cold plate and decorate with strawberries. Serves 6 to 8.

## COEUR À LA CRÈME II

Follow the preceding recipe, but use 2 cups cottage cheese in place of cream cheese, and 1 cup heavy cream instead of sour cream.

## CRÈME SAINT-HONORÉ

This is a very good gelatin dessert. Good enough to serve alone, but very special when accompanied by a sauce.

½ cup cold water
1 envelope unflavored
  gelatin
1 ½ cups flavored Crème
  Pâtissière (see Index),
  hot
6 egg whites
¼ tsp. cream of tartar
⅓ cup sugar
1 ½ tsp. vanilla extract or
  other flavoring
1 cup chopped nuts, cake
  bits, candied fruits
  (optional)

Pour the cold water into the container with the steel blade. Sprinkle gelatin over the water and soak for 10 minutes. Add the hot Crème Pâtissière and blend briefly to dissolve the gelatin. Beat egg whites with the cream of tartar until stiff; gradually add the sugar and flavoring. Fold the flavored meringue into the cooled *crème* mixture. Fold in nuts, cake bits or candied fruits, if using them. Place in a serving dish and chill. Serve with a fruit sauce.

## HELENE'S PUMPERNICKEL DESSERT

3 cups (1-lb. loaf, crusts
  removed) pumpernickel
  crumbs
¼ cup cherry jam or jelly
½ cup kirsch
2 cups heavy cream
2 cans (17 oz. each) sour
  cherries
1 cup sugar

Break the bread into pieces, place in the container with the steel blade, and crumble. Add cherry jam and kirsch. Blend by turning the motor on and immediately off; set aside. Whip the cream with the plastic blade. Place a layer of the crumbs in the bottom of a bowl, then add a layer of drained cherries, sprinkled with part of the sugar. Spoon whipped cream over cherries. Continue to layer, ending with whipped cream. Chill. This is particularly attractive when served in a glass bowl. Serves 6.

# PASTRY DESSERTS

## CREAM PUFFS AND ÉCLAIRS

Cream puffs, éclairs and profiteroles are made with sweetened *pâte à choux* (cream-puff pastry; see Index). They can be frosted or served plain with a sauce. Traditionally, they are filled with Crème Pâtissière. They are also good filled with flavored whipped cream or ice cream. The Italian filling for cream puffs is based on ricotta cheese.

### RICOTTA FILLING

*1 lb. ricotta cheese*
*1 cup sugar*
*2 Tbsp. Crème de Cacao*
*¼ tsp. almond extract*
*2 Tbsp. candied orange peel*
*2 oz. semisweet chocolate*

Put the cheese, sugar, crème de cacao and almond extract in the container with the steel blade, and blend until smooth; set aside. Chop candied orange peel and chocolate with the steel blade. Fold all together. This can also be used as a filling for a *génoise* type of cake or in a ladyfinger-lined mold.

### CRÈME PÂTISSIÈRE

This traditional *crème* filling is a base for many fruit tarts, pastries and pies. It can be lightened with beaten egg whites or whipped cream to fill cream puffs or to layer pastries. It can also be combined with fruit or other solids, cake bits, etc., as in Crème Saint-Honoré (see Index).

*5 egg yolks*
*1 cup sugar*
*¾ cup sifted flour*
*2 cups boiling milk*
*1 tbsp. butter*
*1½ tsp. vanilla extract*
*2 Tbsp. flavoring (rum, liqueur, coffee, pulverized nuts)*

Put egg yolks and sugar in the container with the steel blade, and blend until pale yellow. Add flour and blend again. With the motor running, pour the boiling milk through the tube in a thin stream. After all the milk has been added, place the mixture in the top part of a double boiler over boiling water and cook until thick and smooth, beating continuously. Finish with butter and flavorings.

To use in tart shells, glaze a baked sweet pastry shell with currant jelly or apricot preserves. Spoon *crème pâtissière* over this, and place cooked or fresh fruits on top. Glaze with Jelly Sauce (see Index), preserves or thick vanilla gelatin.

## APPLES IN A BLANKET

*1 cup sugar*
*2 cups water*
*1 cinnamon stick*
*3 baking apples*

*1 recipe Cream-Cheese Pastry (see Index)*
*½ cup cinnamon sugar*
*1 cup Mincemeat (see Index), or canned mincemeat*
*1 egg yolk, beaten*
*2 Tbsp. water*
*whipped cream*
*cinnamon sugar*

Preheat oven to 375°F. Make cinnamon syrup: Cook 1 cup sugar with the water and the cinnamon stick until syrupy. Set aside. Peel and core the apples, and cut into ½-inch-thick slices. Poach apple slices in the cinnamon syrup for 10 minutes. Drain and cool.

Make the pastry. Roll it out ⅛ inch thick, and cut into twelve 5-inch circles. Place a poached apple ring on a square of the dough and sprinkle with a little cinnamon sugar. Spread a thin layer of mincemeat on the apple, and cover with another slice of apple sprinkled with more cinnamon sugar. Moisten the edge of the dough square, place another dough square on top, crimp the edges, and prick the top. Mix egg yolk and water to make egg wash. Brush tops of pastry with egg wash and sprinkle with more cinnamon sugar. Place packages on a shallow pan, and bake in the preheated oven for 15 minutes. Serve with whipped cream flavored with cinnamon sugar, or with Hard Sauce (see Index). Serves 6.

## PRESERVE PASTRIES

2 recipies Basic Piecrust
  (see Index)
1 cup preserves
½ cup chopped almonds
  (optional)
cooking oil

Make the pastry, and roll it out ⅛ inch thick. Cut into 3-inch squares or circles. Spoon 2 tablespoons of the preserves (marmalade, strawberry jam, apricot jam, etc.) on the center of each piece of pastry. Chop almonds in the container with the steel blade, and sprinkle nuts over the preserves. Top with another square or circle of dough. Seal the moistened edges. Fry in oil heated to 375°F. until golden. Drain on paper towels. These can also be glazed and baked in a 350°F. oven for 15 minutes. Serve with Preserves Sauce (see Index). Serves 6 to 8.

———

# PIE FILLINGS AND PIES

## CHIFFON PIE FILLING I

½ cup liqueur (brandy,
  crème de menthe,
  Triple Sec, etc.)
1 envelope unflavored
  gelatin
¾ cup milk, hot
3 eggs, separated
1½ cups sugar
¼ tsp. cream of tartar
1 cup heavy cream
½ cup nuts, chopped
  (optional)

Pour the liqueur into the container with the steel blade. Sprinkle gelatin over the liqueur, and soak for 10 minutes. With the motor running, pour the hot milk through the tube, and blend until gelatin is dissolved. Add egg yolks and 1 cup of the sugar; blend. Chill until mixture is syrupy. Beat the egg whites with cream of tartar until soft peaks form, then gradually add remaining ½ cup sugar. Fold meringue into the gelatin mixture. Whip the cream with the plastic blade, and fold all together, adding nuts if you use them. Spoon into a pie shell and refrigerate until set. This may be frozen. Garnish with chocolate curls, nuts, citrus rind—whatever suits.

## CHIFFON PIE FILLING II

*1 envelope unflavored
  gelatin
⅔ cup sugar
½ cup hot water, liqueur
  or juice
3 eggs, separated
1 cup fresh berries or
  other fruit, or 1 cup
  cooked or canned fruit
¼ tsp. salt
2 tsp. lemon juice
¼ tsp. cream of tartar*

Put the gelatin and ⅓ cup of the sugar in the container with steel blade. Add the hot liquid and blend until gelatin has dissolved. Add egg yolks, fruit, salt and lemon juice, and blend. Chill until syrupy. Beat egg whites with cream of tartar until stiff, and gradually add remaining ⅓ cup of sugar. Fold meringue into the fruit-gelatin mixture, and spoon into a pie shell. Chill until firm. Decorate with more fruit or cream.

## COTTAGE-CHEESE FILLING

*½ cup sugar
4 tsp. butter
¼ tsp. salt
3 eggs, separated
1½ cups cottage cheese
2 tsp. flavoring (lemon,
  orange, rum, etc.)*

Place all ingredients except egg whites in the container with the steel blade, and process. Beat egg whites stiff but not dry, and fold into the cheese mixture. Spoon into a pie shell. Bake in a preheated 425°F. oven for 20 minutes. When the pie is cool, fruit may be arranged on top, or fruit purées or preserves can be spooned over it.

# MOUSSE FILLING

This is particularly good in a nut or a meringue crust. It can also be used as a molded dessert.

*1 pkg. (3 oz.) fruit-flavored gelatin (lemon, raspberry, lime, etc.)*
*2 cups boiling water*
*1 cup confectioners' sugar*
*8 oz. cream cheese*
*1 cup sour cream*
*2 cups heavy cream*
*4 cups fresh, canned or cooked fruit, puréed or finely chopped*

Dissolve the gelatin in 2 cups boiling water, and chill until set. Put into the container with the steel blade half of the following: the set gelatin, sugar, cream cheese and sour cream, and blend; set aside. Blend the other half of these ingredients and add to the first batch; let everything chill. Whip the cream with the plastic blade. Process the fruit with the steel blade, and fold it into the gelatin mixture. Fold in the whipped cream. Place in pie shells, and chill. Serve with additional flavored whipped cream. Makes enough filling for two 8-inch shells.

# MINCEMEAT

*1½ lb. seeded raisins*
*2 lb. apples, cut up*
*1½ lb. dried currants*
*½ lb. citron peel*
*½ lb. candied lemon peel*
*½ lb. candied orange peel*
*½ lb. blanched almonds*
*3 oranges, quartered and seeded*
*3 lemons, quartered and seeded*
*1 Tbsp. ground cinnamon*
*1 Tbsp. ground cloves*
*1 Tbsp. ground allspice*
*1 Tbsp. ground ginger*
*1 Tbsp. grated nutmeg*
*1 Tbsp. grated mace*
*1 cup sherry*
*1 cup brandy*

Assemble all the ingredients except sherry and brandy in a large bowl. Process all the ingredients, 2 cups at a time, with the steel blade; mix well. Stir in the sherry and brandy. Keep well covered, and let age for at least 1 month.

## APPLE CUSTARD PIE

*6 cups apples, unpeeled,*
*    cored and quartered*
*3 eggs*
*⅔ cup sugar*
*½ tsp. salt*
*¼ tsp. grated nutmeg*
*1 cup milk, hot*
*1 cup light cream, hot*
*1 unbaked pie shell, 9*
*    inches*
*nutmeg for dusting*

Preheat oven to 375°F. Slice the cored quartered apples with the slicing disc; set aside in a separate bowl. Place eggs, sugar, salt and nutmeg in the container and blend. With the motor running, add the hot milk and cream through the feeder tube. Combine with the apples, and pour into the unbaked pie shell. Cover with foil, and bake in the preheated oven for 25 to 30 minutes. Remove foil, and continue to bake until a knife inserted in the custard comes out clean. Dust with more nutmeg. Serves 6 to 8.

## SWEDISH ALMOND PIE

*¼ lb. butter (1 stick)*
*¼ cup powdered sugar*
*1 cup flour*
*1 egg yolk*


*⅔ cup blanched almonds*
*5½ Tbsp. butter*
*½ cup granulated sugar*
*2 eggs*
*powdered sugar*

Preheat oven to 300°F. for a large pie or to 375° for tarts. Place ¼ pound butter, cut into pieces, and powdered sugar in the container with the steel blade; blend. Add the flour and egg yolk and blend until smooth. Scrape down the dough. Chill for 1 hour. Pat the dough into a buttered pie tin, or into individual tart shells.

Grind almonds with the steel blade; set aside. Place 5½ tablespoons butter and granulated sugar in the container with the steel blade, and blend until smooth. Add almonds and eggs and process until well blended. Scrape down. Spread the filling evenly over the dough. For a large pie, bake in a 300°F. oven for 30 minutes. Cool in the pan, and sprinkle with more powdered sugar. If smaller tart shells are used bake them in a 375°F. oven for 20 minutes. Check after 15 minutes. Serves 6 to 8.

## SPIRITED PIE

½ lb. butter (2 sticks), cut
up
1 lb. confectioners' sugar
6 eggs
⅓ cup brandy or rum
1 Nut Crust or baked
Sweet Pastry crust
(see Index)

Cream butter and sugar in the processor with the steel blade. Add the eggs, one at a time, with the motor running. Pour in the spirits and mix for 5 seconds. Spoon into the pie shell and freeze overnight. Thaw just before serving. Serves 6.

## LINZERTORTE

1½ cups unblanched
almonds
1 cup butter (2 sticks),
minus 2 Tbsp.
1 cup sugar, sifted
3 egg yolks
grated rind of 1 lemon
¼ tsp. ground cloves
½ tsp. ground cinnamon
1½ cups flour
1 cup raspberry jam
additional jam
powdered sugar

Preheat oven to 400°F. Grind almonds and set aside. Place the butter, cut into pieces, and the sugar in the container with the steel blade, and blend until light. With the motor running, add the egg yolks, one at a time, through the tube. Add the lemon rind, spices, flour and almonds, and blend. Wrap the dough in wax paper and chill for at least 1 hour.

Roll out three quarters of the dough, keeping the rest chilled. Lightly butter the bottom of an 8- or 9-inch false-bottom cake pan, patting the dough over the bottom and sides of the pan to make a shell about ¼ inch thick. Spread jam evenly over the bottom of the shell. Roll out remaining dough and cut it into ½-inch-wide strips. Make a lattice of dough strips over the top of the pie. Bake in the preheated oven for 35 minutes, or until golden brown. When the torte is done, remove the outside ring. Fill the lattice spaces with more jam and sprinkle with powdered sugar.

# DESSERT SAUCES

## FRUIT SAUCES

In the food processor fruits can be puréed into smooth, attractive sauces almost instantly. Place the fruit (fresh, frozen, canned or cooked) in the container with the steel blade, and purée. Then combine with any other ingredients.

*Apricot Sauce*—Use 2 cups dried fruit purée, cooked with 1½ cups sugar until thickened. Makes about 3 cups.

*Cardinal Sauce*—Use 1 cup raspberry purée and 1 cup strawberry purée mixed with 1 teaspoon cornstarch, and cook with 1 cup sugar until translucent. Makes about 2½ cups.

*Jelly Sauce*—Use equal parts of either raspberry or strawberry jelly and currant jelly, blended together and heated until smooth.

*Preserves Sauce*—Combine 2 cups fruit purée (cherry, berry, peach, etc.) with 1 cup of complementary preserves; cook over hot water for 1 hour. Finish with 4 teaspoons liqueur and 1 teaspoon lemon juice. Makes about 2½ cups.

*Honey Sauce*—Mix 2 cups fruit purée with ½ cup honey and 3 tablespoons light rum, and heat until honey has dissolved. Cut-up fruit may be added when the mixture is cool. Makes about 2½ cups.

## HARD SAUCE

Put 3½ Tbsp. softened butter, cut up, 1 cup confectioners' sugar or granulated or brown sugar, and 1 tablespoon rum or brandy in the container with the steel blade, and blend. Refrigerate for 2 hours before serving. For a fluffier sauce, add 1 egg white, slightly beaten. Makes about 1 cup.

## WHIPPED-CREAM SAUCE

*3 egg yolks*
*½ cup confectioners'*
*sugar*
*¼ cup liqueur*
*1 cup heavy cream*

Place egg yolks, sugar and liqueur in the container with the steel blade, and blend until smooth. Whip the cream with the plastic blade, and fold into the egg-yolk mixture. Chill. Magnificent with strawberries or a fruit or liqueur soufflé. Makes about 3 cups.

## MAY'S CHOCOLATE SAUCE

*2 oz. unsweetened*
*chocolate*
*1 Tbsp. butter*
*⅓ cup boiling water*
*1 cup sugar*
*1 tsp. salt*
*2 Tbsp. corn syrup*
*1 tsp. vanilla extract*

Put the chocolate, cut into pieces, into the container with the steel blade, and chop. Add the butter and boiling water and process. Add sugar and salt. Blend and scrape down the sides. Put in the top part of a double boiler over simmering water, add the corn syrup, and cook until sauce becomes shiny. Add vanilla. Whisk the sauce before serving. Makes about 2 cups.

# INDEX

Albanian Meatballs, 68
Allemande Sauce, 37
Almond(s)
  Hollandaise, 40
  Icebox Cookies, 219
  Lace Cookies, 215
  Linzertorte, 236
  Marzipan, 15
  Nut-Mushroom Stuffing (for fish), 130
  Paste, 15
  Pie, Swedish, 235
  Praline Powder, 14
  and Sweet-Potato Croquettes, 169
Anchovy(ies)
  Butter, 51
  Hollandaise, 40
  Jansson's Temptation, 124
  Salad Dressing, 46
  Stuffing (for hard-cooked eggs, cold),
    104
Apple(s)
  Cake, Fresh, 204
  Custard Pie, 235
  in a Blanket, 231
  Muffins, 185
  Pancakes, 199
  and Raisin Stuffing (for poultry), 139
  and Sausage Filling (for entrée crêpes),
    196
Applesauce Bread, 187
Apricot(s)
  Dried Apricots, Pickled, 18
  Finish for Baked Ham, 159
  -Orange Bread, 187
  Prune-Apricot Whip, 227

-Prune Stuffing (for poultry), 139
Sauce, 237
Soufflé, Cold, 226
Artichoke Purée, 92
Asparagus Mousse, 179
Asparagus Purée, Fresh, 92
Aspic Dishes
  Asparagus Mousse, 179
  Avocado Mold, 176
  Chaud-Froid, 45
  Clam and Tomato Aspic, Pale Pink, 176
  Cranberry-Wine Ring, 177
  Cream-Cheese and Ham Mold, 180
  Cucumber Radish Mold, 177
  Curry Ring, 178
  Pepper Rings, Jellied, 179
  Potato Aspic, 178
  Poultry Clam Mold, Jellied, 137
  Red, White and Green Mold, 138
  Seafood Mousse, Cold, 122
  Shrimp Mousse, Cold, 123
  Tongue Mold, 156
  Veal and Liver Loaf in Jelly, 157
Aurore Sauce, 35
Avocado
  Blue Cheese Spread, 64
  Guacamole, 74
  Mold, 176
  -Rum Dip, 74
  Sauce, 44
  Soup, Cold, 97


Bacon
  Biscuit, 185

Bacon (*continued*)
  and Chutney Stuffing (for hard-cooked
    eggs, cold), 104
  -Olive Filling (for tarts), 58
  and Onion Stuffing (for hard-cooked
    eggs, hot), 105
  Pancakes, 199
Bagna Cauda, 73
Banana
  Ginger Banana Muffins, 186
  Mayonnaise, 39
  -Nut Bread, 187
  Orange Cake, 206
Bean(s)
  black beans and rice (Moors and Chris-
    tians), 88
  Black Bean Soup, Cuban, 88
  Black Bean Soup II, 89
  Green-Bean Purée, 92
Béarnaise Sauce, 41
Beauharnaise Sauce, 41
Béchamel Sauce (Cream Sauce), 35
  Fish, 35
Beef
  Beefburgers, 144
  Birds, 153
  Bombay Beefburgers, 144
  Burgundy Beefburgers, 144
  Chopped Beef Roulades, 145
  Consommé, 79
  Corned Beef Loaf, 149
  Empanada Filling, 62
  Filling (for turnovers), 61
  Ground, Cuban (Picadillo), 146
  Mushroom Beefburgers, 144
  Orientale Beefburgers, 144
  Smoked Beefburgers, 144
  Steak Tartar, 67
  Steak Tartar, Scandinavian Style, 68
  Stock, 76
  Tia Juana Beefburgers, 144
  Tuscan Beefburgers, 144
Beer Cheese Spread, 63
Beer Sauce, 146
Beet(s)
  Borscht, Cold, 98
  à la Française, 162
  Hors d'Oeuvre, 71
  Soup, Russian, 82
  in Sour-Cream Sauce, 162
Benne (Sesame Seed) Wafers, 57
Bercy Sauce, 37
Billi-Bi, 96
Biscuits, 183-185
  Bacon, 185

Baking Powder, 184
Blue Cheese, 185
Butter, Little, Brother Bernard's (yeast),
  192
Cheese, 184
Curry, 185
Drop, 184
Ham and Onion, 185
Herb, 185
Orange, 184
Pinwheels, 185
Bisques, 95-96
Blue Cheese, *see* Cheese
Bolognese Meat Sauce, 42
Bombay Beefburgers, 144
Bontemps Sauce, 36
Bordelaise Sauce, 33
Borscht, Cold, 98
Bouchées Anchoise, 57
Bourbon Balls, *see* Rum Balls, 218
Bovril Butter, 51
Brandade de Morue, 125
Brandied Blue Cheese, 64
Brandy Snaps, 214
Brandy Spice Cookies (drop), 213
Brazil-Nut Stuffing (for poultry), 141
Bread Crumbs, 22
  Dried, 22
  Fresh or Soft, 22
  Golden or Toasted, 22
Breads—Quick Breads, 187-189
  Applesauce Bread, 187
  Apricot-Orange Bread, 187
  Banana-Nut Bread, 187
  Benne (Sesame Seed) Wafers, 57
  Cheese Popovers, 189
  Cheese Straws, 54
  Fruit Bread, 187
  Lemon Bread, 188
  Parmesan Cheese Drops, 54
  Popovers, 189
  Prune Bread, 187
  Yorkshire Pudding, 189
  Zucchini Bread, 188
  *see also* Biscuits
Breads—Yeast Breads, 189-192
  Brioche, 191
  Brioche Crust, 191
  Sweet Bread, 190
  White Bread, 189
Brioche, *see* Breads—Yeast Breads
Broccoli Soup, Cold, 97
Broccoli Soup, Potato-Thickened, 86
Brother Bernard's Little Butter Biscuits,
  192

Brown Sugar Cookies, 215
Brown Sauce (Sauce Espagnole), 32
Brown Stock, 77
Brussels Sprouts Purée, 92
Bubble and Squeak, 148
Bulgur, Tabbouleh, 181
Burgundy Beefburgers, 144
Butter Frosting, 209
Butter Thins (drop cookies), 214
Butters—Compound, 50-51
    Anchovy, 51
    Bovril, 51
    Green, 51
    Horseradish, 51
    Piquant, 51
    Shrimp, 51
Butterscotch Chews (molded cookies), 217
Butterscotch Cookies (rolled), 216


Cabbage
    and Apples, 162
    Coleslaw, Ground, 180
    Meatballs in Cabbage, 151
    Red and Green, with Chestnuts, 163
Caesar Dressing, Processor, 49
Cakes, 201-209
    Apple, Fresh, 204
    Banana Orange, 206
    Carrot, 206
    Cheesecake, Baked, 207
    Cheesecake, Mocha, 208
    Cheesecake, Unbaked, 207
    Chocolate, 203
    Cocoa, 203
    Genoa, 208
    Graham Cracker, 205
    Nut Torte, 204
    Pecan Roll, 208
    White, 203
    Yellow, 202
    Zwieback Torte, 205
Caper
    Essence of Caper Sauce, 160
    Salad Dressing, 46
    Sauce, 35
Caraway Squash Bisque, 100
Cardinal Sauce, 237
Carl's Quenelle Canapés, 55
Carrot(s)
    Cake, 206
    Chips, 19
    Crécy, 163
    Crécy Soup, Cold, 101
    Ring, 163

Salad, Pungent, 181
Soup, Potato-Thickened, 86
and Turnip Spread, Raw, 67
Cauliflower Purée, 92
Caviar Salad Dressing, 46
Celeriac (Celery Root)
    Rémoulade, 180
    Salad with Mustard Cream Dressing, 181
    Soup, Potato-Thickened, 86
    Stuffed with Peas, 164
Celery Purée, 92
Celery Soup, Potato-Thickened, 86
Charleston Lamb Breakfast Sausage, 147
Chasseur Sauce, 33
Chaud-Froid, 45
Cheese
    and Almond Fingers, 54
    Biscuit, 184
    Beer Cheese Spread, 63
    Blue Cheese
        Avocado Spread, 64
        and Bacon Dressing, 46
        Biscuit, 185
        Brandied, 64
        Quiche, 116
        and Walnut Stuffing (for hard-cooked
            eggs, cold), 104
    Broiled Cheese Spread, 64
    (and) Chive Sauce, 35
    Cottage Cheese
        Coeur à la Crème II, 229
        Dessert Crêpes, 197
        Filling (for pie), 233
        Pancakes, 199
        Pastry, 25
        Potato Casserole, 168
        and Vegetable Filling (for turnovers),
            61
    Cream Cheese
        Coeur à la Crème I, 228
        Crêpes Grand Marnier, 196
        Filling (for tarts), 58
        Frosting, 210
        and Fruit Mousse, Frozen, 226
        and Ham Mold, 180
        Pastry, 25
        and Peanut-Butter Spread, 64
        Salad Dressing, 50
    Croquettes, 118
    Custard Timbale, 113
    Extra-Light Soufflé, 109
    Fondue, 118
    Green Cheese Soufflé, 109
    Liptauer, 63
    Mornay Sauce, 35

Cheese (*continued*)
  Muffins, 186
  Parmesan Cheese Drops, 54
  Parmesan Omelet, 106
  Popovers, 189
  Ricotta Filling (for cream puffs), 230
  Rounds, 54
  Soft Cheese Soufflé, 108
  Soufflé, 108
  and Sour Cream Dressing, 46
  Spinach Gnocchi, 170
Cheesecake
  Baked, 207
  Mocha, 208
  Unbaked, 207
Chestnut(s)
  with Red and Green Cabbage, 163
  fresh, to shell and peel, 88, 140
  Soup, 88
  Stuffing (for poultry), 140
Chicken
  Basting Sauce for, 159
  Breasts Suprême, 132
  and Broccoli Roulade, 112
  Consommé, 80
  Croquettes, 132
  Cutlets à la Russe, 135
  Egg-Flower Soup, 82
  and Mushroom Soufflé, 109
  Patties Surprise, 135
  Quenelles, 133
  Spread, 65
  Stock, 77
  -Tarragon Spread, 65
  Tarts with Eggs, 134
Chicken Liver(s)
  and Chestnut Balls, 70
  and Florentine Filling (for tarts), 59
  with Pasta, 137
  Pâté, 66
  Timbales, 113
  Toast, 56
  and Water-Chestnut Soufflé, 110
Chicory Soup, Potato-Thickened, 86
Chiffonade Salad Dressing, 46
Chiffon Pie Filling I, 232; II, 233
Chinese Meat Loaf, 149
Chive Cheese Sauce, 35
Chives Stuffing (for hard-cooked eggs, cold), 104
Chocolate
  Butter Frosting, 210
  Cake, 203
  Chip Cookies (drop), 212

Cookies (icebox), 218
Crêpes, 198
Crisps, 216
Filling (for Florentines), 221
Pots de Crème au Chocolat, Quick, 228
Sauce, May's, 238
Soufflé, Hot, 224
Chopping coarse, medium, fine, 7-8
Choron Sauce, 41
Chutney
  -Cheese Filling, 59
  Green Tomato, Grandmother Page's, 17
  Mango, 16
  Pear, 17
  Salad Dressing, 46
Cinnamon-Nut Cookies (drop), 212
Citrus Butter Frosting, 210
Citrus Cookies (drop), 212
Clam
  Bisque, *see* Oyster Bisque, 95
  Poultry Clam Mold, Jellied, 137
  and Tomato Aspic, Pale Pink, 176
Cleaning procedures, 12
Cock-a-Leekie, 81
Cocoa Butter Frosting, 210
Cocoa Cake, 203
Coconut, 15
  To Make Coconut Milk, 15
  To Make Grated Coconut, 15
  To Open, 15
  Tropical Cookies (molded), 217
Codfish, Salt
  Balls, 69
  Brandade de Morue, 125
  Cakes, 128
  Potatoes, Baked, Stuffed with Codfish, 124
Coeur à la Crème I, 228; II, 229
Coffee
  Butter Frosting, 210
  Cookies (drop), 212
  Soufflé, Cold, 225
  Soufflé, Hot, 224
Coleslaw, Ground, 180
Consommé, 79-82
Cookies, 211-221
  Almond (icebox), 219
  Almond Lace (drop), 215
  Bourbon Balls, *see* Rum Balls, 218
  Brandy Snaps (drop), 214
  Brandy Spice (drop), 213
  Brown Sugar (drop), 215
  Butterscotch (rolled), 216
  Butterscotch Chews (molded), 217

Butter Thins (drop), 214
Chocolate (icebox), 218
Chocolate Chip (drop), 212
Chocolate Crisps (rolled), 216
Cinnamon-Nut (drop), 212
Citrus (drop), 212
Coffee (drop), 212
Crystallized Fruit (molded), 217
Drop Cookie Dough I, 212; II, 213
Extra Nutty (molded), 217
Florentines (drop), 221
Icebox Cookies I, 218; II, 219
Jam Pinwheels (rolled), 216
Lemon Drop Thins, 214
Liqueur (rolled), 216
Macaroons (drop), 220
Maple (rolled), 216
Maple Walnut (drop), 213
Molded, 217-218
Nut (molded), 217
Oatmeal Drop, 213
Orange Pecan (icebox), 218
Peppermint (icebox), 219
Pistachio (drop), 213
Rolled, 216
Rose (icebox), 219
Rum Balls (molded), 218
Rum and White Raisin (drop), 213
Shortbread (rolled), 220
Spritz or Press, 219
Sugar (rolled), 216
Surprise (molded), 217
Tender Rounds (molded), 217
Tropical (molded), 217
Wine (icebox), 218
Corn Soufflé (in stuffed peppers), 152
Corn Soup, Cream of, 93
Corn Chips Stuffing (for hard-cooked eggs, cold), 104
Corned Beef, *see* Beef
Cottage Cheese, *see* Cheese
Coulibiac, 127
Coulibiac Filling (for entrée crêpes), 195
Crab Bisque, *see* Lobster Bisque, 96
Crab Croquettes, 128
Cracker Crumbs, 22
Cranberry
  Meat Loaf, 149
  Orange Muffins, 186
  -Wine Ring, 177
Crayfish Bisque, *see* Lobster Bisque, 96
Cream Cheese, *see* Cheese
Cream-Puff Pastry (Pâte à Choux), 27, 57
Cream Puffs, 27, 57, 230

Cream Sauce (Sauce Béchamel), 35
Cream, to whip, 8
Cream, Whipped-Cream Sauce, 238
Crécy Soup, Cold, 101
Crème Pâtissière, 230
Crème Saint-Honoré, 229
Creole Bisque, Cold, 98
Creole Sauce, 41
Crêpes—Dessert, 193-198
  Chocolate, 198
  Cottage Cheese, 197
  Dessert Crêpes I and II, 196
  Grand Marnier, 196
  Mandarin, 198
  Nut Fruit, 197
  Soufflé, 197
Crêpes—Entrée, 194
Crêpes—Entrée, Filled, 195
Cress Sauce, 45
Crisp-Crisp Salad, 182
Croquettes, 128
  Cheese, 118
  Chicken, 132
  Crab, 128
  Lobster, 128
  Shrimp, 128
  Sweet-Potato and Almond, 169
Crouton Frittata, 107
Crumb Shells, 29
Crystallized Fruit Cookies (molded), 217
Cuban Black-Bean Soup, 88
Cuban Ground Beef (Picadillo), 146
Cucumber(s)
  Radish Mold, 177
  and Radishes, Creamed, 164
  Sauce, Cold, 44
  Sauce, Hot, 35
  Soup, Cold, 99
  Sour-Cream Salad Dressing, 48
Curry, Curried
  Biscuits, 185
  Mayonnaise, 39
  Meat Loaf, 148
  Onion Curry Dressing, 46
  Ring, 178
  Sauce, 36
Custard Filling for Quiche, 115
Custard Timbales, 113
Custards and Cream and Gelatin Desserts
  Chiffon Pie Filling I, 232; II, 233
  Coeur à la Crème I, 228; II, 229
  Crème Pâtissière, 230
  Crème Saint-Honoré, 229
  Fruit Whip, Baked, 228

Custard Desserts (*continued*)
  Gelatin Fruit Cream, 226
  Helene's Pumpernickel Dessert, 229
  Mousse Filling, 234
  Pots de Crème au Chocolat, Quick, 228
  Prune-Apricot Whip, 227

Daiquiri Soufflé, Cold, 225
Demi-Glace Sauce, 33
Desserts, *see* Cakes; Cookies; Crêpes—
    Dessert; Custards and Cream and
    Gelatin Desserts; Fillings—Dessert;
    Frostings; Mousse—Dessert; Pastry
    Desserts; Pie Fillings and Pies
    —Dessert; Sauce—Dessert; Soufflé
    —Dessert; *see also* names of fruits
Diable Sauce, 33
Dill Sauce, 44
Dips, 72-74
  Avocado-Rum, 74
  Bagna Cauda, 73
  Guacamole, 74
  Salsa Verde, 72
  South Sea, 74
  Tapenade, 73
  *see also* Spreads
Duxelles, 21
  Chicken and Mushroom Soufflé, 109
  Hollandaise, 40
  Omelet, 106
  and Salmon Roulade, 112

Éclairs, 27, 230
Eggs
  Frittata
    Crouton, 107
    Peasant, 107
    Zucchini, 107
  Hard-Cooked, Stuffed, Cold, 103
    Anchovy Stuffing, 104
    Bacon and Chutney, 104
    Blue Cheese and Walnut, 104
    Chives, 104
    Corn Chips, 104
    Olives, 104
    Sardine, 104
    Shrimp and Water Chestnut, 104
    Tapenade, 104
  Hard-Cooked, Stuffed, Hot, 104
    with Bacon and Onion, 105
    Chimay, 104
    with Ham, 105
    Hungarian, 105
    Parsley, 105

    with Peas and Chicken Livers, 104
    with Smoked Fish, 105
    with Tuna Fish, 105
  Omelets, 105-107
    Duxelles, 106
    Fines Herbes, 106
    Fines Herbes with Cheese, 106
    Ham, 106
    Pancake, 106-107
    Parmesan, 106
    Pimiento, 106
    Plain, 105
    Salmon, 106
    Savoyard, 106
    Sorrel, 106
    Spinach, 106
    Western, 106
  Poached, Chicken Tarts with Eggs, 134
  Whites, to whip, 8
Eggplant
  Caviar, 67
  with Mushrooms, 164
  Stuffed, 150
Emerald Mayonnaise, 38
Empanada, 60
Empanada Filling, 62
Espagnole Sauce (Brown Sauce), 32

Far East Shrimp Balls, 70
Fillings—Dessert
  Almond Paste, 15
  Chiffon Pie Filling I, 232; II, 233
  Chocolate Filling, 221
  Cottage-Cheese Filling (for pie), 233
  Crème Pâtissière, 230
  Mincemeat, 234
  Mousse Filling, 234
  Praline Powder, 14
  Ricotta Filling (for cream puffs), 230
Fillings and Stuffings—Entrée and Hors
    d'Oeuvre
  Apple and Raisin Stuffing (for poultry),
    139
  Apple and Sausage Filling (for entrée
    crêpes), 196
  Apricot-Prune Stuffing (for poultry), 139
  Bacon-Olive Filling (for tarts), 58
  Beef Filling (for turnovers), 61
  Brazil-Nut Stuffing (for poultry), 141
  Chestnut Stuffing (for poultry), 140
  Chutney-Cheese Filling (for tarts), 59
  Cottage Cheese and Vegetable Filling
    (for turnovers), 61
  Coulibiac Filling (for entrée Crêpes), 195
  Cream-Cheese Filling (for tarts), 58

Empanada Filling, 62
Fillings for Hard-Cooked Eggs, Cold, 104
Fillings for Hard-Cooked Eggs, Hot, 104-105
Fillings for Hors d'Oeuvre, Cold, 62-68
Fillings for Tarts and Cream Puffs, Hot, 58-62
Fish Stuffings, 130
Florentine Filling (for tarts), 59
Green Stuffing (for poultry), 141
Ham and Olive Stuffing (for poultry), 142
Mushroom Cream Cheese Filling (for tarts), 58
Mushroom Filling (for tarts), 58
Nut-Mushroom Stuffing (for fish), 130
Pork and Shredded Cabbage Filling (for turnovers), 61
Poultry Mousse Mixture (for entrée crêpes), 195
Poultry Stuffings, 139-142
Seafood Stuffing (for entrée crêpes), 195
Seafood Stuffing (for fish), 130
Shrimp Filling (for turnovers), 60
Spinach Purée (for tarts, and variations), 59
Sweet Potato and Walnut Stuffing (for poultry), 140
Veal Quenelle Filling (for breast of lamb), 154
Zucchini Stuffing (for entrée crêpes), 195
Fines Herbes with Cheese Omelet, 106
Fines Herbes Omelet, 106
Fish
    Béchamel Sauce, 35
    Canned Fish Cakes, 129
    Loaf, Baked, 129
    Pâté, 129
    Potage Bagration, 94
    Pudding, Scandinavian, 123
    Quenelles, 120
    Quenelle Canapés, Carl's, 55
    Smoked Fish and Florentine Filling (for tarts), 59
    Smoked Fish Stuffing (for hard-cooked eggs, hot), 105
    Soufflé (leftover fish), 109
    Soufflé Base, 109
    Soup, Cold, 100
    Stock (Fumet), 78
    *see also* names of fish
Florentine Filling (for tarts), and variations, 59
Florentine Soufflé, 108

Florentines (drop cookies), 221
Flounder, Fish Pâté, 129
Fondue, Cheese, 118
Foyot Sauce, 41
Frostings, 209-210
    Butter Frosting, 209
    Chocolate Butter, 210
    Citrus Butter, 210
    Cocoa Butter, 210
    Coffee Butter, 210
    Cream-Cheese, 210
    Fruit, 210
    Lemon Glaze, 188
    Mocha Butter, 210
    Royal Icing, 210
    Wine Butter, 210
Fruit
    Bread, 187
    and Cheese Mousse, Frozen, 226
    Frosting, 210
    Gelatin Fruit Cream, 226
    Mousse, Frozen, 226
    Sauces, 237
    Whip, Baked, 228
    *see also* names of fruits
Fumet (Fish Stock), 78

Garlic Salad Dressing, 46
Gazpacho, 99
Gelatin Fruit Cream, 226
Genoa Cake, 208
Ginger
    Banana Muffins, 186
    Sherry, 20
    Soufflé, Cold, 226
Gnocchi, Spinach, 170
Gougère, 56
Graham Cracker Cake, 205
Grand Marnier Crêpes, 196
Grandmother Page's Green Tomato Chutney, 17
Grapes, Soufflé Véronique, 109
Grapes, Véronique Sauce, 35
Green Butter, 51
Green Goddess Dressing, 49
Green-Pepper Sour-Cream Salad Dressing, 48
Green Stuffing (for poultry), 141
Gribiche Sauce (Hard-Cooked Egg Mayonnaise), 39
Guacamole, 74

Ham
    and Cream-Cheese Mold, 180

Ham (continued)
  and Olive Stuffing (for poultry), 142
  Omelet, 106
  and Onion Biscuit, 185
  Stuffing (for hard-cooked eggs, hot), 105
  Upside-Down Cake, 150
Hard Sauce, 237
Helene's Pumpernickel Dessert, 229
Herb
  Biscuit, 185
  Broth, 80
  Fines Herbes Omelet, 106
  Fines Herbes Omelet with Cheese, 106
  Sauce, 36
Herring, Kippered Herring Spread, 66
Hollandaise, 40
  Almond, 40
  Anchovy, 40
  Duxelles, 40
  Shrimp, 40
Honey Salad Dressing, 46
Honey Sauce, 237
Hors d'Oeuvre, 53-74
  Albanian Meatballs, 68
  Avocado Blue-Cheese Spread, 64
  Avocado-Rum Dip, 74
  Bagna Cauda, 73
  Beer Cheese Spread, 63
  Beet Hors d'Oeuvre, 71
  Benne (Sesame Seed) Wafers, 57
  Bouchées Anchois, 57
  Brandied Blue Cheese, 64
  Cheese and Almond Fingers, 54
  Cheese Spread, Broiled, 64
  Cheese Straws, 54
  Chicken-Liver and Chestnut Balls, 70
  Chicken-Liver Pâté, 66
  Chicken-Liver Toast, 56
  Chicken Spread, 65
  Chicken-Tarragon Spread, 65
  Codfish Balls, 69
  Dips, 72-74
  Eggplant Caviar, 67
  Fillings for Tarts and Cream Puffs, 58-62
  Gougère, 56
  Guacamole, 74
  Iraqi Meatballs, 69
  Kippered Herring Spread, 66
  Liptauer Cheese, 63
  Meatballs, 68-70
  Mushrooms, Raw, Stuffed, 71
  Parmesan Cheese Drops, 54
  Peanut-Butter and Cream-Cheese
    Spread, 64
  Pirozhki, 60

  Pirozhki or Turnover Fillings, 60-61
  Potato Pancakes, Miniature, 56
  Quenelle Canapés, Carl's, 55
  Salsa Verde, 72
  Scallops with Salsa Verde, 73
  Seafood Balls, 69-70
  Shrimp Balls, Far East, 70
  Shrimp Paste, Baked, 55
  Shrimp Toast, 55
  South Sea Dip, 74
  Spreads and Fillings, Cold, 62-68
  Steak Tartar, 67
  Steak Tartar, Scandinavian Style, 68
  Tapenade, 73
  Taramasalata, 66
  Tarts and Cream Puffs, Hot, 57-62
  Tongue Spread, 65
  Turnip and Carrot Spread, Raw, 67
  Vegetable, Cold, 71-72
  Vegetable Macédoine, 72
  Yankee Meatballs, 69
Horseradish
  Butter, 51
  Mayonnaise, 38
  Sauce, 35
Hot Sauce, 20
Hungarian Eggs (hard-cooked eggs, hot),
  105

Illustrations of machine parts, 11
Indian Patties (lamb), 145
Indienne Mayonnaise, 39
Iraqi Meatballs, 69
Ivory Sauce, 37

Jade Soup, 90
Jam Pinwheels (cookies), 216
Jansson's Temptation, 124
Jelly Sauce, 237

Kotopita, 136

Lamb
  Breakfast Sausage, Charleston, 147
  Breast of, with Veal Quenelle Filling,
    154
  Indian Patties, 145
  Marinade and Basting Sauce for, 160
  Patties, 145
Leek
  and Potato Soup, 89

Purée, 92
Quiche, 116
Legumes, Dried, Purée of, 90
Lemon
  Bread, 188
  Consommé, 79
  Drop Thins, 214
  Glaze, 188
  Soufflé, Hot, 224
Lettuce Soup, Potato-Thickened, 86
Linzertorte, 236
Liptauer Cheese, 63
Liqueur Cookies (rolled), 216
Liqueur Soufflé, Hot, 224
Liver(s)
  (beef) and Veal Loaf in Jelly, 157
  (calf's) Pâté Maison Middleton, 159
  Chicken
    and Chestnut Balls, 70
    and Florentine Filling, 59
    Noelle's Pâté, 158
    with Pasta, 137
    Pâté, 66
    Pâté de Campagne Bleu Rieumailhol,
      158
    Timbales, 113
    Toast, 56
    and Water-Chestnut Soufflé, 110
Lobster Bisque, 96
Lobster Croquettes, 128
Louis Sauce, 39
Lyonnaise Sauce, 33


Macaroons, 220
Macaroon Soufflé, Cold, 225
Madeira Sauce I and II, 33
Maltaise Sauce, 40
Mandarin Crêpes, 198
Mango Chutney, 16
Maple Cookies (rolled), 216
Maple Soufflé, Hot, 224
Maple Walnut Cookies (drop), 213
Marzipan, 15
Mayonnaise, 38
  Banana, 39
  Curry, 39
  Emerald, 38
  Hard-Cooked Egg (Gribiche Sauce), 39
  Horseradish, 38
  Indienne, 39
  Louis Sauce, 39
  Mustard, 38
  Piquant, 39
  Rémoulade Sauce, 39

Tartare Sauce, 38
Tomato Anchovy, 38
May's Chocolate Sauce, 238
Meat, *see also* Meatballs; Meat Loaves
  Coating for Roasted Meat, 160
  Cold Meat Dishes, 155-157
  Frills and Fancies, 159-160
  Ground Meat Roulade, 112
  Ground Meats, 143-146
  Meat-Filled, 153-155
  Sauce Bolognese, 42
  Soufflé (leftover meat), 109
  Soufflé Base, 109
  *see also* Beef; Ham; Lamb; Pork; Sau-
    sage; Veal; Liver(s); Tongue
Meatballs, 68-70
  Albanian, 68
  in Cabbage, 151
  Iraqi, 69
  Sauerkraut Balls, 146
  Yankee, 69
Meat Loaves, 148-150
  Basic, and Variations, 148
  Chinese, 149
  Corned Beef, 149
  Cranberry, 149
  Curried, 148
  Ham Upside-Down Cake, 150
  Mexican, 149
  Munich, 149
  Sauerbraten, 149
Mediterranean Casserole, 174
Meringue Crumb Shell, 30
Mexican Fish Sauce, 43
Mexican Meat Loaf, 149
Mincemeat, 234
Minestrone, 84
Mint Sauce, 34
Mocha Butter Frosting, 210
Mocha Cheesecake, 208
Moors and Christians (black beans and
  rice), 88
Mornay Sauce, 35
Mousse—Dessert
  Filling (for pies), 234
  Fruit and Cheese, Frozen, 226
  Fruit, Frozen, 226
  *see also* Soufflé—Dessert, Cold
Mousse—Entrée
  Asparagus (cold), 179
  Poultry, with Pecans (hot), 133
  Seafood, Cold, 122
  Seafood, Hot, 122
  Shrimp, Cold, 123
Mousseline Sauce, 40

Muffins, 185-186
    Apple, 185
    Cheese, 186
    Cranberry Orange, 186
    Ginger Banana, 186
Munich Meat Loaf, 149
Mushroom(s)
    Beefburgers, 144
    Broth (Consommé Forestière), 81
    Cream-Cheese Filling (for tarts), 58
    Duxelles, 21
    with Eggplant, 164
    Filling (for tarts), 58
    Ketchup, 19
    Nut-Mushroom Stuffing (for fish), 130
    Purée, 93
    Quiche, 117
    Raw, Stuffed, 71
    Sauce, 37
    see also entries under Duxelles
Mussels, Billi-Bi, 96
Mustard
    Cream Salad Dressing, 46
    Mayonnaise, 38
    Sauce, 33

Nantua Sauce, 37
Noelle's Pâté, 158
Nut(s)
    Cinnamon-Nut Cookies (drop), 212
    Cookies (molded), 217
    Crust, 30
    Extra Nutty Cookies (molded), 217
    Fruit Crêpes, 197
    -Mushroom Stuffing (for fish), 130
    Soufflé, Hot, 224
    Torte, 204
    see also names of nuts

Oatmeal Drop Cookies, 213
Oil and Vinegar Dressing, 46
Olive and Ham Stuffing (for poultry), 142
Olives Stuffing (for hard-cooked eggs, cold), 104
Onion(s)
    Curry Salad Dressing, 46
    Purée, 92
    Sherry, 20
    Soup, Light, 83
    Sour-Cream Salad Dressing, 48
    Stuffed, 165
Operating procedures, 10
Orange
    Apricot-Orange Bread, 187

Biscuits, 184
Consommé à l'Orange, 79
Cranberry Orange Muffins, 186
Mandarin Crêpes, 198
(or)-Lemon-Grand Marnier Soufflé, Cold, 225
Pancakes, 199
Pecan Cookies (icebox), 218
Sauce (entrée), 34
Soufflé, Hot, 224
Orientale Beefburgers, 144
Oyster Bisque, 95

Pancakes, 198-199
    Apple, 199
    Bacon, 199
    Cottage Cheese, 199
    Orange, 199
    Pecan, 199
    Pfannkuchen, 199
    Potato, Miniature, 56
    Western, 199
    see also Crêpes
Paprika Sauce, 36
Parmesan Cheese, see Cheese
Parsley Eggs (hard-cooked eggs, hot), 105
Parsnips with Sherry, 165
Pasta with Chicken Livers, 137
Pastry—Basic
    Cottage-Cheese Pastry, 25
    Cream-Cheese Pastry, 25
    Cream-Puff Pastry (Pâte à Choux), 27
    Crumb Shells, 29
    egg glaze or wash, 26, 190, 191, 192, 231
    Meringue Crumb Shell, 30
    Nut Crust, 30
    Pâte Brisée, 26
    Piecrust, Basic, 28
    Piecrust, Flaky, 28
    Quiche Shell, 114
    Stay-Crisp Pastry, 24
    Sweet Pastry (Pâte Sucrée), 29
    to bake tart shells before filling, 23
    to make cocktail turnovers, 23
    to make pastry shells, 23
    to make pinwheels, 24
    Turnover Pastry, 26
Pastry Desserts, 230-236
    Apples in a Blanket, 231
    Cream Puffs, 27, 57, 230
    Éclairs, 27, 230
    Preserve Pastries, 232
    see also Pie Fillings and Pies—Dessert

Pastry—Entrée and Hors d'Oeuvre
  Bouchées Anchois, 57
  Gougère, 56
  Tarts and Cream Puffs, Hot (for hors d'oeuvre), 57-62
  *see also* Pies and Tarts—Entrée and Hors d'Oeuvre
Pâte
  Brisée, 26
  à Choux (Cream-Puff Pastry), 27
  Sucrée (Sweet Pastry), 29
Pâtés, 158-159
  de Campagne Bleu Rieumailhol, 158
  Chicken-Liver, 66
  Fish, 129
  Maison Middleton, 159
  Noelle's, 158
Pea Purée, Fresh (Soup Saint-Germain), 87
Peanut Butter, 14
Peanut Butter and Cream-Cheese Spread, 64
Peanuts, *see* Banana Mayonnaise, 39; Bombay Beefburgers, 144; Chutney-Cheese Filling, 59; Curry Biscuits, 185; Ham and Olive Stuffing, 142
Pear Chutney, 17
Peasant Frittata, 107
Peasant Soup, 85
Pecan(s)
  Banana-Nut Bread, 187
  Pancakes, 199
  Roll, 208
  Rum Balls, 218
Pepper(s)
  Green-Pepper Sour-Cream Salad Dressing, 48
  Hot Sauce, 20
  Rings, Jellied, 179
  Stuffed (with corn soufflé), 152
Peppermint Cookies (icebox), 219
Périgourdine Sauce, 33
Pfannkuchen, 199
Picadillo (Cuban Ground Beef), 146
Pickles and Relishes
  Carrot Chips, 19
  Dried Apricots, Pickled, 18
  Green Tomato Chutney, Grandmother Page's, 17
  Mango Chutney, 16
  Mushroom Ketchup, 19
  Pear Chutney, 17
  Pumpkin Chips, 18
  Zucchini-Raisin Pickle, 19
Pie Fillings and Pies—Dessert, 232-236

Almond Pie, Swedish, 235
Apple Custard Pie, 235
Chiffon Pie Filling I, 232; II, 233
Cottage-Cheese Filling, 233
Crème Pâtissière, 230
Linzertorte, 236
Mincemeat, 234
Mousse Filling, 234
Piecrust, Basic, 28
Piecrust, Flaky, 28
Ricotta Filling, 230
Spirited Pie, 236
Pies and Tarts—Entrée and Hors d'Oeuvre
  Chicken Tarts with Eggs, 134
  Coulibiac (salmon), 127
  Kotopita (poultry), 136
  *see also* Fillings for Tarts, Hot, 58-62; *see also* Quiche(s)
Pimiento Omelet, 106
Pimiento Salad Dressing, 48
Pineapple-Currant Sauce, 150
Pinwheels (biscuits), 185
Piquant Butter, 51
Piquant Mayonnaise, 39
Piquante Sauce, 34
Pirozhki, 60
Pirozhki Fillings, 60-61
Pistachio Cookies (drop), 213
Pistou, 83
Pistou Soup, 83
Plum Sauce (entrée), 43
Popovers, 189
Popovers, Cheese, 189
Pork
  Basting Sauce for, 159
  Sausage Meat, 147
  Scrapple, 147
  and Shredded Cabbage Filling (for turnovers), 61
Potage, *see* Soups
Potato(es)
  Anna, 166
  Annette, 167
  Aspic, 178
  Baked, Stuffed with Codfish, 124
  Casserole, 168
  Dauphinoise, 166
  Galette, 167
  and Leek Soup, 89
  à la Normande, 166
  Pancakes, Miniature, 56
  Quenelles, 167
  -Thickened Vegetable Soup, 86
  Voisin, 167
Pots de Crème au Chocolat, Quick, 228

Poulette Sauce, 37
Poultry
  Clam Mold, Jellied, 137
  Kotopita, 136
  Mousse with Pecans, 133
  Mousse Mixture (for entrée crêpes), 195
  Stuffings, 139-142
  Volaille Mornay, 134
  see also Chicken
Praline Powder, 14
Preserve Pastries, 232
Preserves Sauce, 237
Prune
  Apricot-Prune Stuffing (for poultry), 139
  -Apricot Whip, 227
  Bread, 187
Pudding, Fish, Scandinavian, 123
Pudding, Yorkshire, 189
Pumpernickel Dessert, Helene's, 229
Pumpkin Chips, 18
Pumpkin Purée (Purée Potiron), 87

Quenelle(s), 120
  Canapés, Carl's, 55
  Chicken, 133
  Fish, 120
  Potato, 167
  Shellfish, 120
  Veal Quenelle Filling, 154
Quiche(s), 114-117
  Blue Cheese, 116
  Custard Filling, 115
  Firmer Filling, 115
  Leek, 116
  Mushroom, 117
  Shell, 114
  Spinach, à la Grecque, 116
  White, 115
  Zucchini, 117

Radish (and) Cucumber Mold, 177
Radishes and Cucumbers, Creamed, 164
Raisin and Apple Stuffing (for poultry), 139
Raisin, White, and Rum Cookies (drop), 213
Ravigote Dressing, 50
Red, White and Green Mold, 138
Rémoulade Sauce, 39
Rose Cookies (icebox), 219
Rothschild Soufflé, Hot, 224
Roulade, Chopped Beef, 145
Roulade Soufflé, 111
Royal Icing, 210

Rum Balls, 218
Rum and White Raisin Cookies (drop), 213
Russian Beet Soup, 82
Rutabaga Soufflé, 168


Salad
  Asparagus Mousse, 179
  Avocado Mold, 176
  Carrot, Pungent, 181
  Celeriac, with Mustard Cream Dressing, 181
  Celeriac Rémoulade, 180
  Clam and Tomato Aspic, Pale Pink, 176
  Coleslaw, Ground, 180
  Cranberry-Wine Ring, 177
  Cream-Cheese and Ham Mold, 180
  Crisp-Crisp, 182
  Cucumber Radish Mold, 177
  Curry Ring, 178
  Pepper Rings, Jellied, 179
  Potato Aspic, 178
  Red, White and Green Mold, 138
  Tabbouleh, 181
  Vegetable, Raw, 182
Salad Dressing, 46-50
  Anchovy, 46
  Blue Cheese and Bacon, 46
  Caesar, Processor, 49
  Caper, 46
  Caviar, 46
  Chiffonade, 46
  Chutney, 46
  Cooked, 47
  Cream-Cheese, 50
  Creamy, 47-48
  Cucumber Sour-Cream, 48
  Garlic, 46
  Green Goddess, 49
  Green-Pepper Sour-Cream, 48
  Honey, 46
  Mayonnaise, see Mayonnaise
  Mustard Cream, 46
  Oil and Vinegar, 46
  Onion Curry, 46
  Onion Sour-Cream, 48
  Pimiento, 48
  Ravigote, 50
  Siennese, 47
  Sour-Cream, 48
  Sour-Cream and Cheese, 46
  Tropical, 47
  Vermouth Sour-Cream, 48
  Vinaigrette Sauce, 47
  Watercress, 46

Salmon
  Canned Fish Cakes, 129
  Coulibiac, 127
  and Duxelles Roulade, 112
  and Florentine Filling (for tarts), 59
  Omelet, 106
Salsa Verde, 72
Sardine Stuffing (for hard-cooked eggs, cold), 104
Sauce
  Allemande, 37
  Almond Hollandaise, 40
  Anchovy Hollandaise, 40
  Apricot Finish for Baked Ham, 159
  Aurore, 35
  Avocado, 44
  Avocado-Rum Dip, 74
  Basting, for Pork or Chicken, 159
  Béarnaise, 41
  Beauharnaise, 41
  Béchamel (Cream), 35
  Béchamel, Fish, 35
  Beer, 146
  Bercy, 37
  Bontemps, 36
  Bordelaise, 33
  Brown (Espagnole), 32
  Caper, 35
  Chasseur, 33
  Chaud-Froid, 45
  Cheese Chive, 35
  Choron, 41
  Coating for Roasted Meat, 160
  Cream (Béchamel), 35
  Creole, 41
  Cress, 45
  Cucumber, Cold, 44
  Cucumber, Hot, 35
  Curry, 36
  Demi-Glace, 33
  Diable, 33
  Dill, 44
  Duxelles Hollandaise, 40
  Egg-and-Oil-Based, 38-41
  Espagnole (Brown), 32
  Essence of Caper, 160
  Fish Béchamel, 35
  Foyot, 41
  Gribiche (Hard-Cooked-Egg Mayonnaise), 39
  Herb, 36
  Hollandaise, 40
  Horseradish, 35
  Hot Sauce, 20
  Ivory, 37
  Louis, 39
  Lyonnaise, 33
  Madeira I and II, 33
  Maltaise, 40
  Marinade and Basting, for Lamb, 160
  Mayonnaise, 38-39; for details *see* Mayonnaise
  Meat, Bolognese, 42
  Mexican (for) Fish, 43
  Mint, 34
  Mornay, 35
  Mousseline, 40
  Mushroom, 37
  Mustard, 33
  Nantua, 37
  Orange, 34
  Paprika, 36
  Périgourdine, 33
  Pineapple-Currant, 150
  Piquante, 34
  Pistou, 83
  Plum, 43
  Poulette, 37
  Rémoulade, 39
  Salsa Verde, 72
  Shrimp Hollandaise, 40
  Suprême, 37
  Tartare, 38
  Tuna, 155
  Vegetable, for Meat or Poultry, 42
  Velouté, 36
  Véronique, 35
  Vinaigrette, 47
  White, 34
  White Butter, 45
  *see also* Butters—Compound; Dips; Salad Dressing; Spreads
Sauce—Dessert, 237-238
  Apricot, 237
  Cardinal, 237
  Chocolate, May's, 238
  Hard, 237
  Jelly, 237
  Honey, 237
  Preserves, 237
  Whipped-Cream, 238
Sauerbraten Meat Loaf, 149
Sauerkraut Balls, 146
Sausage, 147-148
  and Apple Filling (for entrée crêpes), 196
  Bubble and Squeak, 148
  Crouton Frittata, 107
  Lamb, Breakfast, Charleston, 147
  Peasant Frittata, 107
  Sausage Meat, 147

Savoyard (pancake) Omelet, 106
Scallops with Salsa Verde, 73
Scandinavian Fish Pudding, 123
Scandinavian Style Steak Tartar, 68
Scrapple, 147
Seafood
  Balls, 69-70
  Medallions, Pojarski, 126
  Mousse, Cold, 122
  Mousse, Hot, 122
  Soufflé, 110
  Soufflé Base, 109
  Stuffing (for entrée crêpes), 195
  Stuffing (for fish), 130
Sesame Seed (Benne) Wafers, 57
Shellfish Quenelles, 120
Sherries, Flavored, 20-21
  Ginger, 20
  Onion, 20
  Super Hot, 21
Shortbread, 220
Shredding blade, 9
Shrimp
  Balls, Far East, 70
  Bisque, Cold, 100
  Bisque Creole, Cold, 98
  Bisque, Hot, see Lobster Bisque, 96
  Butter, 51
  Croquettes, 128
  Filling (for turnovers), 60
  and Florentine Filling (for tarts), 59
  Hollandaise, 40
  Mousse, Cold, 123
  Paste, Baked, 55
  Toast, 55
  and Water Chestnuts Stuffing (for hard-
    cooked eggs, cold), 104
Siennese Dressing, 47
Slicing blade, 9
Sole, Turban of, 121
Sopa Verde, 84
Sorrel Omelet, 106
Sorrel, Potage Germiny, 89, (recipe) 95
Soufflé—Dessert, Cold, 225
  Apricot, 226
  Coffee, 225
  Daiquiri, 225
  Ginger, 226
  Macaroon, 225
  Orange-Lemon-Grand Marnier, 225
Soufflé—Dessert, Hot, 224
  I, 224; II, 225
  Chocolate, 224
  Coffee, 224
  Crêpes Soufflé, 197

  Lemon, 224
  Liqueur, 224
  Maple, 224
  Nut, 224
  Orange, 224
  Rothschild, 224
Souffle—Entrée, 108-110
  Base (vegetable, meat, or seafood), 109
  basic procedures, 108
  Cheese, 108
  Chicken and Mushroom, 109
  Chicken-Liver and Water-Chestnut, 110
  Corn (in stuffed peppers), 152
  Extra Light, 109
  Fish (leftover), 109
  Florentine, 108
  Green Cheese, 109
  Meat (leftover), 109
  Roulade Soufflé, 111
    Chicken and Broccoli, 112
    Duxelles and Salmon, 112
    Filling, 112
    Ground Meat, Seasoned, 112
    Tongue and Spinach, 112
  Rutabaga, 168
  Seafood, 110
  Soft Cheese, 108
  Succotash, 110
  Vegetable, Basic Recipe, 171
  Véronique, 109
  without Sauce Base, 110
Soup
  Avocado, Cold, 97
  Beef Consommé, 79
  Beet, Russian, 82
  Billi-Bi, 96
  Bisque Creole, Cold, 98
  Bisques, 95-96
  Black-Bean, Cuban, 88
  Black-Bean, II, 89
  Borscht, Cold, 98
  Broccoli, Cold, 97
  Caraway Squash Bisque, 100
  Chestnut, 88
  Chicken Consommé, 80
  Chicken Egg-Flower, 82
  Clam Bisque, see Oyster Bisque, 95
  Cock-a-Leekie, 81
  Cold Soups, 97-101
  Consommé Forestière (Mushroom
    Broth), 81
  Consommé Madrilène, 80
  Consommé à l'Orange, 79
  Consommé Paysanne, 81
  Consommé Vert-Pré, 80

Corn, Cream of, 93
Crab Bisque, *see* Lobster Bisque, 96
Crayfish Bisque, *see* Lobster Bisque, 96
Cream Soups, 91-93
Crécy, Cold, 101
Cucumber, Cold, 99
Fish, Cold, 101
garnishes, 75
Gazpacho, 99
Herb Broth, 80
Jade, 90
Lemon Consommé, 79
Lobster Bisque, 96
Minestrone, 84
Mushroom Broth (Consommé Forestière), 81
Onion, Light, 83
Oyster Bisque, 95
Pea Purée, Fresh (Saint-Germain), 87
Peasant, 85
Pistou, 83
Potage Bagration—Fish, 94
Potage Bagration—Veal, 94
Potage Crécy, *see* Potato and Leek, 89
Potage Germiny, 95; *see also* Potato and Leek, 89
Potato and Leek, 89
Pumpkin Purée (Purée Potiron), 87
Purée of Dried Legumes, 90
Purées, 85-90
Shrimp Bisque, Cold, 100
Shrimp Bisque, Hot, *see* Loster Bisque, 96
Sopa Verde, 84
Thick Soups, 85-90
Thin Soups, 79-82
Tomato Bouillon, 79
Tomato, Cream of, 93
Vegetable, 82-85
   Cream, 91
   Potato-Thickened, 86
   Purées, 87-90
Veloutés, 94-95
Vichyssoise, *see* Potato and Leek, 89
Wine Consommé, 79
Winter Squash Purée, 87
Sour Cream
   and Cheese Salad Dressing, 46
   Cucumber Salad Dressing, 48
   Green-Pepper Salad Dressing, 48
   Onion Salad Dressing, 48
   Salad Dressing, 48
   Vermouth Salad Dressing, 48
South Sea Dip, 74

Spinach
   Balls, 170
   Florentine Filling (for tarts), and variations, 59
   Florentine Soufflé, 108
   Gnocchi, 170
   Niçoise, 169
   Omelet, 106
   Purée (for soup), 92
   Purée (with cream, for tarts), 59
   Quiche à la Grecque, 116
   Soup, Potato-Thickened, 86
Spirited Pie, 236
Spreads, Cold, 62-68
   Avocado Blue-Cheese, 64
   Beer Cheese, 63
   Blue Cheese, Brandied, 64
   Cheese, Broiled, 64
   Chicken, 65
   Chicken-Liver Pâté, 66
   Chicken-Tarragon, 65
   Eggplant Caviar, 67
   Kippered Herring, 66
   Liptauer Cheese, 63
   Mushroom, Raw, 71
   Peanut-Butter and Cream-Cheese, 64
   Steak Tartar, 67
   Taramasalata, 66
   Tongue, 65
   Turnip and Carrot, Raw, 67
Squash
   Caraway Squash Bisque, 100
   Winter Squash Casserole, 174
   Winter Squash Purée, 87
Stay Crisp Pastry, 24
Steak, *see* Beef
Steel blade, 9
Stock, 76-78
   Beef, 76
   Brown, 77
   Chicken, 77
   Fish (Fumet), 78
   to clarify, 76
   Veal, 77
   Vegetable, 78
Stuffings, *see* Fillings and Stuffings— Entrée and Hors d'Oeuvre
Succotash Soufflé, 110
Sugar Cookies (rolled), 216
Super Hot Sherry, 21
Suprême Sauce, 37
Surprise Cookies (molded), 217
Swedish Almond Pie, 235
Sweet Bread, 190
Sweet Pastry (Pâte Sucrée), 29

Sweet-Potato and Almond Croquettes, 169
Sweet Potato and Walnut Stuffing (for poultry), 140
Swiss Chard and Zucchini Casserole, 173

Tabbouleh, 181
Tapenade, 73
Tapenade Stuffing (for hard-cooked eggs, cold), 104
Taramasalata, 66
Tartare Sauce, 38
Tender Rounds (molded cookies), 217
Tia Juana Beefburgers, 144
Timbales, 112-114
  Based on Béchamel Sauce, 114
  Cheese Custard, 113
  Chicken-Liver, 113
  Custard, 113
  Vegetable Custard, 113
Toasts
  Cheese and Almond Fingers, 54
  Chicken-Liver, 56
  Shrimp, 55
Tomato(es)
  Anchovy Mayonnaise, 38
  Bouillon, 79
  and Clam Aspic, Pale Pink, 176
  Green Tomato Chutney, Grandmother Page's, 17
  Soup, Cream of, 93
  Vegetable-Stuffed, 172
Tongue
  Mold, 156
  and Spinach Roulade, 112
  Spread, 65
Torte, see Cakes
Tropical Salad Dressing, 47
Tropical Cookies (molded), 217
Tuna Fish
  Canned Fish Cakes, 129
  Sauce, 155
  Stuffing (for hard-cooked eggs, hot), 105
Turban of Sole, 121
Turnip and Carrot Spread, Raw, 67
Turnover Fillings, 60-61
Turnover Pastry, 26
Tuscan Beefburgers, 144

Veal
  Birds, 153
  Breast of, Stuffed, Rolled, 153
  and Liver Loaf in Jelly, 157

Patties, 145
Potage Bagration, 94
Quenelle Filling, 154
Stock, 77
Vitello Tonnato, 155
Vegetable(s)
  and Cottage-Cheese Filling (for turnovers), 61
  Cream Soup, 91
  Custard Timbale, 113
  Hors d'Oeuvre, Cold, 71-72
  Macédoine, 72
  Meat-Filled, 150-152
  Mediterranean Casserole, 174
  and Potato Purées, 171
  Purées (soups), 87-90
  Purées for Cream Soups, 91-93
  Salad, Raw, 182
  Sauce for Meat or Poultry, 42
  Soufflé Base, 109
  Souffléed, Basic Recipe, 171
  Stock, 78
  -Stuffed Tomatoes, 172
  see also names of vegetables
Veloutés (soups), 94-95
Velouté Sauce, 36
Vermouth Sour-Cream Salad Dressing, 48
Véronique Sauce, 35
Vichyssoise, see Potato and Leek Soup, 89
Vinaigrette Sauce, 47
Vitello Tonnato, 155
Volaille Mornay, 134

Waffles, 200
Walnut
  and Blue Cheese Stuffing (for hard-cooked eggs, cold), 104
  Maple Walnut Cookies (drop), 213
  Nut Fruit Crêpes, 197
  and Sweet-Potato Stuffing (for poultry), 140
Watercress
  Cress Sauce, 45
  Purée, 93
  Salad Dressing, 46
  Soup, Potato-Thickened, 86
Western Omelet, 106
Western Pancakes, 199
Whipped-Cream Sauce, 238
White Bread, 189
White Butter Sauce, 45
White Cake, 203
White Quiche, 115

White Sauces, 34
Wine
  Butter Frosting, 210
  Consommé, 79
  Cookies (icebox), 218

Yankee Meatballs, 69
Yellow Cake, 202
Yorkshire Pudding, 189

Zucchini
  Bread, 188
  Filled (with meat), 152
  Frittata, 107
  Quiche, 117
  -Raisin Pickle, 19
  and Sour-Cream Casserole, 172
  Stuffed with Peas, 173
  and Swiss-Chard Casserole, 173
Zwieback Torte, 205